The Gladiators

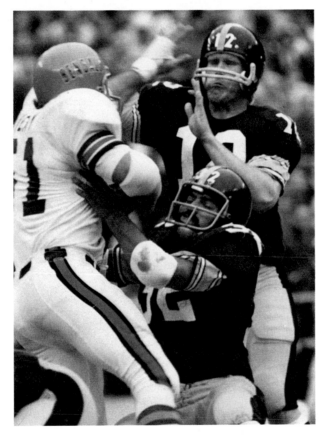

The Gladiators

A Rutledge Book
Prentice-Hall, Inc. Englewood Cliffs, New Jersey

Fred R. Sammis: Publisher
John T. Sammis: Creative Director
Doris Townsend: Editor-in-Chief
Allan Mogel: Art Director
Jeanne McClow: Managing Editor
Jeremy Friedlander: Associate Editor
Gwen Evrard: Associate Art Director
Arthur Gubernick: Production Consultant
Margaret Riemer: Editorial Assistant
Sally Andrews: Editorial Assistant

Library of Congress Catalog Card Number: 72-82980
ISBN: 0-13-357087-8
Prepared and produced by Rutledge Books, 17 East
45th Street, New York, N.Y. 10017
Published in 1973 by Prentice-Hall, Inc., Englewood Cliffs,
N.J.
Printed in Italy by Mondadori, Verona

CONTENTS

1
"IT'S THE MEN WHO PLAY THE GAME" by Tex Maule 9

2
THE FIRST SEASON by Jim Terzian 16

3
A LONG WAY BACK TO THE BENCH by Lee Hutson 48

4
THE THIRD TEAM by Norm Schacter 112

5
FOOTBALL AT 1/500 134

6
THE BETTER WAY by Skip Myslenski 186

7
THRESHOLDS by Steve Taylor and Mercer Field 208

8
THE NEW BREED by Patrick Russell 240

1
"IT'S THE MEN WHO PLAY THE GAME"

by Tex Maule

It has, in recent years, become fashionable to ascribe the burgeoning popularity of professional football to certain factors. The growth of television and its intelligent use first by Commissioner Bert Bell and then by his successor, Pete Rozelle, are two such factors, and certainly valid ones. Some feel also that professional football, a contact sport, thrives particularly well in a climate of violence, which these times supply in overflowing measure. Prosperity and more leisure to devote to sports help provide the vast pro football audience too. But the people who advance these theories are overlooking the primary factor accounting for the popularity of the game.

Pro football survived the scant early years, entrenched itself during the building years and finally became the premier spectator sport of this country because of the extraordinary men who have played it all along. Men made the game when George Halas, Jim Thorpe, Red Grange and Johnny Blood played during its Neanderthal Age. And men make the game what it is today.

Today it is a big business. When Halas both owned and played for the Chicago Bears back in the early twenties, he took home the team's proceeds from the games in a small black satchel. The custodian of the satchel, more often than not, was George Trafton, the meanest Bear of the era. Trafton played center and linebacker for the club, and did so with such unrestrained gusto that when the Bears were playing on foreign soil, the crowds usually came out of the stands after him when the game was over.

Halas, having thoughtfully collected the Bear share of the gate at half-time, would take Trafton out a few seconds before the final whistle so that he might have a reasonable head start and give him the bag on the theory that a man running for his life is not apt to be caught. It worked.

Trafton played for Halas for 13 years, never losing a footrace to a crowd and earning all-pro honors several times. His reputation as a brawler earned him two pro fights: one against Primo Carnera, the other against Art Shires, a baseball player with a similar reputation.

Carnera knocked George out in one round, although Trafton later maintained that to save his life, he had taken a dive, since a member of the Capone gang was at ringside with a pistol trained on him to insure his defeat. The fight with Shires was not much more rewarding. They fought for three rounds, and when the third round ended, neither of them could lift a hand from exhaustion, and neither of them had done noticeable damage to the other. The referee called it a draw, but no one who saw it even called it a fight.

Trafton, for me, bridged the gap in time from those early days to the period just after World War II, when I became publicity director of the Rams. He had remained in pro football as an assistant coach and was serving in that capacity for Clark Shaughnessy, who was then head coach of the Rams.

It was Trafton, in fact, who first pointed out to me that it was the players who made pro football successful. This was when television was just beginning to take hold; the Rams had sold home television rights to Hoffman Television in exchange for a guaranteed break-even gate. The deal eventually cost Hoffman $600,000 and proved rather conclusively that televising home games, even in Los Angeles with no weather problem, would destroy the home gate.

"I think Dan [Reeves, the Rams' owner] is making a mistake," Trafton said when he heard of the deal. "He's got the right idea with the scouting, because it's the men who play the game who will bring the people out to see it. We got some of the best in the world, but you can't give away their talent, and that's what he is doing."

Trafton was busy that year, 1949, trying to create a carbon copy of what he had been when he had played. The term is appropriate, because the rookie linebacker he was working with was Tank Younger, the first black man drafted from an all-black college, Grambling.

Younger had been discovered by Eddie Kotal, the chief scout of the Rams. When he had reported to sign his contract, Shaughnessy had taken him out to UCLA to see for himself whether Younger had the skill to play for the pros.

It would be difficult to imagine a more unfair test than the one the coach gave Tank. He stationed Younger as a defensive halfback—he had been a running back at Grambling—and then had Tom Fears, an all-pro receiver, run patterns at him while all-pro Bob Waterfield, under no pressure, threw. Younger, of course, never got within rifle shot of Fears, and several times Fears's fakes forced him to cross his legs and fall down.

"If that man's a football player, I'll eat him," said Shaughnessy.

"You may have to," Trafton told the Old Man.

He had to eat his words, at any rate. Late during the training period, Younger was on the verge of being cut when Trafton put him into a scrimmage as a linebacker. Tank came close to doing serious damage to blockers and ballcarriers before Trafton took him out. He made the club and played both fullback and linebacker with distinction.

Younger was one of the first of many great black running backs. When he joined the Rams, there were very few other blacks in the NFL. "Yet I never had any racial problem," he said recently. "Not from the players on the Rams or from the players on the other teams. We had an all-pro tackle from Tennessee named Dick Huffman. I remember once when we were playing the Green Bay Packers and they had Ed Neal at middle guard, I tried to block him on a punt. He hit me in the nose with his elbow, and the next thing I knew, I was on the sideline with my nose all over my face. And it was Huffman who came over and asked me who had done it and told me he'd take care of Neal for me. He didn't, but he tried, and I guess it was then I knew I was a part of the team, color or not."

The decade of the fifties saw the most dramatic growth in the nationwide interest in professional football. The NFL was truly national with the Rams and the 49ers in California, and television aerials were sprouting like odd mushrooms from rooftops all over the nation. And the players in the league became the stars of what was to become the nation's most popular sports program—pro football on Sunday afternoon television.

During this decade there were, of course, fewer teams; consequently, individual stars were actually spotlighted more than they are now. On the Rams alone, there were running backs such as Deacon Dan Towler, Younger and Dick Hoerner—three fullbacks who each weighed over 230 and could run the hundred under 10 seconds. Vitamin Smith set a league record returning kickoffs for touchdowns, and the Ram wide receivers were Elroy (Crazylegs) Hirsch and Tom Fears. Fears broke Don Hutson's record for passes caught in a single season, and Hirsch broke Hutson's record for yards gained receiving passes.

The 49ers had Hugh McElhenny, quite possibly the most spectacular broken-field runner of them all, plus John Henry Johnson and Joe Perry, who was to play an incredible 15 years at fullback, a position that has a normal career expectancy of about one-third of that.

Then there were Doak Walker, Hunchy Hoernschemeyer and Bobby Layne at Detroit, exercising a hypnotic spell over a Cleveland team that included Otto Graham, Marion Motley, Dante Lavelli, Mac Speedie, Dub Jones and Paul Brown as coach. It was Brown and Clark Shaughnessy who opened the game up so that these players could display their considerable talents.

Of course, Brown and Shaughnessy had the quarterbacks to implement their imaginative and innovative offenses. The Rams had Bob Waterfield and Norm Van Brocklin, and Brown had Graham. "The Dutchman" (Van Brocklin) came from Oregon as a rookie in 1949, an impatient, outspoken young man

with absolute confidence in himself. Once, early in his career, when Waterfield was handling most of the chores at quarterback, Van Brocklin told Shaughnessy (on one of the rare afternoons when Buckets was off), "Put me in, coach. I'll break every passing record in the book for you."

Many of the stars of that time have continued in pro football as the coaches of today, providing a pleasing continuity to the game and a lasting allegiance to the past. Van Brocklin is as crusty a coach as he was a quarterback, badgering players, sportswriters and friends with equal asperity.

When he was playing for the Rams, he developed a strong dislike for the late Maxwell Stiles, then a columnist for the Los Angeles *Daily Mirror*. Stiles, as outspoken as Van Brocklin, had been a Waterfield supporter when the Ram fans were split into Waterfield and Van Brocklin camps. Stiles never missed a Ram practice during training camp, usually coming to the morning workout in his bedroom slippers.

One day, seeing Stiles on the sideline and practically on the field, Van Brocklin called a wide sweep toward him that carried over the sideline, upending Max and knocking him out of his slippers. Van Brocklin tossed the slippers over the fence nearby. When Stiles finally came to and found them, he said, "Look how hard they hit me! They knocked my shoes right over the fence."

The next day, he appeared at practice wearing a jersey with the number 39.

"Why number thirty-nine?" someone on the team asked him.

"You guys never have been able to hit this number, so I figure I'll be safe wearing it," Stiles said. It was Hugh McElhenny's number.

Van Brocklin's last year as a player was 1960, when he took the Philadelphia Eagles to the world championship. His retirement coincided neatly with the beginning of a new decade and a new look for the game. Lamar Hunt had started the American Football League, and the long and, for the league owners, costly war between the leagues began.

The war was a profitable one for the men who played or came into the game while it was going on. There was considerable fear that with the addition of so many more teams, the talent would be so diluted that the quality of the game would suffer irreparable harm. Indeed, for a few years the new league, with few exceptions, played on a level several notches below the old. Now, however, the teams, whatever their origin—NFL or AFL—are on a par, and there has been no extraordinary dilution of talent. Actually, the men playing professional football today are much bigger and a good deal faster than those of 25 years ago. They would dwarf many of the players who made up the Chicago Bear team that defeated the Washington Redskins, 73-0, in 1941.

Of course, there were giants a couple of decades ago too. Neal, the middle guard who smashed Younger's nose, played at about 325, and so did Les Bingaman, his counterpart with the Lions. Neal was an enormously strong man who was a Texas blacksmith in the off-season; he customarily opened a beer bottle by flipping the top off with his thumb and broke the empty over a rock-hard forearm. But he had little lateral mobility; the position of middle guard was phased out of pro football when Paul Brown split his guards wide on offense, taking the defensive tackles with them and isolating the big, stationary middle guards in protecting against up-the-middle rushes.

Some of the stars of the old days, even though their positions are played now as they were then, would not be drafted today. Ed Sprinkle, the notorious defensive end for the Bears, weighed around 200 pounds and was neither as quick nor as fast as Deacon Jones, who weighs 250. Hal Dean, an all-pro guard for the Rams, weighed 196; it is doubtful that he could do more than make Merlin Olsen, the 270-pound all-pro defensive tackle of the Rams today, break stride.

So the physical dimensions of the players, in almost every position, have changed. The common denominator which links the old and the new is courage; no physical cowards played football then, and none do now.

Aside from this common trait, the players, by position, share certain temperamental characteristics. Vincent T. Lombardi tailored his personality to fit the player he had to deal with. "Offensive linemen have to have disciplined personalities," he once said. "I can take an average good athlete with discipline and teach him to be an excellent offensive guard or tackle. He doesn't need imagination—just retention."

The great Green Bay offensive lines of the Lombardi era included men like Jerry Kramer, Fuzzy Thurston and Forrest Gregg, all preeminent at their positions. At least one of them—Kramer—has imagination as well as retention. He has written two books since his block cleared the way to a Green Bay championship a few years ago and prompted the publication of his best seller, *Instant Replay*. But in the Green Bay offense, the offensive linemen performed, precisely, the tasks that Lombardi set for them.

"They have to be people who prefer to know beforehand what they are going to do," Lombardi said. "An offensive lineman in the Lombardi system should never make a mental error. It is the unforgivable sin."

Of course, Lombardi was not much given to forgiving defensive errors either. But he considered defense to be a game of reaction; there were certain rules to be followed, but the defenders—line, linebackers and secondary—had to have a different personality from the blockers.

"I'm not downgrading my offensive line," he said. "But, generally, it takes a better athlete to play defense. What he does is always predicated upon what the offensive player does first, so he's always a split second behind. He has to make that up with his reaction, physically, or his head, mentally. That's why it's so important to put a player in the right position. Henry Jordan and Willie Davis were perfect examples of that."

Lombardi acquired Davis and Jordan from the Cleveland Browns by trade in his first season as head coach of the Packers. Both had been offensive linemen at Cleveland; he converted Jordan to a defensive tackle and Davis to a defensive end, and both were all-pro at their new positions.

"The fact that I changed them is no criticism of Paul Brown," Lombardi said. "Paul is one of the great coaches of our time. But he happened to be loaded on the defensive line, and he needed help on offense, and he tried to fit them in there. Both of them were natural defensive players. They didn't take discipline too well. That's why I had to get on Henry so much."

Lombardi may have been right, although it is doubtful that many offensive linemen would agree with him. The offensive line is, in most cases, a faceless unit whose rare satisfactions come hidden in the traffic generated by a running play off tackle, where only the back with the ball and the tackle blocked know what the offensive guard accomplished.

The meticulous, comprehensive scouting systems that assist the NFL clubs in their selection of the best of the college seniors each season discover and evaluate the physical potential of the players available in computer detail. In fact, all this data is stored in a computer in most cases. The one ineluctable facet of a player's character is his response to stress—to actually performing on the field.

Tex Schramm, the president of the Dallas Cowboys, learned scouting techniques under Dan Reeves, who put the Rams far ahead of the field in the late forties and early fifties. Schramm tried to work out a questionnaire that would tell him which players would have the psychological motivation necessary for a good pro football player. His computer had refined the physical requirements already. He called in psychologists, IBM and computer experts and had some 300 questions that he thought might winnow the information for him.

Understandably enough, most college seniors did not want to take time to answer 300 questions in writing. The list was finally reduced to some 50.

"We tested it for a long time," Schramm said not long ago. "We tested it with rookies and with the veterans, and it never worked." For instance, it showed that Lee Roy Jordan (the fine middle linebacker for the Cowboys) really had no strong desire to hit people, a rather useful trait in a middle linebacker. But he wanted so much to be a member of the group that he hit people very hard anyway. Probably a psychological profile of Dick Butkus would show extremes just the opposite of Jordan's. So in the tenuous area of psychological profiles, players at any position can achieve excellence for totally different reasons.

A look at quarterbacks will demonstrate this point well.

When Waterfield and Van Brocklin were the quarterbacks of the Rams, they represented as schizophrenic a pair of signal callers as can be imagined. Waterfield was a very cool—some called him cold—calculating type, hard to get close to, unemotional during a game, friendly but distant with his fellow players. Van Brocklin was volatile, emotional and quick to yell at his blockers when they executed what he called a "Look out!" block—one in which the offensive lineman missed his target, then turned and hollered "Look out!" to the quarterback. Waterfield, under the same situation, would only eye the culprit very coldly.

But both systems worked. The team played as well for Waterfield as it did for Van Brocklin. Both of them were leaders as well as master technicians. A parallel today could be cited at Washington, with Sonny Jurgensen and Bill Kilmer, or at Dallas, with Roger Staubach and Craig Morton.

Joe Namath, the quarterback of the New York Jets, is a free soul. His life-style is a swinging one. He wears his hair long. He is a fixture in the singles bars on New York's East Side; he owned one until Rozelle made him get rid of it. Some experts would say that he is the best quarterback of the sixties; others would opt for either Bart Starr, now the quarterback coach of the Green Bay Packers, or John Unitas, who now owns all the career records for quarterbacks.

Starr is a quiet, very religious and very dedicated man. His hair is reasonably short. His sideburns stop short of his earlobe. And he was as good a quarterback as Namath, if not better. Unitas for a long time wore a crew cut. He is a quiet, self-sufficient man who seldom says a word more than he needs to say to get across his point. Namath is an ebullient

man who, in his book, wrote that he felt that sex on Saturday night before a game relaxed him. He has, on occasion, been known to have a small drink. Starr almost never drinks. Unitas drinks, but mostly during the off-season. Starr is a thoughtful, well-read man. Unitas reads little. And Namath probably doesn't have time to read.

Van Brocklin is, off the field, a conservative man. Early in his coaching career, when he had the Minnesota expansion team, he played the Rams in Los Angeles. The Rams had acquired Claude Crabb from the Vikings; Crabb was a defensive back, and the only players the Vikings had enough of were defensive backs. Previously, at the Viking training camp in Bemidji, Minnesota, Van Brocklin had insisted that Crabb, like all other Viking players, keep his hair cropped short and his sideburns minimal.

The Rams whomped the Vikings, as they should have. Coming out of the ramp leading to the dressing rooms, Van Brocklin saw Crabb, who by then had let his hair grow almost to shoulder-length. They talked for a moment, and then Van Brocklin pointed to the Ram bus. The players getting on almost all had hair as long as Crabb's.

"What a bunch of pansies," he said to Crabb. He looked at the Viking bus. "Look at my club," he said. "You don't see any long hair on any of them."

Crabb looked at the Vikings climbing on the bus for a moment, then nodded. "Yeah, coach," he said. "That's the most clean-cut looking bunch of one-and-five ballplayers I think I ever saw."

Ironically, Starr, in his first season as a coach, is coaching another quarterback from Alabama. Scott Hunter, like Starr, was drafted late; Bart was taken on the seventeenth round by Green Bay when he came up, and Hunter, in a year in which Jim Plunkett, Archie Manning and Dan Pastorini were available, was skipped over until the seventh round. But Hunter's personality more nearly resembles Namath's (another Alabama product) than it does Starr's.

"He must have been the most undisciplined player who ever played for Bear Bryant," coach Dan Devine says of Hunter. "He has a lot of confidence, and he's going to be a great one, but he needed disciplining. As a rookie, he tried to tell the place-kickers what to do. I stopped that, but it was a while before he learned to take instruction."

Hunter is learning discipline under the aegis of Devine and Starr. He is a bright, cheerful, handsome young man, one of the rising young generation of quarterbacks who are the Starrs, Namaths, Waterfields and Unitases of the future.

Like all the rest, he has his own style. He watched Starr and Namath on television, checking their moves and their releases, but he does not think that he has patterned himself on any of them. "They're all different," he says. "Sure, I used to watch how Bart set up and Joe's release, and I know Joe pretty well. He has a place in Alabama, and I go by there now and then during the off-season, and we talk. He's a nice guy, but I'm like Scott Hunter, not like anyone else."

Quarterbacks, because of the requirements of their position, are completely various. The throwing motion, like the baseball windup, is not stereotyped or restricted to one style; quarterbacks deliver the ball in as many different ways as there are quarterbacks. Sonny Jurgensen sometimes looks like a side-arm pitcher, but he completes passes. Bobby Layne's passes occasionally tumbled end over end, but they hit the target.

Probably the quality any quarterback must have in spades is the ability to adjust to the situation. Van Brocklin, who could do that superbly when he played the position, took a while to learn to adjust as a coach. As a player, he may have been the least likely runner who ever came down the pike. He ran with the speed and grace of a pregnant hippopotamus. This was no great handicap for the Dutchman; he had an exceptionally quick release, so that he could use the quick gun to negate a rush, instead of quick feet, a la Fran Tarkenton.

Tarkenton was his first quarterback when the Dutchman took over the Minnesota Vikings in their first year. Van Brocklin never really adjusted to having a scrambling quarterback. "When you got a quarterback like the Peach [short for Georgia Peach], you better work up a pretty good third and forty offense," he said sourly. "I don't know any coaches with that kind of offense."

By the time he took over the Atlanta Falcons, he had adjusted to reality. With Bob Berry, another small quarterback who runs occasionally, Van Brocklin has put together a contender.

The day of the quarterback who, in Van Brocklin's phrase, ran only from sheer terror, is probably over. The new breed—quarterbacks like Roger Staubach of Dallas, Greg Landry of Detroit, Jim Plunkett of New England, Bobby Douglass of Chicago and Hunter—all run, but not from terror. The quarterbacks, significantly, have grown bigger and faster to answer the need for another back to carry the ball when pass coverage blankets the targets.

The game itself changes from year to year and from decade to decade, influenced by coaches, by developments in the college game, by changes in the rules. The flood of new players arrives from the colleges with different skills; soccer-style place-kickers, for instance, are playing a bigger and bigger part in the general scheme of things. This is a minor area of the game, but not so minor as it might seem at first blush. Not only is the soccer-style kicker valuable for the three points he can put up with long-range field goals; he can also help the defense considerably by booming kickoffs out of the end zone, which cannot be returned.

The kickers, soccer-style or otherwise, are a breed apart. At most practices, they spend a lonely time by themselves perfecting their specialty, working with the rest of the team only when the coaches call drills for the special teams.

Most of them are philosophical about their rather distant relationship with the other players on the club. Said one foreign kicker, after he had kicked a game-winning field goal, "I have kick a touchdown, and that is what I get pay for. Is no need for me to know more. Is also no need for me to know all players, even."

The game has changed other than in the acceptance of soccer-style kickers, of course. In 1972, the hash marks were moved in, thereby creating more opportunity for pass receivers to whipsaw the zone and a wider variety of routes for the running backs to negotiate. But the men catching the passes and the men running the routes did not change. Maybe the defensive backs grew a bit grayer over the season and the linebackers more worried, but basically the players were the same. They haven't changed all that much since the game began.

Pro football players have reflected, faithfully, the change in society; now there is more rebellion and less conformity among their ranks. There are players who quit the game and write bitter books about how it brutalized them; they usually write the books after they have played in the league long enough to earn the money to take the time to write the books.

"I don't like them talking for me," says Mike Curtis, the middle linebacker for the Baltimore Colts, who is an independent soul himself, as are most middle linebackers. "I haven't been brutalized by pro football. It has been a rewarding thing for me. I play hard on the field, but I don't try to hurt anyone. If Dave Meggyesy and his friends feel that way, let them talk for themselves."

And, of course, as a result of the escalation of salaries, pro football players are more prosperous today than they used to be. In the heyday of the Rams in 1950, Dick Huffman, the all-pro tackle who tried to reprimand Ed Neal for his ill treatment of Tank Younger, went to Canada. He had been all-pro for three years, and he was earning $6,500 per year.

He was offered $7,000, wanted $7,500. The Rams refused to budge, so he left. Today, he would earn something in the neighborhood of $30,000.

The players coming into the league today seem to have a clearer idea of their future than did the old-timers. They play with the same desire and with more speed and strength, but at the same time, most of them are preparing for when they will play no longer. (Hunter, in his second season in the league, is already looking ahead; he majored in finance at Alabama, and is casting about for a job in the off-season which will advance his career when his playing days are over.) They have good examples of the success a good pro football career can breed in other fields. Probably no other group of professional athletes can match the postsport careers of pro football players. This has been the case for quite a long time.

For starters, Whizzer White, who was a great running back for the Detroit Lions, is Justice Byron White of the Supreme Court. One of the best surgeons in the Los Angeles area, Danny Fortman, once played guard for the Chicago Bears.

Gino Marchetti was one of the most punishing defensive ends who ever played professional football, but most people did not consider him a genius otherwise. In fact, once when the Baltimore Colts were playing in San Francisco and their bus went by San Francisco University (now San Francisco State), where Gino had played college football, Artie Donovan pointed the school out to the other players.

"That's where Gino played," he said in the high, piping voice that went so strangely with his defensive tackle's bulk. "When he left school, they retired his grades."

But Marchetti, helped by the Colt owner at the time, Carroll Rosenbloom, went into business with two other players to build Gino's Hamburger Huts. Today Gino is worth something over ten million dollars, and his business is growing steadily.

Frank Ryan, the ex-Cleveland, ex-Los Angeles quarterback, took his PhD in mathematics at Rice University while he played pro football and is now a teacher. Charley Johnson, quarterback for St. Louis, Denver and Houston, also has a doctor's degree.

Fuzzy Thurston and Max McGee, former Packers in the days of Packer glory, own a string of restaurants in Wisconsin called the Left Guard. Fuzzy was the left guard, Max a wide receiver. When you stop to think about it, you can understand why they named all the restaurants the Left Guard; would anyone a little overweight want to eat in a place called the Wide Receiver?

The list of pro football players who have been successful after their playing days have ended is a long one. The qualities that made them good pro football players are the qualities that made them good competitors in any other field. When Schramm was trying to work out a computerized profile of the psychology of the successful football players, several other industries were looking over his shoulder with considerable interest. They reasoned that if he could work out a test that would predict success, other than physical, in pro football, the formula would, of course, work in any other field of endeavor requiring aggressive perseverance.

Schramm did, finally, come up with a test to determine the qualities of a man that guarantee success in most endeavors. Unfortunately, however, the best test is longer than the one he postulated. It sometimes takes as long as 20 years, as in the case of George Blanda. But once a man has proved his ability as a player in the tough competition of professional football, the odds are very big that he will succeed in anything else he tries.

The men make the game, and to an extent, the game makes the men.

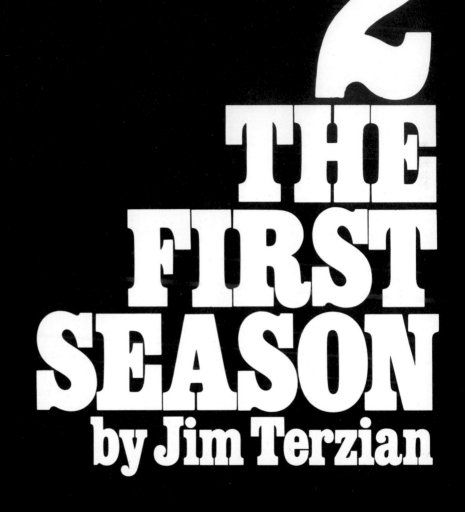

2
THE
FIRST
SEASON
by Jim Terzian

The pro football year begins in the long hot weeks of summer when 26 individual armies train for one purpose—to develop maximum hand-to-hand attack capabilities and ferocious defenses. It is the first season, complete unto itself, with its own rewards and penalties, its own life-style.

For those who play, coach or administer the game of professional football, the competitive year is divided into three parts: the training period, the league games and the play-offs leading to the Super Bowl. Each segment is a season unto itself, with its own time span, its own rules, its own rewards and punishments, its own life-style on and off the field.

Of the three, the most structured—and certainly the most regimented—is the training period, extending from mid-July to mid-September, when league play begins.

During the 9 or 10 long, hot summer weeks of this "first season," 26 individual armies (each an NFL team) will train for battle. Comprising each army, some 150 men—players, coaches, scouts, trainers, equipment men and administrative personnel—will work and live together for a common purpose: to maximize offensive and defensive capability in literal hand-to-hand combat. And before the training has ended, each army will have waged six exhibition battles against rival armies under full combat conditions. Casualty lists are high. Subpar performances can bring discharge. Some of the old soldiers will fade away. By the time the first season ends, 40 warriors and 7 reserve players per squad have honed to battle-ready pitch.

The cast into military terminology is not accidental. NFL camps are marked by class distinctions, orders of the day, drills, punishments, pain, curfews, isolation, self-denial, family disruptions and career displacements over which an individual has little or no control as long as he agrees to live within the pro football establishment. There's even a draft.

But eventually the analogy gives way to civilian options. Induction into pro football is voluntary. A draftee can refuse his orders without undue penalty or hold out for better terms or pursue an altogether different career if he so desires. Nor is he forced to stay in the ranks after he reports; he can ask to be traded—a practice more common among established players—if such a move is acceptable to all parties. He can even go over the hill without the dire consequences that follow such a move in the military. The pay is better, too.

The first season puts enormous pressure on individual-player careers. For veterans it means beating down bids by younger rivals eager to take over their starting roles and the high salaries that go with them. For second-year men it means having to prove that their initial pro success was no fluke; meanwhile they too keep wary eyes on talented rookies looking to displace *them*. For rookies training camp is a fateful, frequently lonely struggle against long odds waged under conditions guaranteed to

Executed in unison and to a count, grass drills resemble preparation for a ballet.

19

Getting into shape at my age is work. I hate it.

grind body and soul into pulp. They may have been all-Americans in college; in camp they're pro football's noncitizens—"piss-ants," in the words of one veteran. Rookies suffer this inferior role until they—a fortunate few—either make the squad, at which time they are initiated into the lofty brotherhood that separates regulars from low-caste pretenders, or fail and leave camp, bringing their summer torture to a merciful end.

Among established players there is a pervasive dislike for camp routine, especially the man-killing, two-a-day workouts under a broiling sun, orchestrated by whistles and sharp-tongued coaches to whom pity is just another four-letter word. One former Navy man, now a blocking back with the Washington Redskins, calls the training period "boot camp and you can shove it!" Another, a New York Giant defensive end, admits, "I hate two-a-day drills. Getting into

When asked whether weight lifting might be less exhausting prior to workouts, Jethro Pugh, all 265 pounds of him braced under a 300-pound bar bell, lets out a sweaty grunt and says, "Man, who wants to die before goin' out there."

shape at my age is work. I just hate it." Others complain that the first season is too long or that teams play too many exhibition contests, even though, by agreement between the Players Association and club owners, they draw extra pay—anywhere from $92.88 a game for second-year men to $340.56 for those with five or more years of service. Rookies, as befits their status, get nothing except their salaries and a per diem allowance of $13.42 plus room, board and laundry, as do all other men on the club roster.

Some participants, however, find no fault with the long weeks of preparation. One all-pro linebacker, approaching his mid-30s, has little patience with complainers: "I grew up on a farm and picked cotton and peanuts, harvested corn and raised hogs and

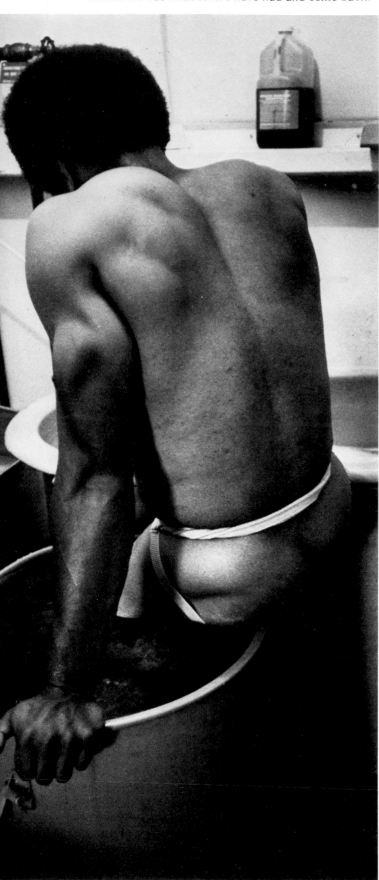

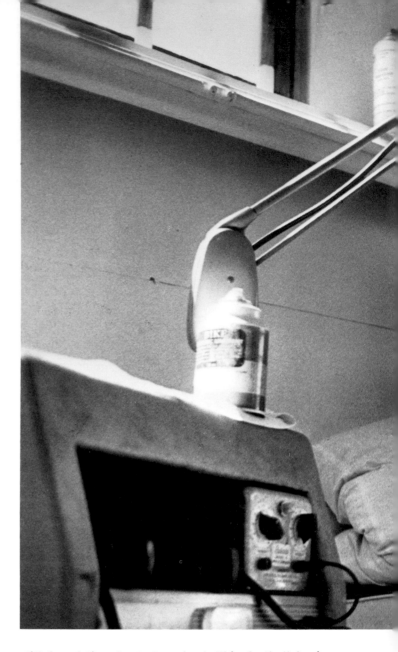

still found time to go to school. This football business—" he winced from a pulled hamstring "is like a day off compared to what I did on the farm as a youngster." Coaches, naturally, stress the advantages of training. They insist that the quality and quantity of events during the first season—conditioning, play execution, timing, development of new talent, team depth, trades, injuries, especially injuries!—supply the key to the balance of the competitive year.

Head coach Tom Landry of the Dallas Cowboys is a particular advocate of training camp. That the Cowboys lost starting quarterback Roger Staubach through a shoulder separation on August 12, 1972, meant moving backup quarterback Craig Morton to the starting slot and getting an experienced quarterback to back *him* up—veteran Jack Concannon of the Chicago Bears, who joined the club late in August. "In our September 4 exhibition loss [20–10] to Kansas City," Landry recalls, "he [Concannon] just

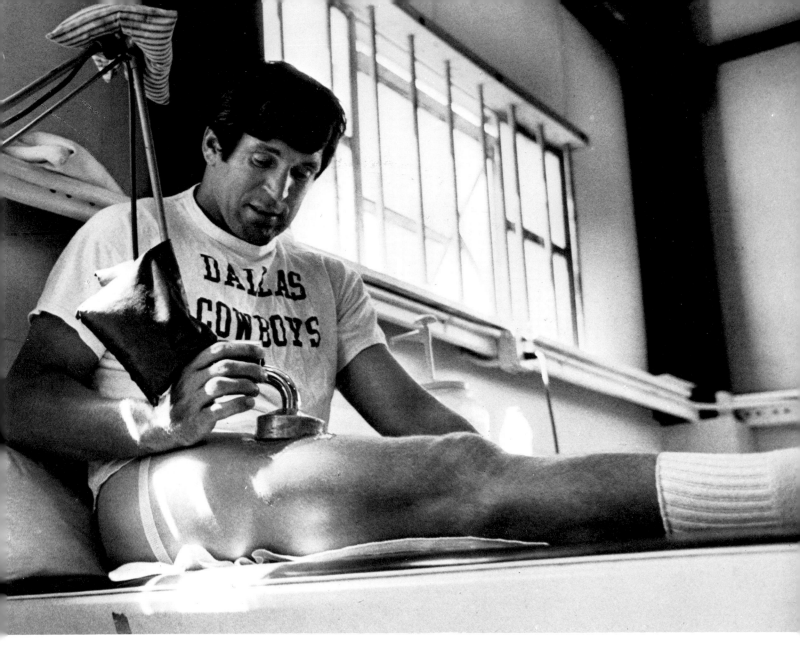

didn't do anything. He looked like a guy two weeks into training camp when everyone else has been there seven weeks." Actually, Concannon was just exactly that.

Landry had other problems in 1972. Early in August, the temperamental Duane Thomas was traded to San Diego for running back Mike Montgomery and wide receiver Billy Parks. Breaking in the new men held up Landry's team plans. So did injuries to running back Calvin Hill, flanker Lance Alworth, all-pro defensive end George Andrie (who had a back problem all summer long) and promising rookie defensive back Bill Thomas. Add the unfamiliarity with team plays of three all-star rookies who didn't report until July 29, and you have Landry's understated analysis that "all these things prevent you from executing real well. We will eventually. But it takes time."

From the point of view of assistant coaches,

training camp is a team's only chance to put together a complex attack and defense organization without worrying about next week's game. It's a time to experiment, teach, trade, test old injuries, see who's lost a step or gained a pound. Once league competition starts, you can't whistle back a play.

However reluctantly, players ultimately agree with this assessment. They know that for 18 out of 26 NFL teams their divisional finish out of the money will mean watching the dollar-rich play-offs on television instead of sharing in the long, fresh green reaped from the third season.

Pride, too, plays a big part. One seasoned safety with the Detroit Lions welcomes the challenge of training camp. "It's me against the system," he says quietly. "What all that gut-busting does, day after day, is give me the chance to go another round. I mean, if you let up on the drills or cut training camp to a couple of weeks, some bouncy kid will be playing

The Cowboys are in Thousand Oaks to get in shape for winning football, not for a rest cure.

in my place while I'm still unbuttoning my corset. No, I need all the work I can get to show I can do my job as well as anyone around, maybe even a bit better." Another veteran, a topflight San Francisco running back with impeccable field credentials and an off-season corporate job, has a psychological approach to camp: "People lay it on me when I'm not playing ball. My family, my boss, my friends—they all make demands on me, which is what life is all about, I suppose. But when training starts, I drop out of the home scene. I kiss my wife good-bye, put the kids in her care and tell my boss I won't be holding any more client meetings for a while. To me, training camp is a retreat, a chance to put my head together."

Rookies generally aren't so philosophical. "With all them cats out there on the field, how's a coach gonna get a line on what you can do?" one high draft choice despairs. "One guy I know came here same day I did, took his physical, ran ten laps, showered off and was let go before lunch!" Another first-year man boggles at the emphasis placed on drills: "How'm I goin' make the team kissin' grass? I'm number one in push-ups, but does that give me a fair shot at tight end? What I need is more contact work—hit, run an' catch. Only way I get that is for camp to last until Thanksgiving Day. I won't mind."

These disparate reactions to the first season are prevalent in all 26 NFL camps from Massachusetts to California. But nowhere, perhaps, are they more freely expressed than in the training camp of a team that has just come off a winning year, as the Dallas Cowboys did in January, 1972, when they were crowned champions of professional football.

Where It's At

Conejo Valley is a semi-arid rolling plain about an hour's northward drive by freeway from the Los Angeles International Airport. In Spanish *conejo* means rabbit, and early settlers dubbed the area "The Valley of the Rabbits" because of the hordes of cottontails and jacks that still infest the countryside. But during summers, it's better known as the "Valley of the Cowboys," after the Dallas club which for the past decade has been training near Thousand Oaks, California, in the heart of the valley.

Actual training site is California Lutheran College (CLC), a small, spankingly modern school whose green playing fields and well-watered lawns sparkle like emeralds among the sun-browned hills that cradle the campus. The weather is dry, with hot, sunny days and cool nights. A prevailing breeze blows in from the Pacific Ocean, some 20 miles to the west.

"If I *have* to suffer through training," one well-traveled Cowboy concedes, "let it be here. I've been to a half-dozen camps. The worst is where the Saints train, in Hattiesburg, Mississippi."

Life-style at Thousand Oaks for players, coaches and even president Tex Schramm is set by head coach Tom Landry, a quietly intense man who's been at the club's helm since its entry into the NFL in 1960. Easy to approach but difficult to know, his emotional barometer is hidden behind an eternally dour visage. "The Great Stone Face" is the way the team's official press guide puts it. But behind the facile portrait sketch is a warm, very human person, so soft-spoken that to stand upwind of him during a press conference is to risk losing his words.

In a sport where tempers flare and emotions range, Tom Landry retains a maddening composure even in defeat, though he hates to lose as much as any man in football. Conversely, his commitment to winning football is total, best exemplified by his club's 12-year struggle to reach the top after an initial year in the NFL in which the Cowboys did not win a single game. He's also a committed Christian, a practicing Methodist and an active supporter of evangelist Billy Graham.

Planning is Landry's bag, perfect play execution his goal. Toward this end he has a tendency to drive himself single-mindedly, apparently unaware of time or effort expended. Sportswriter Frank Luksa of the Dallas *Times Herald* quotes all-pro defensive tackle Bob Lilly on Tom Landry during a 1970 losing streak: "Coach Landry punished himself physically and mentally, working 20 hours a day. He was trying to make everything perfect. . . . I had the feeling he was trying to coach everybody." Luska, a frank observer of the Cowboy scene, then quotes Lilly on how his head coach, after a humiliating 38–0 loss to St. Louis in the middle of the 1970 season, eased up and delegated some of his field authority to his assistants. Landry then became, in Lilly's words, "the team coordinator, though he still worked 20 hours a day."

Coincidentally, that's when Dallas began to win consistently. Sweeping their next five league games, the Cowboys went all the way to the 1971 Super Bowl only to drop a 16–13 heartbreaker to Baltimore. They reached the Super Bowl again the following year, this time walking off with the championship as they walloped the Miami Dolphins, 24–3.

In the same interview, sportswriter Luksa himself provides what may well be the definitive personality profile of the man as well as the team: "One thing the Cowboys know about Landry . . . he feels motivation should come from within the individual player, not the head coach." This thoroughly mature approach pervades the Cowboy training camp at

Rooms are simply furnished. Simplicity extends to
dining facilities. There are diversions to
keep the players occupied. Walt Garrison whittles.

29

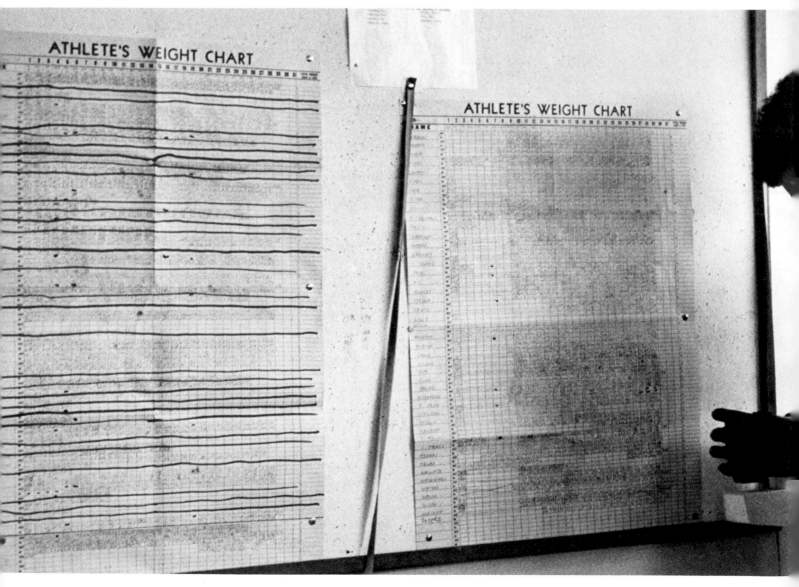

*All players are then put through a series of stamina
tests: a mile run against time, 40-yard sprints,
etc. That overweight players are also fined hurts even more.*

Thousand Oaks—in the daily schedule, in the workouts, at mealtimes, in the camp's facilities and in the
public image of Cowboy coaches and players. Landry
insists that there be minimum distraction during
camp, which he considers a time of constant learning and adjustment. Courteous to visitors and news-
men, he draws the line on activities that in his opinion disturb player concentration. Accordingly, he
places locker rooms, players' living quarters and
team meetings out of bounds to visitors, even to the
press, except on rare occasions. It's been said, with
some justification, that it's more difficult to get into
the Cowboy locker rooms at CLC than it is into the
Rockettes' dressing rooms at Radio City Music Hall.

Apparently, luxury is also a distraction to Landry. Living quarters in camp are Spartan. Everyone from Tex Schramm, club president and general
manager, to the lowest rookie beds down in a
large two-winged dormitory. As top VIP, Schramm
enjoys a two-room suite. Landry occupies a single
room, as do his assistants. Players live in one wing
of the dormitory, coaches and management staff in
the other. A large common room, used for general
team meetings and off-hour television viewing, separates the two wings. Curfew is inflexible—11 P.M.
except for Saturdays, when it extends to midnight.
Bed checks are the rule, not the exception, as are
morning roll calls. The dormitory also houses a communication center for news media, a press lounge,
a telephone switchboard, a mail drop and rooms for
small meetings and motion picture viewing of the
day's training activities.

All players sleep two in a room. Veterans may
choose their roommates; if they express no prefer-
ence, like positions room together—tackle with
tackle, guard with guard, back with back—on the
theory that such pairings encourage football homework. Rookies are assigned rooms in alphabetical
order without regard to position, size or color. Sometimes they may have to triple up, depending on the
camp's population. But no one complains. A first-year
man would sleep on a window ledge, if he had to,
just to stay on the roster.

You can't ring for bellboys or waiters in the
camp; there are none. A crew of college boys and
girls makes up the rooms and performs other house-
keeping chores. The dorm's population, except for
daytime hours, is all male. The rooms themselves
are simply furnished, as though Landry, an industrial
engineer by education, had designed them himself.
Furniture is contemporary dorm: hard, narrow beds;
pine dressers and built-in study desks plus whatever
amenities players can scrounge. Physical giants like

31

George Andrie and Ralph Neely rent oversize beds. The others do with what's available. Each suite of two rooms, uncarpeted and adjoining, are separated by a shower bath, a john, a couple of sinks and a large walk-in closet accessible from both sides. "Caesar's Palace it ain't," quips safety Cornell Green, resident expert on the good life. "But after a ton of workouts, it's home-sweet-home to me."

Simplicity extends to dining facilities. The entire Cowboy contingent eats in the student cafeteria, about a long-field-goal try from the dormitory. Everyone stands in the chow line—players, coaches, the administrative staff, even visiting VIP's—and carries his own tray to the table. There is segregation in the dining room—but in kind, not color. Veterans gen-

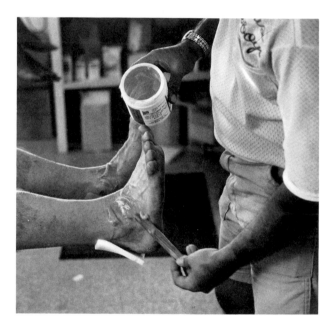

erally sit together, apart from the first-year men, whom they haze unmaliciously at meals, as in making the rookies stand and sing their alma mater songs. (But a rookie has yet to make the squad on the strength of either his singing ability or his performance at the annual rookie show, another camp tradition, in which he gets the chance to sling back a few barbs at the vets and coaches.) The food is robust and of high quality, with meat, vegetables, fruits, milk and desserts in abundance. Breakfasts are huge; lunches as big or as small as players want to make them; dinners are varied and ample, though hardly in the *cordon bleu* tradition. There's a "fat man's table" too, for those who must watch their calories.

But where the first season is really at for the Cowboys is on the playing fields of California Lutheran College. With a strong football program during the school year, CLC (some misled students call it "Jock A&M") boasts three superbly maintained athletic fields, a couple of running tracks, an outdoor apparatus area, a fenced-in weight-lifting yard and two large locker rooms. The purposeful manner in which players and coaches use these training facilities during the summer says it all: the Cowboys are in Thousand Oaks to get in shape for winning football, not for a rest cure.

Privilege and Penalty

As 1972 Super Bowl champs, the Cowboys earned the dubious privilege of facing the College All-Stars in the annual *Chicago Tribune* Charity Game July 28—dubious because a victory by the top NFL team is assumed. Anything less would be a calamity for the pros, which is exactly what happened in 1963, the last time the All-Stars whipped their big brothers, 21–17. The losing team? The Green Bay Packers, coached by Vince Lombardi. Cowboy cornerback Herb Adderley, then with the Packers, remembers that game well: "The press wouldn't let us forget it. Neither would Lombardi. He worked our tails off the rest of the year."

Tom Landry at the start of the 1972 campaign had no intention of letting such history repeat itself. He called for camp to open July 7, a week early. Except for the 3 draft choices on the all-star squad, all the rookies came first, almost 40 of them. Some 40 veterans came five days later; there was the usual scattering of holdout-late arrivals, including the moody and silent Duane Thomas, last year's Cowboy running star. With the All-Star Game less than three weeks off, Landry put the squad into high gear.

Cowboy camp begins with physicals for all players, a protective measure against team liability for old and hidden hurts. Roster pruning starts with the first suspicious X ray, the first substandard blood count. All players—veterans included—are then put through a series of stamina tests: a mile run against time, 40-yard sprints, chin-ups and weight lifting. Those who don't measure up are penalized with body-punishing drills aimed at shoring up muscles and trimming blubber. Like the public stocks of old, these penalties are posted for all to see. "Rodney Wallace, seven penalty days," reads a typical notice on the club's hot line in the dormitory main entrance.

Penalty periods consist of 20 minutes of nonstop calisthenics. Immediately after gruelling two-hour workouts, they're about as popular with players as jock itch. That overweights are also fined hurts even more. Safetyman Cornell Green drew a $50 fine

A typical camp day for the Cowboys begins with breakfast at 7:30, after which rookies report for taping; veterans get taped later, after they've read the news.

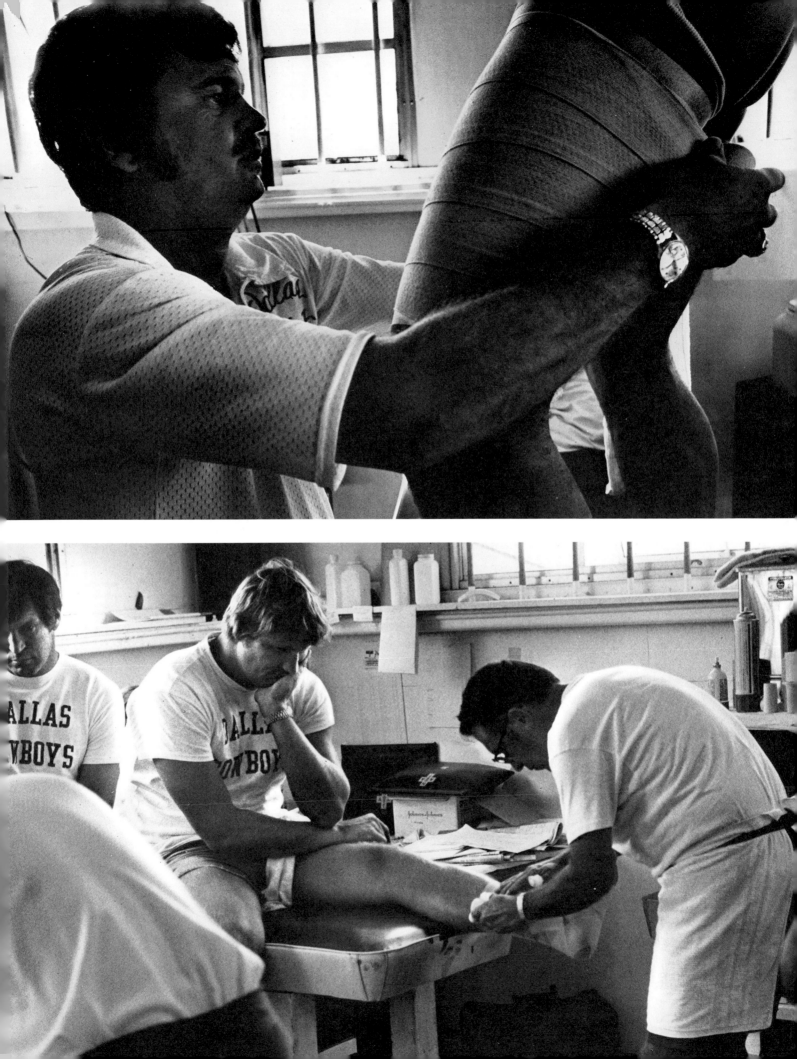

for reporting a pound over his 208 playing weight. "I'm now down to two-oh-five," he announced two weeks later. "At these rates, I figure the club owes me a hundred fifty bucks."

A typical camp day for the Cowboys begins with breakfast at 7:30, after which rookies report for taping; veterans get taped later, after they've read the financial news and sports pages. Following a general meeting and roll call at nine—anyone failing to show without permission is fined—the players head for adjoining locker rooms. There are two: one for the veterans, another for the rookies. Just so no one misses the point, there's a sign prominently displayed over the veterans' door: "Varsity Locker Room. No Rookies Allowed!"

Posted schedules give details on the uniform of the day. Full gear means helmet, pads, jerseys, pants and cleats—prelude to a heavy workout. Plastic jackets are mandatory for weight watchers. Sweats and sneakers mean a less strenuous routine. The offense wears white, the defense blue. Each player is assigned a number according to his position; veterans usually get the same number they had the year before.

By 10 A.M. all Cowboys except the halt and the lame are jogging around the quarter-mile track that rings the south practice field. Coaches too jog to guard against pulled muscles or worse. On the second day of camp, special teams coach Bobby Franklin, lacking a proper warm-up, broke an ankle demonstrating agility drills.

At 10:10 a blast from Landry's whistle lines up the squad for calisthenics. "Okay, left arm! Roll 'em forward . . . fifty times! One, two, three—" a voice barks. Assistant coaches take turns as drillmasters; sometimes team captains lead the exercises. That Landry himself goes through the paces accounts for his trim lines; he's no more than five pounds over the playing weight he maintained as a defensive back for the New York Giants in the fifties. "Hit the deck an' gimme a spread! Right leg . . . way out!" the drillmaster commands. Players flop in the grass, left legs doubled back, right legs stretched out. "Now

bend an' reach! Reach an' . . . hold it . . . hold it . . . hold it!" Executed in unison and to a count, grass drills resemble preparation for a ballet, if not the ballet itself.

Team-units drills are next. In front of the north goalposts, quarterbacks "hut!," fade and pass the ball under the direction of offensive backfield coach Dan Reeves, at 31 the youngest full-time assistant in the NFL. "Lead your man, Roger, lead your man!" he exhorts. "He'll get clobbered waiting for the ball!" A little way apart from the quarterbacks, offensive line coach Jim Myers puts behemoths like tackles Bob Asher and Ralph Neely, centers Dave Manders and John Fitzgerald and guards Blaine Nye and John Niland through their paces. You sense the field tilting under the ponderous charge; not a man on the Cowboy front line weighs under 245.

Meanwhile, some eight or nine defensive line candidates jump at the hoarse commands of line coach Ernie Stautner. In his late 40s and built along the proportions of a massive tree trunk, this Hall of Famer can still demonstrate how to charge past an opposing 260-pound lineman. "Like this," he explains to rookie Brian Goodman. "Get him low, like this— ur-rhunk!" You can hear the whack clear across the gridiron.

Similarly, defensive backfield candidates work out under coach Gene Stallings. At a sharp yelp— "left, deep an' out!"—individual cornerbacks snort and backpedal furiously to simulate pass-interception plays. Two remarkable actions catch the eye: the speed at which they cut and run backwards and the zap with which the 37-year-old Stallings can throw the football.

No one stands around except the spectators. Coach Ray Renfro works with the receivers, and

Bobby Franklin hobbles about in a cast, coaching the punters and place-kickers. Meanwhile, special assistants Ermel Allen and Sid Gillman give a hand where needed. Still another unit, made up of half a dozen rugged linebackers, performs under coach Jerry Tubbs, for eight years a middle linebacker for

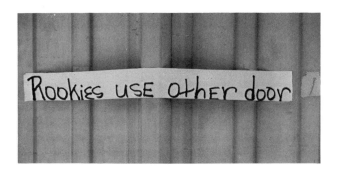

the Cowboys. Three of the current linebacking crew —Chuck Howley, Lee Roy Jordan and Dave Edwards —are his former teammates. It's not easy to be critical of old friends, but Tubbs doesn't mince words: "Ah called a red dawg, Chuck! What you doin' behind the line?"

Howley, a canny 14-year veteran but flagrantly out of position on the previous call, grins and puts it on. "Yo' Texas drawl, man! How you s'pose a West Virginny boy like me goin' dig that hog holler?"

The predominant language pattern among the Cowboys is pure Texan. Even Northerners like Stautner (raised in Albany, New York, attended Boston College and played for Pittsburgh), Dave Manders (a Milwaukeean) and Larry Cole (from Minnesota) speak with Texas accents. Among the veterans only Yale's Calvin Hill and Navy's Roger Staubach have resisted the drawl.

Unit activity continues under a warming sun. Moving in and out of the various groups, Landry, a golf cap protecting his balding head, seems to see everything on the field—from the booming punts of Marv Bateman to the deft defensive cuts of Mel Renfro—even when some action occurs out of his line of vision. "Sunavagun if he don't!" agrees Cowboy cameraman Bob Friedman, high atop the 40-foot tower from which he films the practice sessions. "Yesterday, while Tom was talking to Reeves about running keys, he asked me if I got a shot of Alworth doing down-and-outs. And dammit if his back wasn't to pass drills all along!"

Friedman has a precise schedule of what to shoot and when, worked out minute by minute and area by area by Landry himself. Later, in the coaches' quarters, the rushes are viewed and reviewed as the basis for the evening skull sessions or, more fatefully, for deciding who stays on the squad and who doesn't.

By 10:45 the various units, which have up to now been working in splendid isolation, converge. The day's practice sheet tells the story: end run force (defense); strongside drill, pass defense, POA (point of attack) for tackles, pass protection. (Pro football terms are among the most colorful in the English lan-

guage, their meanings equally so. For example, there's the *forearm shiver,* which the Cowboy playbook understates as "a method of neutralizing a block by delivering a blow with a forearm." There's the *banjo eye opener*—a "pass coverage between two or three defenders responsible for one, two or three receivers." And there's the poetic *jet call,* which takes place "any time outside linebacker has inside responsibility on run; no containment, flow away.") A whistle signals. For the first time that morning, football as a game becomes recognizable to the layman. Two uniformed elevens—one blue-shirted, the other white—face each other at midfield and put into team play the intricate maneuvers of the preceding hour.

"Hut one! Hut two! Hut, Hut!" The quarterback clutches the ball from the center, fades back, hands off or fakes or throws. Bodies clash. One blocking hit with both feet on the ground is all that's allowed, and players make the most of it. Tackling in dummy drills is forbidden. When a defensive man touches the ballcarrier, the play is whistled dead. To minimize the jarring effects of body contact, players on defense often wear large rubber pads fastened to their forearms. Sweaty and helmeted, standing their ground in the heat and dust of the simulated battlefield, they resemble nothing so much as shield-bearing Roman gladiators engaged in combat.

Meanwhile, on the sidelines players cheer their teammates on. "Way to go, Mel!" shouts a blue shirt at an interception. But when fullback Walt Garrison comes out of the backfield and muffs a pass, the raucous cry of "Oh, you sweet pea!" is heard from across the field. Nevertheless, field discipline prevails. When a player is removed from the lineup, he *runs* to the sidelines. His replacement *runs* in, whether for the first time or the twentieth. As another readiness reminder, no player dare drop his helmet during practice. If he does, it costs him $25.

The morning workout finally ends, not at 11:50, as expected, but 15 minutes later. "Weakside drill was off," Landry tells the coaches responsible for the execution. "Jerry, Wanda's not moving with the key. Meg had to shift over twice." The teams go over the maneuvers—again. Parenthetically, Wanda and Meg are not Cowboy concessions to women's liberation. They're names used by many pro teams to identify areas covered by the weakside linebacker (Wanda) and the middle linebacker (Meg). The strongside linebacker (Sara) covers that part of the offensive line which, having an extra man, is the stronger side.

Landry finally blows an end to the workout, but still it isn't over for the offensive squad, whose players have to wrestle with barbells and weights before they can shower. The defense is not being

overlooked; they go at the weights in the afternoon. When asked whether weight lifting might be less exhausting prior to workouts, Jethro Pugh, all 265 pounds of him braced under a 300-pound barbell, lets out a sweaty grunt and says, "Man, who wants to die *before* goin' out there!"

Other forms of camp punishment include the two-man and seven-man blocking sleds, heavy steel structures against which linemen charge with straining shoulders and churning legs. Running backs have their own torture instrument, the blaster, a set of padded tension bars, built much like swinging doors, that runners must literally blast through to get to the other side. "It teaches a man to run with his head down," coach Myers explains. "Otherwise the blaster gives him a friendly headache, even when he's wearing a helmet."

The knee-high rope maze is another challenger. Players run through it at top speed, placing one foot and then the other in the squares formed by tightly stretched ropes. Nimble defensive backs take the maze in stride; even Tody Smith, at 6-5 and 245, runs through it with amazing grace. Not so Rodney Wallace. At 6-5 and obviously overweight, he stumbles over the ropes and crashes painfully to the ground. Usually, a practice goof like this is good for laughs from teammates eager for any diversion. But when Rodney falls, there are only murmurs of sympathy for the big guard candidate.

"Right on, Rod!"
"Get 'im, stud!"
"Give it a go!"

Nobody laughs because Rodney Wallace, only 23 and in his second year with the Cowboys, is in the painful throes of a comeback. "Is he ever!" agrees Dick Mansperger, director of Cowboy player personnel. "He was at two eighty-six, thirty pounds over his playing weight. Doc Knight [team physician] put

Two uniformed elevens—one blue-shirted, the other white—face each other at midfield and put into team play the intricate maneuvers of the preceding hour.

him on a diet of tea, toast, dry meat and juice. Period. And the coaches piled it on with double penalty drills. Maybe too much, because after a couple of days of this, Rod up and quit camp."

But the Cowboys didn't quit on Rod. They sent a scout to find him, and three days later the beefy youngster was back in camp. "I told the coach I was ready to work," Wallace recalls, with only a slight shudder. "Diet, penalty periods, fines and all. The first day back, they assign me to pass blockin' the whole defensive line—alone. Then they make me run a quarter, then some wind sprints. A half-hour into practice, I'm ready to faint."

Just before the All-Star Game, Rodney Wallace,

of wives in camp on the theory that domesticity and down-and-outs don't mix, not when a man is struggling for his football life. Another drawback is the hours. With two workouts a day and skull sessions that last until 9:30 or 10 P.M., a man has little time, and probably less energy, for marital pleasures. At best, he may settle for a quick fly-in visit from his wife—provided that he's still on the roster by the time she gets there.

The absence (or presence) of sex partners seems to be less of a problem for bachelors and rovers who, whether in camp or on game trips, manage to keep lines of communications with local females open. Conveniently, training camps act as sexual magnets,

weight down to 270, has his 255-pound goal well in view. "I'm gonna make it, too," he says quietly. "Or else go back to bein' a janitor, which would make me look pretty stupid. You don't see many guys my size pushin' brooms around."

Diversions

Take 60 or 70 superbly conditioned young men. Work them hard and continuously. Confine them in semi-isolation for as long as two months. Segregate them during this time from their wives and/or girl friends. Guess the number-one topic of conversation.

One practical idea, it would seem, would be for married players to bring their wives to camp. Of the 43 Cowboy veterans listed in the initial 1972 press guide, 35 are married, and most have children. But the Cowboy management discourages the presence

drawing to the scene scores of attractive young women. These camp followers sit in the stands during practice sessions or wander along the fringes of the field, raising their siren voices just loud enough to be overheard by players supposedly preoccupied with blitz dogs and area clues. Their knowledge of plays and players is often acute. At one scrimmage, a straight-haired, blue-jeaned, braless girl, watching a receiver muff a pass thrown directly to him, remarked with some bitterness, "I think that's the first time he's ever dropped anything he got his hands on!"

The players themselves try to be circumspect, at least during duty hours. At Thousand Oaks they're warned against fraternizing with college coeds working on campus, but there's no rule against signing their autograph books, even if "Alfredo's 9 P.M. Sat." appears as part of their signatures. "We're sup-

In the coaches' quarters the rushes are viewed and reviewed as the basis for the evening skull session or, more fatefully, for deciding who stays on the squad and who doesn't.

posed to oblige all fan requests for autographs," one rookie says with a straight face.

In pro football, as in any other sport where whites and blacks mix freely, sex and race are very much in tandem. In camp, when it's a question of a night out or casing local rock joints for fun and games, black players will usually band with blacks and whites with whites, although sometimes an interracial group will do the town together. When this happens, it's no big deal. Anyone who makes it one, pro or con, draws more attention to himself than to the event.

Besides, there are diversions other than girls to keep the players sufficiently occupied. Card games, when there's time, abound. Television offers a variety of sports shows. Many players read, Walt Garrison whittles and a few play chess. In fact, the Spassky-Fischer match drew intense interest, perhaps because football players, like most athletes, relate other confrontations to their own sport. Coming off the playing field one day after a murderous afternoon workout, sweat dripping from their dirt-caked faces, Calvin Hill and Blaine Nye argued the finer points of the previous day's World Championship chess match.

"Never," Hill insisted. "Spassky should never have played queen to bishop two. It's like leaving a running back open while you're covering an ineligible receiver. It'll kill you every time."

The Long Voyage Home

The odds that a rookie will survive the training period and make the team are discouragingly low. The odds that a rookie free agent—one invited to camp without being drafted—will do the same are awesomely low. Of the 37 rookie Cowboys on the 1972 roster, 15 were draftees. The other 22 were free agents. Of the latter, only one—Benny Barnes,

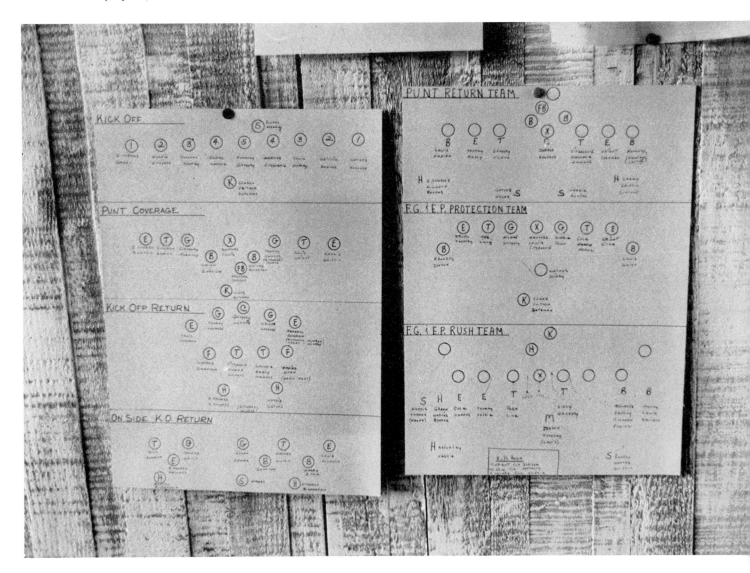

The morning workout finally ends, not at 11:50 as expected but 15 minutes later. "Weakside drill was off," Landry tells the coaches responsible. "Jerry, Wanda's not moving with the key."

a cornerback from Stanford University—survived.

The mathematics of the situation for all NFL clubs work out something like this (the dates are for 1972):

By August 6 a club must cut its roster to 60 players from whatever the figure was at the start of training camp.

By August 29 this number must be further reduced to 49.

By September 4—to 44.

And by the week of September 11, just before the first league game, no NFL squad may carry more than 47 players—40 on the varsity plus 7 reserves, the so-called taxi squad from which players can be moved back and forth. Even here there is restriction: a club is allowed to make only 12 moves for the entire playing season.

What, then, are the determinants which decide which rookies stay and which are cut?

"Size, speed, ability, intelligence, yes, even attitude," says Dick Mansperger, player personnel director for the Cowboys. "If, in the opinion of the coaching staff, a rookie lacks one or more of these pro football essentials, we have to let him go sooner or later." Disappointment at being released, according to Mansperger, is often softened by the fact that first-year men know all along how slim their chances are, not only because of sheer numbers but also because "deep down they know they don't have the total equipment to make it with the pros. Some

departing rookies thank us for having given them a tryout. Others leave obviously hurt, but silent. Some break down. This year only one of them cried. A few bitch it out."

Bobby Smith neither cried nor bitched. A free agent cornerback candidate from New Mexico State with a large 38 on the back of his blue jersey, the 23-year-old Smith must have known his hours in camp were numbered when, a few days before the All-Star Game, he was sent behind the end zone to retrieve field goal attempts, a task usually assigned to ballboys. The next day, defensive backfield coach Gene Stallings called him aside. "Coach Landry wants to see you," Stallings said. "And bring your playbook."

The playbook is the umbilical cord that ties a player to the squad. To take it away is to sever him from the mother club. That's one camp job nobody wants. After an exit interview with Landry, who always makes it a point to talk to departing players, Bobby's next stop was the medical office, where he was given an outgoing physical. The last club official he saw was Joe Bailey, the team's business manager. The failed rookie stepped into Bailey's office, his bags packed, his face as long as the dormitory corridor from where he had just come.

"Hi, Bobby." Bailey's greeting was subdued. "Let me have your forwarding address, okay? You got a copy of this?" The business manager reached for a W-2 form. As a free agent, Smith had been

signed for the minimum $10,000-a-year salary. Sadly for him, his job lasted just a little over two weeks. ". . . so the balance of your salary comes to ninety-three forty, right?" the business manager said.

The response was barely audible. "Seventy-eight sixty-four, after taxes."

"Sure, after taxes. Now here's your plane ticket home . . . we got the right airport?"

An answering nod.

"And cash allowance for ground transportation from the airport to your home. Sign right here, Bobby."

In the silence of pre-parting, the ball-point pen scratching on the piece of paper sounded like an express train tearing through the office.

"Now, one more receipt, Bobby. Team owes you for two days per diem at thirteen forty-two per. Want it in cash? Fine."

The money changed hands. The ceremony, old and familiar to Bailey, new and painful to Smith, was almost over. There remained only the final obligatory question. "What do you plan to do now, Bobby?"

The shoulders squared perceptibly. "Gonna

teach if I can. Got my certification in physical ed. I'm gettin' a tryout—" He paused, wincing quickly at his "slip." "An *interview* with the board of education in Pomona tomorrow."

Bailey got up, smiling encouragement, shaking hands. "Good luck, Bobby."

"Yeah, thanks." The ex-rookie stopped at the door. "And good luck to you all against the All-Stars." Then he was gone, walking down the narrow hall, out the back door and into the waiting airport car for the start of his long voyage home.

According to Mansperger, not all rookies wait for the club to cut them. "Some do it on their own. Take Mixon Robinson, a big tight end from Georgia, where he ran up a three point six average as a pre-med. He cornered Tom Landry one day and asked right out if he had a chance to make the squad. Landry answered he didn't think so. With nine receivers in camp, seven of them veterans, it didn't look good for Robinson. But the coach said he'd put in a good word for him with another team.

" 'No, thanks, Mr. Landry,' the kid answers, 'I'll

Like positions room together—tackle with tackle, guard with guard, back with back—on the theory that such pairings encourage homework.

play for the Cowboys or nobody. You've made my decision easier. I'm going on to med school. Thanks for the tryout.' "

Mansperger pulls on his cigar. "That kid's gonna be a helluva doctor someday," he says. "Letting him go may have been one of the best decisions the Cowboys ever made."

One first-year free agent who came close to making the squad was Maury Daigneau, a quarterback from Northwestern. He seemed to have everything going for him—size, speed, intelligence, a good arm and purpose. After surviving the first cut on August 6, Daigneau found himself one of only three quarterbacks in camp, right behind starter Roger Staubach and backup Craig Morton.

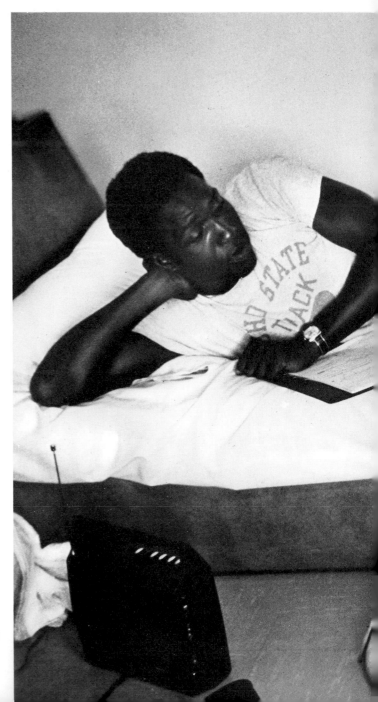

Then, on August 12, the shoulder injury that put Staubach in the hospital boosted Daigneau's chances sky high—a case of one man's tragedy serving as another man's potential triumph. Overnight, the rookie from Northwestern found himself in contention for the number-two quarterback slot. The other man being considered for the job was coaching assistant Danny Reeves, who had filled that post the year before as a player-coach. However, Danny's knees are crisscrossed with scars from half-a-dozen knee operations; his legs are in even worse shape than Morton's.

The Cowboy management weighed the dilemma: to go with Morton as starting quarterback and take a chance with an untested rookie behind him, or to activate a tough, smart, but near-crippled coaching assistant as backup? "We had one more choice," Dick Mansperger points out, "and we took it. We signed nine-year quarterback John Concannon, who'd played out his option with the Chicago Bears. We also prayed for Staubach to heal fast and get back in the lineup." With Concannon's arrival, there was no place for the rookie quarterback on the Cowboy roster. Cut on August 29 after almost two months with the club, Daigneau returned home to Evanston, Illinois, to become a stockbroker—and to prepare for his forthcoming marriage, to take place in January, just before Super Bowl VII.

Not all the heartbreak in camp belongs to rookies. Veterans too have their share, made all the more poignant by records and relationships built up over

the years. At the end of the 1972 training season, Lee Roy Caffey, an all-pro linebacker who had come to the Cowboys in a trade the previous year and helped them to an 11–3 season and a Super Bowl victory, was placed on waivers. At 32, the 10-year veteran, who had played in four NFL championships and three Super Bowls, was perilously close to the end of his career. Another veteran, 33-year-old George Andrie, for 11 years a stalwart on the Cowboy defensive line but hampered by a bad back for the last 3, was moved to the taxi squad just before league play started, his place on the varsity taken by Pat Toomay, 8 years his junior.

Jack Concannon, who had come to the Cowboys with such high hopes only a few weeks earlier, failed to adjust quickly enough to their multiple offense and was also taxied. Player-coach Dan Reeves replaced him. Two other veterans—field-goal kicker Mike Clark, a 10-year veteran who had scored over 1,000 points for three NFL teams, 720 of them for the Cowboys, and punter Ron Widby, a 5-year team regular—were traded. What hurt Clark particularly was moving from a title contender to Buffalo, a team considered to have no chance for the play-offs. To make the trade even more painful, Clark broke an arm during his first exhibition game with the new team.

Most tragic of all, perhaps, was the defection of Duane Thomas, an explosive runner who, in the opinion of many pro football observers, combined the power of Jimmy Brown with the speed of Gale Sayers. Moody, unpredictable and uncommunicative, Thomas reported late to Thousand Oaks, remained in self-imposed Coventry, and was traded to the San Diego Chargers midway in the training season. "He has such great talent," Tom Landry said upon being informed that Thomas might not play again. "He could do great things for himself and his family if he played. That's the tragedy of the whole thing . . ."

Still, there's more to the first season than disappointments, injuries, defections and the physical agony of getting into shape. For the players—those who make the squad—training camp is a taste of the good life to come, a prelude to team camaraderie that grows with the playing year, a sense of belonging to a well-primed unit which has an attainable goal in view: victory and all it can mean in prestige and money, both in and out of football.

Even for those who fail—by actual count more than half who reported to training camp didn't survive the final cut—it may be solace enough to be able to say, "I had a tryout with the Dallas Cowboys."

*He was gone, walking down the narrow hall,
out the back door and into the waiting airport car
for the start of his long trip home.*

3

A LONG WAY BACK TO THE BENCH

by Lee Hutson

There are some 1,400 professional football players. They form an exclusive club. Many of them feel, as Sammy Baugh did, that they have "the best job on earth."

There are no easy positions and no job security. There is always some young bull looking to replace you. There is the constant threat of injury and, the knowledge that you'll only be around a few years.

Still, almost without exception, the men who play the game do so because they love it.

This chapter takes a good look at the positions and the men who play them. It is not a "how to," nor is it a treatise on the human condition. But it is an attempt to discover what it takes to play pro football as seen through the eyes of the players and coaches. An offensive tackle, for example, is only the barest microcosm of man and sport. But anyone who has seen a professional offensive tackle walk off the field after a game, watched him unwrap his soiled and bloodied body and looked into his eyes—anyone who has done this knows that he has witnessed a testimony to struggle and a tribute to spirit.

THE HEAT MEN:
Defensive Linemen

A professional football coach once said, "If a rookie lineman walks into my office and starts out by saying 'Excuse me, sir,' I put him down for offense. On the other hand, if he strolls in, puts one foot on my desk and spits on the floor, I figure him for defense."

What differentiates the men, particularly the linemen, who play on offense from those who perform for the defense? Temperamentally, defensive linemen are just not as polite as offensive linemen; some would go as far as to call them mean. "Yeah, I guess so," agrees former Detroit Lion defensive tackle Alex Karras. "But what the hell, it was my living, and we weren't out there to play patty-cake." The four men up front on defense work in an area affectionately called "The Pit." No less an authority than Joe Willie Namath has said that the modern game has evolved into a basic struggle between the quarterback and the front four. This may smack of oversimplification, but the fact remains that in the last decade the defensive lineman has emerged as a star of the first rank. And it has also been said that football in the National Football League is a game of defense—and defense, without question, begins with the front four.

What, then, does it take for a man to play defensive tackle or defensive end in the National Football League?

"There is no simple yardstick," says Jack Patera, the defensive line coach of the Minnesota Vikings who formerly coached the Los Angeles Rams' front four (the "Fearsome Foursome") and played for the Baltimore Colts during the middle fifties, when the Colts' mammoth defense tormented and dominated the league. "There is an awful lot to it . . . more than meets the eye," Patera adds.

What usually meets the eye is a large man thrashing and slashing his way to the quarterback. When he succeeds and the quarterback is sacked, you

"When you play a Deacon Jones or a Rich Jackson or a Carl Eller, you know they'll be just as mean and just as tough in the fourth quarter as in the first."

have seen one of football's spectacular plays. But there is much more to playing the defensive line than the attention-getting grabs at the passer. The front four must absorb the initial blow of the offense. They must shut down the run and unsettle, if not stop, the pass. They attack the inner machinery of an offense —the blocking patterns—and an outstanding defensive line can control a game by destroying the opposition from the inside out.

"There was a time," says Patera, "when the primary emphasis in considering a defensive line prospect was on his size. A trend was created when people saw what a man like Big Daddy Lipscomb could singlehandedly do to any offense . . . and everyone—scouts, coaches and fans—all thought that in order to play a defensive line position, you had to be a giant."

Pro football's single-minded pursuit of giants to play defense turned up some wonderful football players—huge men who were also gifted athletes. It also brought in hundreds of big rookies who left camp a short time after the first dummy drill.

"What we look for now," Patera continues, "is a man who 'plays big.' Men like Alan Page on our team or John Elliott of the New York Jets or Cincinnati's Mike Reid. These are not especially large men, not in the context of professional football players. Page plays at two forty-five, and I believe Elliott and Reid are about the same. What we care about is whether or not the man is big enough to control his area on the line of scrimmage. If he can do that, he's big enough."

A candidate for a professional front four needs strength and stamina. "The great defensive ends," says Oakland offensive tackle Bob Brown, "are the

ones that keep coming. When you play a Deacon Jones or a Rich Jackson or a Carl Eller, you know they'll be just as mean and just as tough in the fourth quarter as they were in the first."

A defensive tackle or defensive end, to be good, must be quick. "Hell, I'm bigger by twenty or thirty pounds than just about anybody I go against," says Buck Buchanan, the Kansas City Chiefs' 6-foot 7-inch, 280-pound tackle. "And sometimes I'll go straight at them just to let them know I'm there. But there's no way I can count on overpowering my man. Just no way. Those dudes are big, and they're strong, and the good ones are smart. They're foxy. Try to overpower them every time and they'll either cross-block or trap you to death.

"I take pride in my quickness. No one makes all-pro if he's not quick. I give head fakes and shoulder

fakes. Fake left and zoom, I'm gone to the right. 'Course, you do some grabbing and slapping, but you've got to be quick."

Straight-ahead speed is fine, but for defense, the key is quickness. Quickness has replaced bulk as a defensive lineman's essential physical asset.

The lineman's stance has been refined over the years into a picture of dynamic grace. There was a time—lasting about three decades, in fact—when defensive linemen used to arrange themselves like so many frogs waiting for a fly. It was head up, tail down and aesthetics be damned. The most burning question was which tackle to run at. It was slam, slam, slam into the ruck at the tackle hole, and if you didn't make 10 yards, which you usually didn't, that was okay because you'd just punt and let the other guy try his luck, knowing that he probably wouldn't make it either. It was a game calling on big men, the bigger the better, assembled shoulder to shoulder along a line six, seven or even eight men wide.

Today, the defensive lineman takes a sprinter's stance. His tail is high, and his weight is forward of his body's center of gravity. In the old stance a player's first move was to raise his head. In the new stance his first move is straight ahead at full speed. This is the era of the attacking defense.

For most teams defense is a matter of attacking while reading the offense while retaining the ability to react. It is a combination of ingredients that makes experience so valuable for a defensive lineman. The more experienced he is, the closer to the line of scrimmage he can line up. A rookie may tend to charge too fast and get too far into the opponent's backfield before he understands the play. It is better for him to line up a yard or so off the ball and give himself more time. A veteran, because he can "read" faster, can afford to crowd the ball, thus bringing himself closer to the play before the snap and, just as important, reducing the blocking angle for the offensive lineman.

As each play unfolds, the two lines pound together. In practice all week long, coaches in every pro camp shout, beg, swear, promise and threaten, all in a never-ending effort to get their linemen—on offense and defense—off with the snap of the ball because, when the two lines come together, it is the lineman who gets across the scrimmage area first who enjoys the advantage.

A good defensive lineman charges into his blocker low and hard. He attempts to get underneath the blocker's shoulder pads and win the individual battle by assuming the position of greater leverage. At the least, he must stalemate the blocker. At the worst, he is turned and levered out of the way. A defensive lineman can never let up, for if he does, he will be blown out of the play. One of the most typical of rookie mistakes is the attempt to shed every block and make every tackle. What the rookie must do is to learn to control his instincts, curb his zest and remember that his most important job is not making the tackle but controlling his particular area of the scrimmage line.

In a good defense each man up and down the line controls his area and leaves problems in other areas up to the people who are responsible for them. Of course, his greatest delight is in tackling the passer. The only trouble with smashing a quarterback before he can get the ball off, as far as the defense is concerned, is that it doesn't happen often enough. The best rush lines in the game only garner 45 to 50 sacks a year, and the average line gets closer to 30.

But the important statistic in rushing the passer is not how often you dump him. As pointed out, the best rush line will manage to tackle the quarterback only three or four times a game. The big idea is to pressure him. Hurry him. Scare him, if you can. Foul up his timing. "We're the heat men," says Deacon Jones. "We put the heat on . . . that's our job."

"A defensive lineman's job," says Patera, "is to collapse the quarterback's pocket and crowd him into inaccuracy." Patera doesn't take much stock in a lot of faking and "juking" along the line. His theory is that from the snap his man should be off the ball and pressuring, pressuring, pressuring everything back into the quarterback's face.

A pass rusher does not have a great deal of room in which to work. There is an imaginary "lane" about two yards wide in which he can maneuver on his way to the quarterback. If a defensive end, for example, leaves his lane to get around his blocker, he will either stumble over a teammate beside him or circle out so

As each play unfolds, the two lines pound together. When they come together, it is the lineman who gets across the scrimmage area first who enjoys the advantage.

wide that he can't get to the quarterback in time. Forrest Gregg, when he was with Green Bay, and Ron Mix, when he was with San Diego, come quickly to mind as offensive tackles who were masters at riding the defensive end wide to the outside.

The rusher must also live with the knowledge that even when he beats his blocker, he'll probably pick up another one. Both running backs and the center are often assigned to pick up rushers who have broken free. Rushing the passer is a tough business. Deacon Jones says that there are times when teams will assign four men to block him. "It can get discouraging," Jones says. "But you have to remember that you are tying up several guys, and one of your teammates is probably going to be no worse off than one-on-one. And when a defensive lineman is one-on-one with an offensive lineman, the man on defense is going to win. At least he should."

It is also the job of the defensive line to shut down the run. The oldest shell game in offensive football is the choice between running and passing, and the defensive lineman must recognize almost instantly which one he is facing. Is it a pass, or is it a run? Is it a draw, or is it a screen?

The defensive lineman makes his decision by "reading." He "reads" the motion of the play, usually watching the man in front of him. The man he watches is known as his "key." It is an intricate assignment, and it takes experience as well as ability. "The first couple of years I was in this league, they handled me like a baby," says Deacon Jones, the man who was voted defensive player of the decade. "I didn't know what in the hell I was doing. I was big and strong and faster than anyone near to my size, and still they handled me. It was embarrassing."

Most coaches agree that a defensive lineman must learn to play the run before he can become an effective pass rusher. It often happens that a rookie coming into the league is, like Jones, big and fast and strong and not the least bit bashful. He probably puts his foot on the coach's desk and spits on the floor. And he's heard and read where, in the pros, rushing the passer is the whole ball game. So he works on his fakes and his slaps and thinks that he's ready to dismember any passer. Then, in the first scrimmage, the quarterback runs the ball right at him, traps him, sweeps him and screens him, and by the time the first real pass is thrown, the rookie can't get off the line of scrimmage because he's too worried about what the run has been doing to him.

Developing instantaneous response to the various patterns of run blocking usually takes several years of experience. But when the learning is complete, a good defender is so sensitive to the move-

For most teams defense is a matter of attacking while
reading while reacting. It is this combination of
ingredients that makes experience so valuable to linemen.

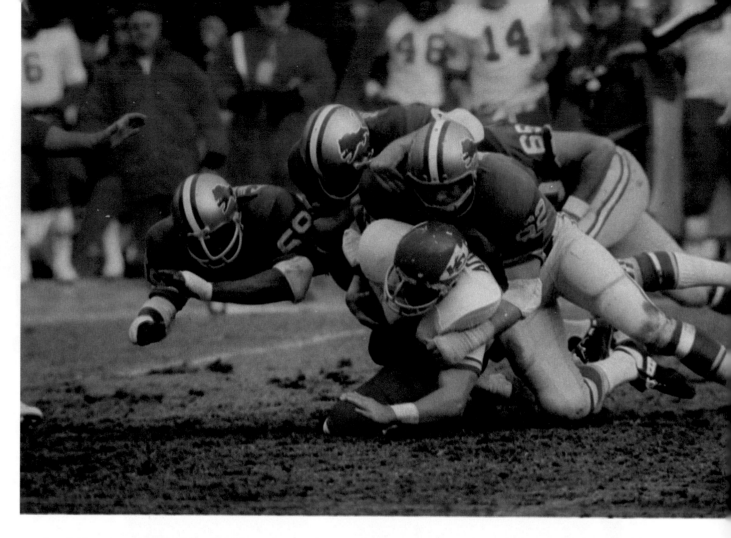

ments of his opponents that he functions automatically. A successful defensive line has more going for it than just four able and well-trained athletes. It has four men who function in coordinated response to every offensive gesture, no matter how subtle.

Ray Jacobs was never an all-pro. He played for the Houston Oilers, the Denver Broncos and the Miami Dolphins. In 1967, he was voted the Dolphins' outstanding lineman. Jacobs was a strong tackle who, by his own admission, spent too many of his early years "just knocking the hell out of people," without fully understanding why. "After a while, though," Jacobs says, "I got on to reading, and suddenly everything became more fun. It was more fun because I was better.

"It's a lot of little things. Some guards lean forward more when they're going to blast you for a run or when they're going to pull. On the other hand, some of them tend to sit back more when they're going to pass block. Those are little things, but they sure as hell help."

"Some offensive linemen will try to 'influence block,'" says Merlin Olsen, the perennial all-pro tackle of the Los Angeles Rams. "They try and push you left, knowing that you'll push back to the right. When you do, they'll let you because they wanted

you over to the right all along. Very clever, some of those guards. Very, very clever."

"You know, I played defensive end for eighteen years in the pros," says Doug Atkins. "It's not the same as being a kicker or a backup quarterback. At defensive end if you don't cut it, you're on your butt in a hurry. I loved it. When I was young, I was big and strong and never got tired, and I had a helluva good time. Later, say after ten or twelve years, I probably slowed down a bit, but I was so much smarter. You don't have to be too awful fast to do your job if you're smart. It was still fun . . . more fun in some ways. I only kept at it as long as I did because it was fun . . . and because I couldn't make that kind of money anywhere else . . . and because I loved the life . . . and because it sure beat working for a living."

"One of the best things about coaching defensive linemen," Patera says, "is that, as a group, they have more fun. They are a different personality type than, say, offensive linemen. They aren't as disciplined . . . not only as football players but as men. They tend to be free-spirited. And on the defensive line there is more opportunity for personal expression. A man can innovate a little more, free-lance somewhat, where the offensive lineman doesn't dare. In some ways it's tougher to play offense."

60

A defensive lineman can never let up,
for if he does, he will be blown
out of the play. His most important
job is not making the tackle but
controlling his area of scrimmage line.

A MATTER OF PRIDE:
Offensive Linemen

"You damn right it's tougher to play offense," says Oakland's Ron Mix, who, during his 10 years with the Chargers, was the premier offensive lineman in the American Football League. "And the thing that gets to you is that no one seems to know how tough it is, and you almost never enjoy the popular recognition of a quarterback or a runner or a defensive lineman."

It has been said that when a man wants to hide out in this country, there is no better place than in the offensive line of pro football. Let him become an offensive tackle, guard or center, and odds are, no one will ever know who he is. The lack of acclaim and recognition is curious. When you consider the importance of the quarterback, and then consider the importance of the front four in their peculiar and homicidal relationship to him, it seems incredible that the offensive line—the only thing separating the precious quarterback from the rapacious front four— should go so unrecognized.

It is also the offensive line, or the front five, that escorts runners on sweeps, takes a beating to create running room up the middle, unselfishly protects the high-priced offensive stars and takes much of the blame when something goes wrong. "It's frustrating," summarizes Walt Sweeney, San Diego's all-pro guard.

Frustrating, indeed. How, then, does a coach keep up the spirit on an offensive line when, all around, the other players are making more money and receiving greater acclaim? How does a coach motivate, let's say, an offensive tackle?

Joe Madro is the offensive line coach of the Houston Oilers. Before that, he coached the offensive line in San Diego, and before that, he coached for the Rams. He's been in pro football a long time, and he is a matter-of-fact sort of fellow. "I tell my men," says Joe, "to look around. I tell them they're lucky to be offensive linemen. There are five offensive linemen.

It seems incredible that the offensive line—the only thing separating the precious quarterback from the rapacious front four—should go so unrecognized.

That gives my men five chances for a starting job on a team in the National Football League. Okay, so they aren't the quarterback or the fullback or some of those guys who get all the press and the big bucks. I tell them this: 'First off, if you think you can play quarterback or flanker or halfback, then go try. Quit wasting my time and go try. Tell the quarterback coach that you think you can beat out Roman Gabriel or John Hadl or our kid here, Pastorini.' Well, of course, they can't. Then I tell them to look at how long an offensive lineman can last. If he's good and takes care of himself and has a little luck, he can play ten, twelve, even fifteen years. Now except for quarterbacks and place-kickers, who can play that long? So I tell them to stop worrying and start learning their profession."

Bob Reynolds is in his second decade as an offensive tackle for the St. Louis Cardinals. He is one of the best. "Nobody ever sees an offensive tackle," Reynolds says. "The center gets to run out there over the ball. The guards pull on sweeps. But the tackles, man, nobody ever notices the tackles. It's a funky situation. You just have to learn to live with it."

The offensive lineman conducts his own personal war. For him it is a matter of pride. "I know," says Sweeney, "that when I go up against a tackle like Merlin Olsen, I am in for a very rough afternoon. I know Olsen is strong, smart, experienced. I know he is the complete football player. No weaknesses. So I am challenged. I want Merlin to respect me. It's a matter of pride.

"The coaches want you to take game films home, watch your man, pick up some pointers. I hate to do it. I almost never do it. If I'm going to play an Olsen, I don't need any film. Watching him could scare a man. I just need to think about it. About playing him. All week, I think about it, and it builds. If I time it right, I'm ready by the day of the game. Ready, hell— I'm obsessed."

"Every player has his own way of getting ready," Madro says. "Sweeney has so much natural ability that he doesn't need to do what a man of lesser ability may have to do. I used to coach Sweeney, and I know he hates to study. But I also know he'll be ready to play when I need him.

"The greatest I ever saw for getting himself prepared was Ron Mix. He was absolutely fantastic. Before a game, he would sit in the locker room and just stare at the floor. For a long time he'd sit there, silent and staring. Then he'd get up and go out onto the field, and no man was ever more ready than Mix. He has a great mind, and his concentration is amazing. I never did know what he thought about, but it worked. I nicknamed him 'Intellectual Assassin.' "

"The center gets to run out there over the ball. The guards pull on sweeps. But the tackles, man, nobody ever notices the tackles. It's a funky situation."

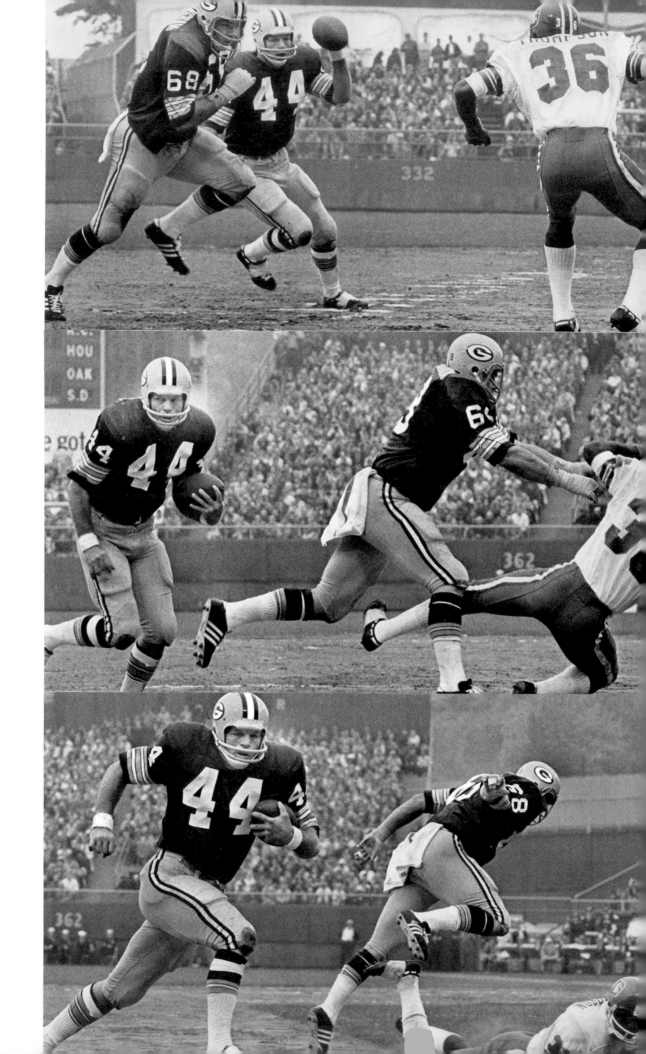

Mix believes that you have to think in order to survive on the offensive line. "You have to concentrate," he says. "The defensive lineman has every advantage but one. He can use his hands and slap and move around and all that. But you know where the play is going. You have to use that knowledge. You have to be thinking out there. And you have to stay cool. It's easy to lose your temper when some guy who weighs two hundred and sixty pounds is beating on your head and you can't beat back."

Offensive line play is more given to technique than is defensive line play. As long as an offensive linemen meets the minimum requirements of size, strength and body balance, he can pretty much think his way through a game. There are many fine tackles, guards and centers playing the game today who struggled for years before they came into their own. Charlie Cowan and Joe Scibelli lead a first-rate offensive line in Los Angeles. Both men are Pro Bowl performers. Both have been in the league over 10 years. But when they were rookies and sophomores, they were part of what was generally considered one of pro football's worst offensive lines. Ten years later, with some of their physical skills no doubt tarnished, both the men and their line are superior.

Another example of the cerebral tackle is Ernie McMillan of St. Louis. Tall and slim for a lineman, McMillan doesn't have the bulk or the pure strength usually associated with a tackle. But he is many times an all-pro. "Ernie may have less pure physical talent than any other star in the league," says Bob Reynolds, McMillan's teammate and friend. "But he is a master. Nobody can pass block any better than Ernie. He does the job with his mind. He has shown me that mental preparation is the most important part of offensive football."

When McMillan talks about his blocking techniques, the discussion sounds a little like a lesson in applied geometry. His key phrases include "center of gravity," "body control" and "efficient angles." When he translates these concepts into an on-the-field performance, the results are nearly perfect. One season, his coaches graded him an astounding 96 percent on pass-blocking—he performed 415 successful blocks in 430 attempts.

But even among offensive linemen, there are those who rely less on technique than on confidence in their ability to match strength with any man and line. Gale Gillingham, the Green Bay Packers' fine guard, is one such lineman, and Bob Brown, Oakland's giant tackle, is another.

"I try to overpower my man," says Gillingham. "I try to stick my helmet under his chin and move him back. He doesn't have to get past me to win, he

"His job is to penetrate, and my job is to stop him. I am not prepared, emotionally or in any other way, to stand there and let some big dude beat up on me."

only has to push me backward a yard or two. His job is to penetrate, and my job is to stop him. I am not prepared, emotionally or in any other way, to stand there and let some big dude beat up on me. I go after him."

Bob Brown, too, plays an *offensive* offensive tackle. He can be seen literally attacking defensive ends, popping them, knocking them over, hurting them. As one coach explained, to do what Brown does requires great quickness, great strength and great self-confidence. Few men have such a combination of assets. Bob Brown does. Mix, Brown's teammate on the Raiders, says, "Everything about Brown is bigger than life—his size, his talent, his intelligence, his sensitivity. He is one of a kind."

Offensive linemen tend to herd together. At some level, they resent their role. It's not that they don't like playing football, and it's not that they resent

fate's having slipped them into the offensive line. What they do resent is the general lack of appreciation they receive. Running backs and even quarterbacks praise their efforts at every opportunity, but then, as one offensive tackle put it, "Why in the hell shouldn't they . . . they get all the money and all the fame. If we don't do our job, they're dead and they know it."

"Offensive tackle is probably the worst job in professional sport," says Mix. "On every play, I don't care what it is, even if it's in a controlled scrimmage, the tackle makes contact. Its pound, pound, pound, and nobody knows except you, the guy you are pounding and maybe your coach."

"I play guard," said the 49ers' Howard Mudd, "because I love playing football, and a guard is what I am. It's true that you don't get much recognition, but your teammates usually know and appreciate the

"Playing in the line is a very personal matter. It is intimate. You are working in very close quarters with teammates and against opponents. There is a great deal of mutual respect."

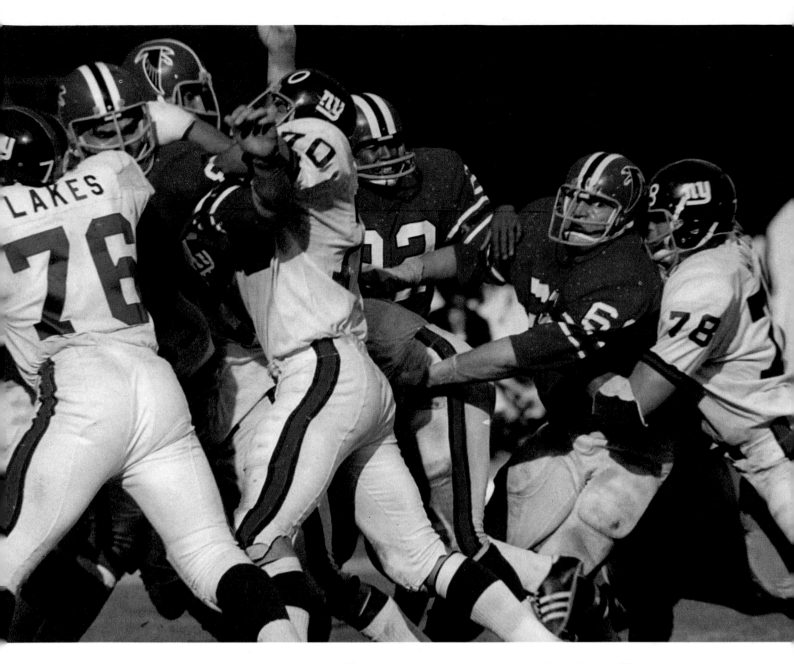

job you do. And peer group recognition is more important to me than popular acclaim.

"Playing in the line is a very personal matter. It is intimate. You are working in very close quarters with teammates and against opponents. There is a great deal of mutual respect. And in how many jobs do you find that?

"And another thing is the personal satisfaction. The satisfaction is real because it is uncluttered and immediate. You either did the job on that block or you didn't. You were either beat or you won. Football is one of the few jobs where the rewards, the satisfactions, the results are clear-cut and immediate. And boy, you can feel them. When was the last time you saw a bunch of salesmen or lawyers or butchers jumping up and down and hugging each other and damn near crying with joy over a sale or winning a case or carving a side of beef?"

Says Bengal coach Paul Brown, "To be an outstanding offensive lineman—and I think almost every lineman in the National Football League is outstanding—a man must be a self-starter. He must be able to motivate himself, and he must take pride in his performance. He can't be a man who needs glory. Some of the finest men I have known in my lifetime have been offensive linemen. They have courage, they have discipline and they have character. The first man I drafted when we started the Cincinnati Bengals was an offensive lineman, our starting center Bob Johnson."

Washington Redskin coach George Allen sums up offensive linemen like this: "You want men with the physical skills, of course. You want good balance, good short distance, quickness, good leg strength, all of that. But regardless of their physical attributes, offensive linemen must be sold on playing in the line."

THE CONSUMMATE ATHLETES:

Running Backs

Then too, there have been some running backs—only a handful to be sure—who did an awful lot with only a minimum of help. Every runner needs a block, but it's what he does with it that separates the great ones from the rest. "I don't know what it is that makes one man run better than another," says Red Grange. "I've been asked a thousand questions about running, and I've given it quite a bit of consideration. When you're running with the ball, you aren't thinking about it. You're just doing it. It is pure instinct.

"The woods are full of straight-ahead runners, the kind you depend on for two or three yards when you really need it, and they'll block for you. It's that kind of player that wins more football games than most people know. But for excitement, for maybe winning a game here and there that you wouldn't otherwise win, I like the broken-field runner.

"I know how that sounds, coming from me, but I honestly believe one runner like Larry Brown or O. J. Simpson is worth a dozen straight-ahead runners. Simpson, I think, ran track, so you know he's fast. But I don't believe speed is all that important. I mean, you can't be out-and-out slow, but I think balance and timing are much more important than speed. And I think peripheral vision is a great asset too. Speed is overrated. Hell, some of the worst football players I've seen were track stars with all kinds of speed. I'd say a great runner needs that natural instinct, great balance, a sense of timing, peripheral vision and a strong body, and he's got to have stamina.

"The best thing about being a running back is that you can be a little lazy if you want to be. I mean during practice. God, I used to hate practice. I never was crazy about football anyway, but I hated practice. The game was fun, but I'm not sure it was worth a week of grueling practice in order to have two hours of fun on the weekend."

"I'd say a great runner needs that natural instinct, great balance, a sense of timing, peripheral vision and a strong body, and he's got to have stamina."

National Football League running backs are the best athletes in the world—they combine strength, stamina, balance, agility, speed and courage. The greats have it all.

"I'll tell you something," says Hugh McElhenny, one of the finest running backs of all time. "I hated practice too. I was probably at my peak when I was in high school. No one is going to believe that, not unless you saw me in high school, but I was better in high school than in college or in professional ball."

McElhenny played for the San Francisco 49ers until the dog days of his career, when he played for the Minnesota Vikings, the New York Giants and the Detroit Lions. "I probably stayed around too long, but I loved the game," he says. "I just didn't want to quit. In high school, I was pretty good, all-state and all that, and the coach never bothered me very much. He saw to it that I got the ball, and I'd just take off. I was pretty big even then, a little over six feet and about one-eighty, and I was a hurdler, and ran the hundred in nine-six, so I just ran and had a great time. Later, with some coaching, I began to think about what I was doing, waiting for my blockers, and I lost some of my spontaneity. A pro doesn't wait for his blockers because he'll run better—he waits for them because if he doesn't, he's apt to have a short career."

The case has been made that as a collective whole, National Football League running backs are the best athletes in the world—they combine strength, stamina, balance, agility, speed and courage. Some are known for their power, some for their speed and some simply for their style. The great ones usually have it all.

"In this league," says George Allen, "a running back must do a lot of things besides run. He must block, he must catch and he must be dependable. If he can block and catch, his running is a bonus."

"Some men," says Miami coach Don Shula, "sit on the bench even though everyone knows they can run with a football. I don't care how well a man can run—he can go the forty in three seconds and have all the moves—he won't play much in this league if he doesn't block or if he busts plays."

"It was a vicious circle," says Willie Ellison. A Ram running back, he rushed for 1,000 yards in 1971, 247 of them in one game—the league record. Ellison now with K.C., had, under coach George Allen, been on the Los Angeles bench four previous years. "The man said I needed to improve on this and that," he continued. "Well, you can only do so much without playing. To improve, you got to play. When Prothro came in [Rams' ex-coach Tommy Prothro], he had a different philosophy. He wanted a man who could run, maybe even break off a long run now and then. I became a starter. I ran well, I don't think I made too many mistakes and I know the rest of my game picked up."

Another man who had to overcome doubts is

"Every time I go on the field, I feel I've got to prove myself again. But that's okay, because I've been having to do that for most of my life."

Denver's Floyd Little. Little is not a big man, not in pro football. He stands 5 feet 10 inches, and he weighs 190 pounds. But last year, his fifth in the NFL, little Little led the league in rushing. He scampered and scurried for 1,133 yards. "Everyone told me I was too small for the pros," he recalls. "Hell, I still hear it . . . even after five years and leading the league. So every time I go on the field, I feel I've got to prove myself again. But that's okay, because I've been having to do that for most of my life.

"To keep going in this game, you've got to have pride and you've got to be able to make the distinction between pain and an injury. I've played with a broken clavicle. I've played with a broken back. It just kills me not to play. I had broken transverse processes in my back the last two games in 1970. The transverse process is a piece of the vertebrae where the muscles attach. I had so much pain I couldn't even get into a three-point stance. I played both of those games into the third quarter before the pain got so bad I had to come out. I'm not bragging about anything. A lot of guys play with pain. It's what football is all about . . . doing the best job you can while you're able."

Little, a great small back, takes a beating.

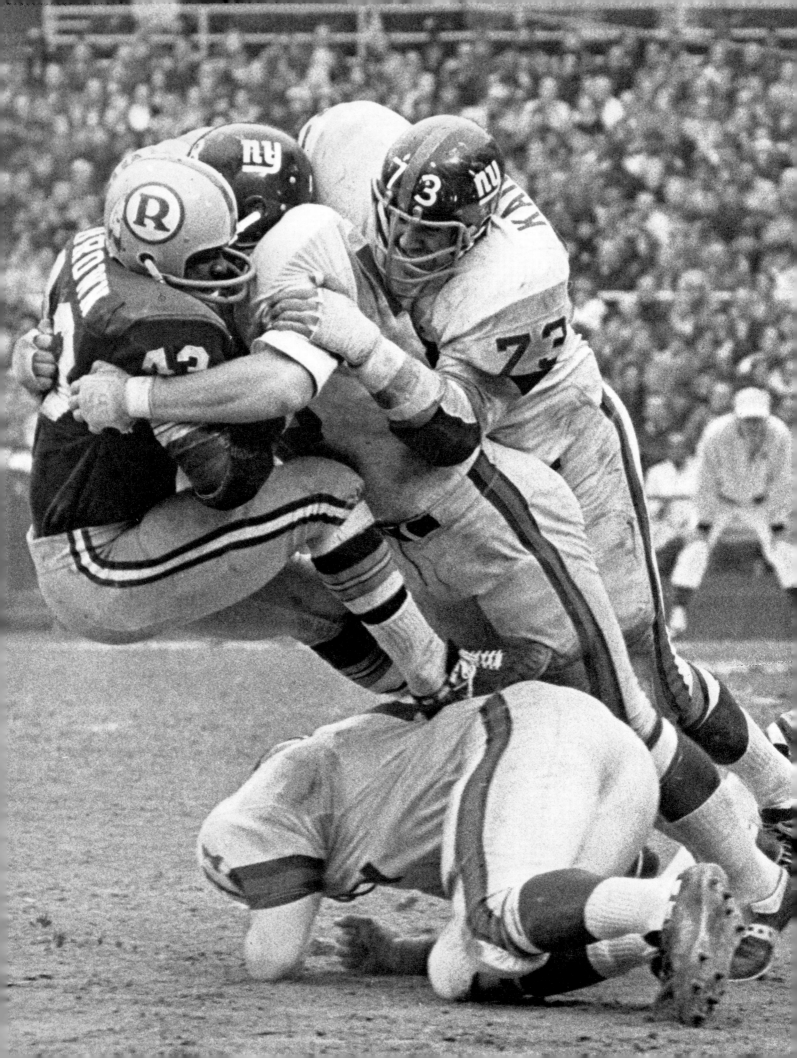

Miami's Larry Csonka, a great big back, gives a beating. "There seems to be a trend to larger backs around the league," Csonka says. "Marv Hubbard, Steve Owens, John Brockington, John Riggins, Norm Bulaich, Franco Harris . . . these are big, young, strong backs. It helps to have size.

"I don't think great speed is as important as maybe it once was. You don't see that many all-the-way runs anymore anyway, not even by the guys with enough speed to do it. Hell, our Mercury Morris is one of the fastest runners in the league . . . but the defense cuts him off too. There is a lot of speed on every defense, and they're set up to take advantage of the angles. Today, a twenty-yard run is long, and a forty-yard run can turn a game around. And you don't need great speed to go twenty or thirty or even forty yards, provided you have some power and, of course, some blocking.

"I think a power runner can intimidate the defense. At least, you can sting them once in a while. Hell, those linebackers spend their whole careers nailing ballcarriers who are usually twenty or thirty pounds smaller than they are. So it helps to even up things a bit when backs come along who are as big as the linebackers.

"Running is a natural thing. There are things you learn about running, but basically it is natural. Either you can do it or you can't. The hard part about being a running back, even a big running back, is learning to block. Blocking can be a bitch. Jim [Jim Kiick, Csonka's running mate in the Miami backfield] and I block well for each other, but that's only because we work on it. We started out as rookies together, and we agreed to block our heads off for one another, and it has helped us both."

One great runner started his career as a blocking back. Or, more accurately, he was a blocking back in college, and he started his career as an eighth round draft choice. Larry Brown, the Redskins' great running back from Kansas, probably gets to the line and through the hole quicker than any other back today.

"I think a running back's greatest asset," Brown says, "is getting to the line before the holes close and before the linebackers can converge. Look at Leroy Kelly. He's been a star for years, thanks to his quick start. Kelly isn't all that fast, but he gets his speed in two steps, and he has strong legs. I like to think I'm a little bit like that."

Ron Johnson has been up and Ron Johnson has been down. He came from a poor family. But because his father worked hard, Ron and his brother Alex, the former American League batting champion, had time to play ball. Their father saw to that. Ron was All-American at Michigan. He was a number-one draft choice of the Cleveland Browns. In Cleveland he sat on the bench. He went to New York in a trade. In New York he's been all-pro, and he's been crippled and on the sidelines. The 1972 season found him healthy again and running well.

"I've heard that hitting a baseball is the most difficult skill in sports," Ron Johnson says, "and there's some truth in that. But I also think that playing running back in the National Football League is no snap. In fact, next to quarterback, I think running back is the toughest position.

"Most other players on the field—the linemen and receivers and defensive backs—are primarily concerned with the one man opposite them. But a runner has to see the whole play and be concerned with all the players . . . he has to know where the defenders are, and he has to know where his help is. Before the play begins, you build a list of alternatives in your mind covering all the ways the play might work out, but when the play starts you don't have time to stop and think. You have to make the right move immediately. Every piece of your thinking machine has to be concentrated on the situation.

"I don't completely accept this 'running is a natural thing' theory that most guys talk about. A lot of running is natural, of course, but there are a lot of things you can learn too. For instance, how to run under control and how to use your blockers. Leroy Kelly is a master at this. He stays so close to his blockers, he looks like he's hiding . . . then pow, he's gone. His quickness is natural, but he's learned to use his blockers and control his speed.

"There are a lot of problems out there for a runner. A lot of big people take some good shots at you. But I'll tell you this—when I'm running well I get a tremendous feeling of dominance and authority. Running with the ball is simply gorgeous."

"I think a power runner can intimidate the defense. At least you can sting them once in a while. Hell, those linebackers spend their whole career nailing ballcarriers."

THE HIT MEN:

Linebackers

Professional linebackers have been described in a variety of ways. Largely, though, the descriptions lean toward flattery mixed with awe. Linebackers have been called the best athletes on the team, they have been called the meanest "hit men" in the game and they have been called the brains of a defense.

"To be a great linebacker," says Tommy Prothro, "you must have strength and speed, and enough concentration to always be fully aware of the situation. Then you must perform at a high level of intensity all the time you're out there, because you are constantly being challenged." Prothro believes that a linebacker must have speed, particularly on the outside, in order to shut off the big play. "I'll even sacrifice experience if, everything else being equal, the younger fellow has more speed," he says.

This theory conflicts with that of George Allen, Prothro's predecessor in Los Angeles. Allen likes age and experience. "Good linebackers," Allen says, "are a major factor in the success of the great defensive teams in the National Football League. Linebacker is an extremely difficult position to play. It takes experience. The linebacker has to be the best all-around athlete on the defensive team. He has to be fast enough to cover passes and strong and big enough to stop the run. I look for a player about six-two and two twenty-five. I feel this is just about the right size for an outside linebacker. Now, if he isn't that big, he can still play and do a good job. Chris Hanburger is an outstanding linebacker who only weighs about two fifteen. The middle linebacker should weigh about two forty-five, and should be about six-three. Dick Butkus is pretty much an ideal size for his position.

"Anyone who plays in the secondary, and I consider linebackers as part of my secondary, must have quick feet. They have got to be quick-starting, whether

*"To be a great linebacker, you must
have strength and speed, and enough concentration
to always be fully aware of the situation."*

they are red-dogging or coming out of their coverage or getting to their 'hook spots.' They must have first-step quickness, and must be able to move well laterally and backward. I think a linebacker should have the footwork of a boxer.

"The linebacker must be able to read a play almost instantly, but never commit himself too soon. This is why I want my linebackers to have experience. The middle backer has to be awfully strong, and yet he should be quick enough to rush the passer on a 'dog.' This is usually a shortcoming in most middle linebackers."

Kansas City coach Hank Stram says, "I don't want to get into any discussion about who are my best athletes. I think every man on our team is great. But I will say one thing. If there is a better athlete in football than Bobby Bell, I haven't seen him."

Bobby Bell has been all-pro six times. He was an all-American tackle at the University of Minnesota. "I've played just about everything," Bell says. "I've played in both lines, and I've played fullback and tight end. In high school I played the secondary. But my favorite spot is where I'm playing today—outside linebacker. You are involved in every kind of play. You stop runs, and you stop passes. I love open-field tackles, and I love to hit. It's a great position."

Bell's teammate, middle linebacker Willie Lanier, is a pretty fair athlete himself. A man who's made all-pro, Lanier is an independent thinker with some introspective views of his role as a football player. "I enjoy football," he says. "I enjoy contact. I enjoy the concept of matching my body and my wits against another man's. I respect my opponent. It's like two boxers. They can go at each other for ten rounds and then hug each other and say, 'You're a hell of a man.'

"Remember the game we lost to Miami last year in the playoffs—the long, long game? Well, even though we lost, it was one of the most enjoyable games I ever played. Playing the game is what's important. I try to remove the pressure of winning from my mind and just see how my skills stack up against those of the other players. It's the competition that I really love."

There was a time, not too long ago, when many teams used only two linebackers, preferring a five-man rush line. Even when professional teams copied each other into four-three-four uniformity, the linebacker's principal role was to support the down linemen against the rush. Linebackers were slimmed-down tackles. They weren't too fast, but they were powerful hitters.

Then some offensive thinkers began to put the heat on the linebackers. They started to get even.

"Anyone who plays in the secondary must have quick feet. He must be able to move well laterally and backward. A linebacker should have a boxer's footwork."

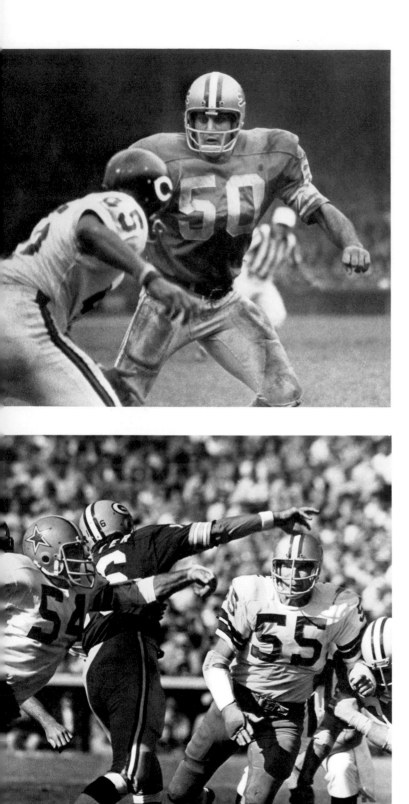

The offense began to send fast halfbacks into short pass patterns, forcing the lumbering linebackers back to cover. They couldn't do it, and almost immediately, coaches began to look for linebackers who had speed and mobility. Today, most linebackers, and all good linebackers, can move. And now that the zone has pretty much become football's standard defensive alignment, the linebackers are valuable adjuncts to the pass defense. In a passing situation, the linebackers sprint back into their zones, usually seven or eight yards ahead of the line of scrimmage.

"Most linebackers sit back in their zone and wait," says Baltimore's Ted Hendricks, who, at 6 feet 7 inches, is a treelike figure in the left side of the Colts' zone. "But I treat the zone more like a man-to-man defense. I get upset at someone who just sits in the middle of his zone and waits for something to happen. When I get back there, I try to look around and see where the action is. A lot of times, if you move with the quarterback's eyes, you'll see what's coming. When I see where the receiver is, I get over to him. What's the use of waiting until he makes the catch?"

Most coaches don't want their zone men to move around that much. "To play the zone well," says Minnesota coach Bud Grant, "players need the discipline to lay back in their own zone even when receivers cross in front of them. If a player leaves his zone, it can be a disaster."

"My coaches tell me that sometimes too," says Hendricks, "and I ask them to tell me when I make a mistake . . . tell me when, by being aggressive, I hurt the team. I'm not hurting the team, or I wouldn't do it. Once you get some experience playing the zone, you can see the patterns and know when it's safe to move. You can't get burned if there's no one there to burn you.

"It helps if we play against a quarterback who is what we call a 'pointer.' You wouldn't think, by the time a man gets to pro ball, that he'd still do something as stupid as point, but some quarterbacks do. A 'pointer' is a quarterback who looks right where he's going to throw all the time he's dropping back. Against somebody like that, you just go where he's pointing. It gets harder when the passer looks you off one way and then comes back the other. Then you have to figure out the pattern. And sometimes they can trap you. Maybe they'll send the wide receiver out and have him curl up on the outside of my zone, right where the numbers are on the field. Then they send a back out to curl up in the middle, on the inside of my zone. Now I'm in a bind. I can't afford to lean either way. Of course, to do that, they have to send a back out into the pattern, and that hurts their protection for the quarterback. I have to hope one of our defensive linemen can break up the play. But say they run that curl to the wide receiver and keep the back in to block. Now there's nobody to hurt me on the inside. I'm not going to stand around in my zone at a time like that. I'm going out there where the receiver is."

Detroit middle linebacker Mike Lucci calls the defensive signals in the NFC's most complicated defense, and he is generally regarded as the man who holds it all together. "Mike Lucci," says Joe Schmidt, Lucci's coach and himself a 12-year all-pro middle linebacker, "is the best middle linebacker in our division. He could be the best in football."

"We play a defense designed by our defensive coach, Jim David," Lucci says. "I've been here as long as Jim has, and our defensive theories have sort of grown up together. Jim's theory is to give the offense a different picture, or 'look,' on every play. In fact, we often give them several different looks while they are lining up. Our line moves from undershifts to overshifts to head to head, and our backers move in and out. The basic idea is, they can't block us if they can't see us.

"The primary responsibility of any linebacker is to get to the ball. I've got to move and be there,

"The linebacker must be able to read a play almost instantly, but never commit himself too soon. This is why I want my linebackers to have experience."

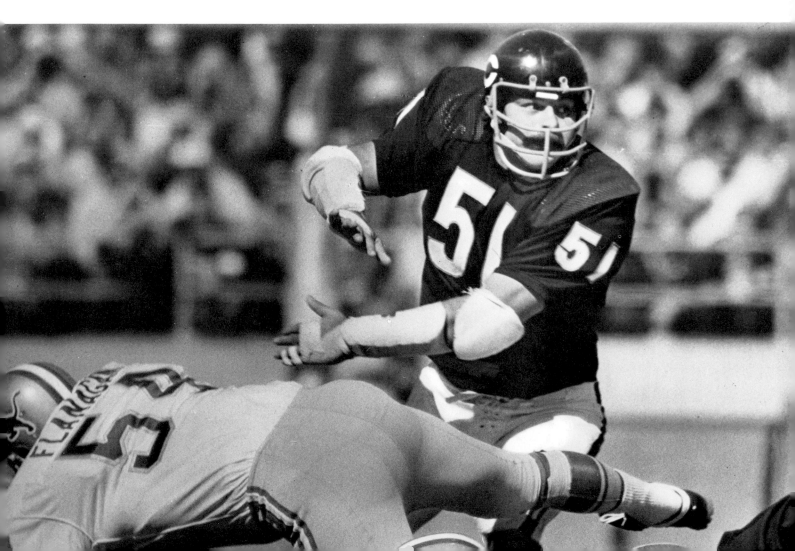

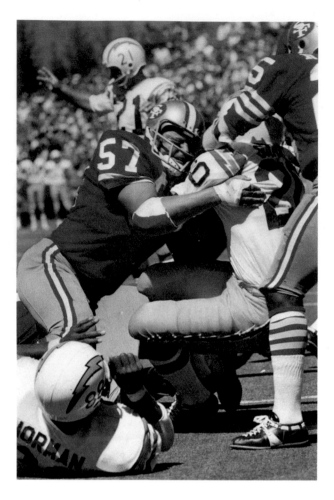

wherever it is. As a matter of fact, all the Lions want to be there. In Detroit we believe in gang tackling. But my basic responsibility is to secure what we call the bubble. That's the term we use for the area I protect when our line is in an overshift or undershift. In an even defense with no shift, our two tackles are head up with the offensive guards, and I'm lined up in front of the center. But when we use an over or under, one of the tackles moves over the center. That leaves a big gap between him and the end. I move over into that gap, opposite the guard, but I'm back off the line. There's a bend in the line there, where I'm off the line, and if you diagram it, it looks something like a bubble.

"Some teams think that the bubble is a weak spot in the defense; many quarterbacks will look at the bubble and audible to run right at it. It's my job to hold the area. If the guard fires out straight at me, I don't have to worry about chasing the ball. I know the ball is coming to me. I know the son of a bitch is coming into my area, and I know I'm going to stop him. I don't hand-fight the blocker, I just try to get anyone who comes busting into that bubble."

"One of the hardest things to learn," says Isiah Robertson, the Rams' sensational rookie linebacker of a season ago, "is to protect your area. I was getting killed by counters, reverses and counter-reverses because I was running all over the field. In school [Robertson attended tiny Southern University] I made most of the tackles. I just ran around and went after the ball. Here you can't do it."

"Robertson has as much, if not more, natural talent than any linebacker I've ever seen," says Tom Catlin, a former Cleveland Browns linebacker and now linebacking coach with the Rams. "But he had a lot to learn. I told him that I was going to be on him from the moment he walked onto the field until the moment he left. He probably thought I was the biggest horse's ass in the world. But he hung in there, kept his mouth shut and worked his butt off."

"Whatever I accomplished last year," Robertson says, "Catlin deserves at least eighty percent of the credit. Hell, I didn't even know how to take a proper stance. Catlin says you learn about eighty percent of what you have to know in your first year . . . but then it takes years and years to learn the rest. It is the great linebackers who know the ninety-two or ninety-three percent of what they have to know. You never know it all, but it's the little things that make the difference."

Probably no linebacker knows more about the "little things" than Miami's Nick Buoniconti. Buoniconti believes that every middle linebacker has basically the same problems. How you go about solving the problems is just a matter of personal choice and your coach's philosophy.

"Once the ball is snapped," Buoniconti says, "different middle linebackers key differently. But before the snap, most of us are looking for the same things. Some linebackers key on the running backs. The way this works is, you key the weakside halfback, or the fullback, and whichever way he goes, you go. But I think most linebackers, especially middle linebackers, key linemen. What you try to do is to key the fellows in front of you, the center and the two guards. Whatever they do is your key, because in most assignments the center is either coming out to get you or blocking back or blocking out. If he blocks back, the guards are probably going to scissor you, and the play is usually going to come up the gut. The best thing to do is to step up and fill the hole.

"Sometimes, they will call a short trap. The center will block the defensive tackle, and the far guard comes over and blocks on the tackle, and what they hope to do is pull the offensive tackle over and have him wipe out the middle linebacker. So

you have to fill the middle and fight off the tackle.

"If you key the center, you really can't go too far wrong. I think you can get confused if you are reading backs, because backs can cross, and sometimes they just get lost behind the line. Still, some teams key backs, so I guess some people see that as the best way.

"On a passing down, when we are in a standard zone, my main assignment is to get back to the weak-side hook zone. The back on that side will either flare in and hook or clear out the zone for a wide receiver coming in on a slant or square-in. They hope I'll go with the back and leave the area vacant for the wide receiver. But I let the back go. I know the safety will pick him up. That's what defense is all about—confidence in your teammates to do their job."

The coordination between the linebackers and the four deep backs is critical—especially to a team using a zone defense or a combination zone and man-to-man defense. The linebacker, as Buoniconti points out, has to know that his rear is being protected, just as the defensive lineman has to know that the linebacker is doing his job and filling all the holes that the front four aren't filling.

"The linebacker has to be the best all-around athlete on the defensive team. He has to be fast enough to cover passes and strong and big enough to stop the run."

85

PALACE GUARDS:
The Secondary

It has only been in football's recent past that coaches began to position their best athletes in the secondary. Paul Brown is generally recognized as the coach who first saw that a gifted athlete could be more valuable stopping touchdowns in the secondary than scoring them for the offense. In the past two decades some of college football's finest offensive stars have been switched to defense. Dickey Moegle, J. C. Caroline, Ed Meador, Johnny Robinson, Clancy Williams, Leroy Keyes, Mel Renfro and Willie Wood come to mind as just a few of the men who were moved to the defensive backfield after outstanding collegiate careers as offensive stars.

The men playing the corners and the safeties are the last line of defense between your opponent and six points in the end zone. They are the palace guards, so to speak. They have to be as good as the men they are guarding against. Of course, it has been said again and again that the best defender cannot hope to cover even an average receiver forever. The deep back's best friend is a strong pass rush. Without it, he is dead. Given enough time, as they say, even your sister can get free.

To help ease the burden on what is an ulcer-giving job—and to help shut off the long and intermediate pass—more and more teams have gone to the zone defense. A few teams, such as Oakland and Kansas City, still play a lot of man-to-man, but they have some exceptional defensive backs and a pretty good pass rush. Of course, the zone too lives or dies with the pass rush.

The basic idea of a zone is deceptively simple. Seven defensive players—three linebackers and four deep backs—each run to a prearranged area, or zone, at the snap of the ball. They stay in the effective center of their zones, more or less regardless of where the receivers go, until the ball is thrown. Once

The men playing the corners and the safeties are the last line of defense between your opponent and six points in the end zone. They are the palace guards.

the ball is in the air, they converge on the intended receiver.

"The zone can be pretty scary," says New England wide receiver Randy Vataha. "You never know where your hit is coming from. You only know that it's coming."

For the defensive back, playing a zone is a completely different experience from playing man-to-man. According to Minnesota's Bud Grant, the two defenses almost require different personality types. "A successful man-to-man pass defender must be a great athlete," says the Viking coach. "He needs great reflexes and great speed. You usually find that these people are very self-confident, even cocky. They're not afraid to go out and challenge anybody.

"But in a zone defense, a back has to subdue those aggressive tendencies. As I said before, he has to have the discipline to stay in his zone even when receivers pass right in front of him. The operative word is *discipline*. Believe me, the zone is not an easy thing to learn."

Johnny Robinson played professional football for 12 seasons. He was several times all-pro. He was a great free safety. He thinks defensive backs have the toughest job of all, zone, man-to-man or any other way.

"The major difference between us [defensive backs] and everybody else," Robinson says, "is the pressure, especially for the cornerbacks. Life out there is perpetual fear. Every play, every snap of the ball can lead to disaster. It's not like that for other players on the field, with the possible exception of the quarterback, and even he gets times when he just hands off the ball. Besides, he's the one calling the play . . . we're the ones in the spot of having to figure out what he called.

"Most players can afford an occasional mistake. A lineman can miss a block, and that just makes it second and ten. Maybe a runner will stumble and fall, but it's the same thing as the missed block. A receiver can run the wrong route or drop a pass. It's not good, but it's not fatal either. But for the cornerback, and to a large extent for the safeties too, a mistake means six points. There is no next time. Teams pass so much now that there are often four or five touchdown passes a game between the two teams. And after every one, I'll guarantee you, some man out there is feeling mighty low."

The hardest job a defensive coach has is to keep up a man's self-confidence after he has been burned for a touchdown pass. "If you can't handle defeat," says San Francisco's all-pro cornerback Jimmy Johnson, "you can't play the corner in this league."

"There is no more emotional moment," Johnny

"A successful man-to-man pass defender must be a great athlete. He needs great reflexes and great speed. You usually find that these people are very self-confident."

Robinson says, "than when that ball is in the air and you are racing your man to get it. It all builds up to that one split second, and it's usually only a question of inches. If you miss, if you get beat and your man scores, it's a long way back to the bench. It has ruined some pretty good players."

Every back agrees about the pressure, but some say that the hardest play is forcing the end run. Herb Adderley, the ex-Packer great now with Dallas, is not a small cornerback. He is 6 feet 2 inches and almost 200 pounds. "Coming up to stop the sweep is a bitch, pure and simple," Adderley says. "Just put yourself in that position. Say you're playing the Dolphins. When they sweep to your side, you only have to contend with Larry Little, one of those big, fast, mean guards who are just looking for you. I mean, they dream about finding cornerbacks out in

"There is no more emotional moment than when that ball is in the air and you are racing your man to get it. . . . If you miss, . . . it's a long way back to the bench."

the open field and driving them about thirty rows up in the stands. And if you somehow avoid Little, you only have to stop a Larry Csonka, who is plenty fast and weighs about two thirty-five and loves to run over people. That's all you have to do. It's a wonder any of us are still alive."

Still, the cornerback's primary job is to break down or, if he can, intercept the forward pass. Cornerbacks are responsible for the wide receivers. The strong or tight safety is usually responsible for the tight end, and the free safety is a rover who goes for the ball.

Coaches stress that cornerbacks maintain what is often called a "good relationship" with the pass receiver. That's a little like a doctor's calling something that really hurts an "exquisite pain." But the "relationship" theory is simply that you stay within

two yards of your man and take away something—either the inside or the outside routes. Which one is determined by such things as the defender's ability to go to his left or to his right and the receiver's ability to do the same and what the tendency charts tell the defender about a particular receiver, a particular quarterback and the game situation.

If, for example, a team is in its two-minute drill and has no more time-outs, the cornerback can pretty much count on outside stuff. In that case, he'll try to take away the outside and give up a little on the inside. Then, of course, the defender must be wary of being set up. Most good receivers will work on a cornerback even when they are out of the play. They will show him their "up" move, for instance, over and over again. And then will come a play in which the defender again sees the move and thinks "up"—

but this time it's an up-and-out, and if he doesn't adjust, it's good-bye.

"Actually, you learn what to expect from teams more than you do from individuals," says Larry Wilson, the all-pro safety of the St. Louis Cardinals, who has been described as the league's most complete football player. It was once said of Wilson that he can fire up his team just by coming on the field to hold the ball for the extra-point kick. "I don't think you succeed only by being smart or fast," Wilson says. "I have a little book. I chart every ball game. Say we play Dallas. I've recorded every game I've played against Dallas and noted what they did against me. Teams do certain things from certain formations, or from certain spots on the field, and you can count on that more than you can the idiosyncrasies of any one player."

91

RUNNING FREE:
Wide Receivers

"The zone has taken a lot of the pressure off the secondary," says Don Shula, "and put it on the wide receiver."

Many observers think that one of Shula's players at Miami, Paul Warfield, may be the best of the many splendid wide receivers currently playing in the NFL. Warfield doesn't like the zone defense. "They're going to have to do something about it," he says. "If teams get good at it, the passing game will become extinct. Everyone knows the zone can shut off the long pass, but what a lot of people don't realize is that zones close off the ten-to-twenty-yard pass too. The linebackers get back in that area with the cornerbacks. It takes a perfect throw to get the ball through all those arms."

Last year Randy Vataha was a rookie sensation with New England. The year before, he had been a sensation in college, when he and his teammate Jim Plunkett led Stanford to the Rose Bowl. "When I was in college," Vataha says, "I used to watch the pros on television. Lots of times on isolated camera I'd see a receiver get open without a fake of any kind. He'd just run a little curl or slant, and *bingo*, the ball would be there. I figured I could do that. In fact, I thought that most anybody could do it. Then, when I ran my first hook in a pro game, I was wide open. And I thought, 'I was right—this is a piece of cake.' Then, the next pattern I ran, they changed their zone on me, and I wound up standing right next to a defender. I began to see the problem. I began to realize that receivers had to be able to read the zones too. It's not as easy as it looks on television, believe me."

"I don't care how they cover me, just as long as it's legal," says Otis Taylor, who feels that he can do his job against a zone, man-to-man, double coverage, bump-and-run or anything else defensive thinkers

"The prime requisite is speed. If a man has speed, everything else opens up for him. An offensive receiver simply has to have the speed to beat those defensive backs."

may come up with. "Most of this game is a matter of instincts. Some have good instincts, and some don't. I can't say I do this or I do that, I just say that I can get to the ball.

"I've worked for seven years now with Lenny Dawson, and he knows what to expect of me. He knows where to find me. On the other hand, if he's in trouble, I know where he'll want me to go. Coordination between the passer and the receiver is very important."

Over the years, some of football's most spectacular players have been wide receivers. It started, in the modern sense, with Green Bay's Don Hutson. He was the prototype. He destroyed defenses. Since Hutson, there has been a steady, growing parade of long-striding, sure-handed pass catchers. From Elroy "'Crazylegs" Hirsch, Harlon Hill and Lenny Moore to Lance Alworth, Charley Taylor and Gene Washington, the gliding, graceful wide receiver has been the glamorous target in football's rapid-fire air attack.

What does it take for a man to play a wide-receiver position?

"In my opinion," says George Allen, "the prime requisite is speed. If a man has speed, everything else opens up for him. An offensive receiver simply has to have the speed to beat those defensive backs. An outstanding receiver will run the forty in four-six or four-seven, and he'll have great hands. He'll be willing to go for the ball in a crowd, and he'll be able to run with it after he catches it."

A man without too much speed can, of course, make it too. The classic example was Baltimore's Raymond Berry. Berry was slow. Berry wasn't too big. But Berry was one of the greatest wide receivers of all time. How? "Easy," says John Unitas, the man who threw all those passes to Berry for all those years. "All Ray had going for him was a bottomless capacity for work, a burning desire for self-improvement and unlimited patience. He simply devoted himself to catching footballs."

If a receiver doesn't have great speed, he will have to work very hard, particularly on timing and precision work, to be able to run his pass routes perfectly. The slow receiver who makes it is the man who stays after practice and works on stops, starts, cuts, catching the ball over his head, catching it while falling out of bounds, catching it while on his head—and then goes home and studies films until, finally, he goes to sleep and dreams of catching footballs. The man who does that, day in and day

"I don't care how they cover me—just as long as it's legal. Most of this game is a matter of instincts. . . . I can't say I can do this or that, but I can get to the ball."

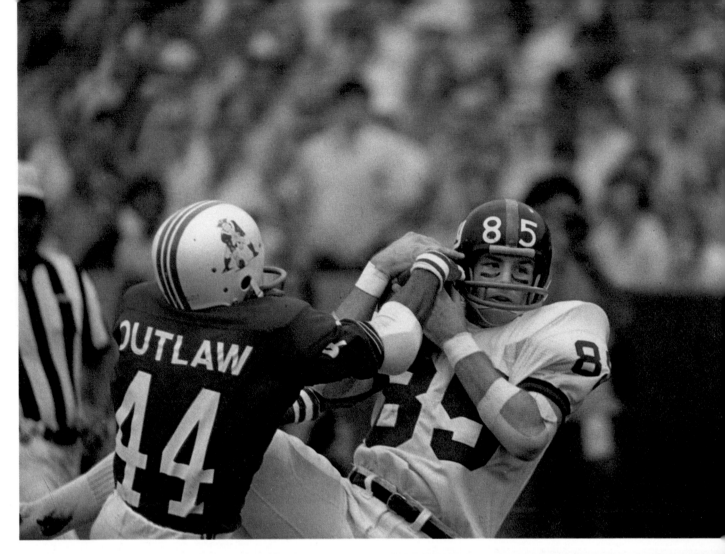

96

out, will make it even if he isn't blessed with speed.

The most important thing in running a pattern is to drive off the defender. If a receiver cannot drive off the defender, all the faking in the world isn't going to help. On the other hand, if the receiver does a good job in driving off the defender, a lot of faking won't be necessary. It is primarily for this reason that speed is such an asset. If a defender respects, or fears, the receiver's ability to explode off the line and race deep, he will be that much easier to drive off. It is this threat that opens up most pass patterns. If the defensive back can just backpedal the way he wants to, he is going to cover most everything the receiver does. Somehow the receiver has to provoke his movement. He must cause the defender to turn in one direction and lose his balance. Paul Warfield and Otis Taylor are both masters at this. Warfield does it with surgically precise pass routes; Taylor does it with instinct.

With good speed and explosive starts, the wide receiver can make the defender "deep-conscious." This can help to create a situation in which the defender will find himself moving backward faster and faster and then getting turned in or out. This is what kills defensive backfield coaches, whose most familiar and plaintive cry is "Don't let them get you turned, whatever you do, don't let those guys get you turned!"

The contest between a wide receiver and a cornerback is one of football's classic vignettes. It is a one-on-one struggle within a narrow corridor of space; the form it will take (out of a limited number of possibilities) depends on the pattern run by the wide receiver.

There are only about six basic patterns. There is a stop or hook or curl-in; regardless of what you call it, you stop, you turn, you catch the ball. There is a sideline or square-out, which means going down and turning out at a 90-degree angle for the sideline. There is an up or fly or streak, which is a matter of outrunning the defender. There is a post, which means running deep and slanting toward the goal post. There is the corner or flag pattern, in which you run to the corner of the end zone. There's the hitch or square-in, where you run five yards and then in. And that's about it. On the basic patterns, there are perhaps 25 variations, and these are where the individual talent comes in.

"Running to get free," says Lance Alworth, one of professional football's all-time-great wide receivers, "is beautiful. It feels good. And then, going for the ball and catching it is pure fantasy. There is nothing else like it. It more than makes up for the beating I get, and for me that's a lot to say."

"Running to get free is beautiful. It feels good. And then, going for the ball and catching it is pure fantasy."

THE RUNAWAY TRUCKS:
Tight Ends

It probably doesn't feel quite as good when you are the tight end. If a wide receiver is likened to a gliding gazelle, a tight end is comparable to a runaway truck careening down a hillside, smashing and crashing as it goes.

The tight end is a creature of the fifties. He was spawned in pro football's air age. He came alive because while quarterbacks wanted still another receiver, runners didn't want to lose another blocker. Ron Kramer at Green Bay and Mike Ditka at Chicago were the early prototypes. Then along came Baltimore's John Mackey. They were a rare breed—large men who could block, yet still possessed the pliant, sure hands of the wide receiver and the speed to bust any reception all the way to six points. Few teams were blessed with such specimens. They were hard to find. Then the college game began to develop tight ends for their own offenses, and after a while, more and more of these extraordinary young men began to show up. Today there is a staggering number of exceptional tight ends. "When you think about what it takes to play the position," says one pro scout, "it seems incredible that there are as many good ones as there are."

There are Charlie Sanders in Detroit and Jim Mitchell in Atlanta and Ted Kwalick in San Francisco and Milt Morin in Cleveland and Jerry Smith in Washington and Jackie Smith in St. Louis and Raymond Chester in Oakland and Bob Klein in Los Angeles and Bob Trumpy in Cincinnati and . . . well, it is a long list. A long list of superb athletes.

"A tight end," says San Diego coach Harland Svare, "has one of the most physically demanding jobs in football. He's got to be big and strong, and he's got to have good speed. He has to be able to catch the ball, usually in a crowd, and he has to be hard-nosed enough to block."

. . . large men who could block, yet still possessed the pliant, sure hands of the wide receiver and had the speed to bust all the way to six points.

Perhaps the epitome of the physical and psychological tight end is the Lions' Sanders. He is 6 feet 4 inches, and weighs 225 pounds. He runs the 40 in 4.8, and he makes leaping, one-handed catches. He likes to block, and he doesn't mind pain.

"Most of the teams around the league," Sanders says, "are using zones or combinations. Well, a zone is okay for a tight end. He can get loose against a zone. But most teams don't zone me. I always seem to get double and even triple coverage.

"I psych myself up all week, watching the strong safety on film and practicing my moves and all that. Then the game begins, and I've got a linebacker chasing me and the free safety coming over. The quarterback sees that, so he throws somewhere else. It gets discouraging. I like to get that ball in my hands and move out."

But for all its problems, Sanders would rather play tight end than wide receiver. He has enough speed to play wide, but he says he wouldn't want to: "I like the inside. I was a defensive end in college until my senior year, and I liked it there. I wouldn't enjoy the game as much out on the flank. Playing tight end, if I miss a pass, I've always got someone to take it out on the next play. Maybe I can unload a dynamite block. But a wide receiver can't do a damn thing when he drops one except mope and moan. And besides, if you're out there like a wide receiver with no one around you and you make a mistake, everyone can see it. That's not for me."

"The best way for a tight end to run his pattern," says Jackie Smith, "is with the threat of force." Smith came to St. Louis in 1963 from Northwest Louisiana State University. At 6 feet 4 inches and 220 pounds, Smith was a hurdler in college. He's been all-pro; he's been around. "There are dozens of variations you can run off your basic pattern," Smith says. "But if you are big, and tight ends are, and if you have decent speed, and tight ends usually do, then the best thing is to run right at your man . . . force him . . . make him turn. When he does, he's been beaten."

"When I came up, I thought I was a wide receiver," says Washington's Jerry Smith, the "other" Smith who plays tight end. "But at that time, the Redskins had a couple of wide receivers named Charley Taylor and Bobby Mitchell. There was no way I was going to get a job out there. They were looking for a tight end, so I moved inside.

"The hard part was the blocking. I was too small for one thing. I was six feet four, but I only weighed two hundred and five. So I went on a weight-lifting, weight-gaining program after the season was over. That was six years ago, and I'm still on it. I weigh two and a quarter now, and I'm strong enough to play inside.

"I caught a lot of passes and scored some touchdowns and all that, but I don't think I was a good tight end until recently. Blocking is partly technique and partly desire. I always had the desire, but I didn't really know what I was doing. I started to learn under Lombardi, and I've learned still more under Allen. It's a tough position, but it's a great place to play—you can make a real contribution."

"The best way for a tight end to run his pattern is with the threat of force. . . . Run right at your man. . . . Force him. . . . Make him turn. When he does, he's beat."

THE MEN WHO PULL THE TRIGGER:
Quarterbacks

How important, really, is the quarterback to a pro football team? Here are some random opinions from some top personalities in pro football.

Hampton Pool, the old coach and master tactician: "Quarterback is football's skill position."

Bob Lilly: "It's the quarterback you have to beat."

Joe Willie Namath: "Football is a struggle between the front four and the quarterback."

Don Meredith: "Quarterback is where it's at, pardner."

Weeb Ewbank: "You can plan and plan, work and work, and it all comes down to the man who pulls the trigger."

Tom Landry: "The quarterback is a part of the whole, and the whole is the sum of all its parts."

Bud Grant: "The quarterback is no more or no less important than the ten guys he's got with him."

John Ralston: "What I look for in a quarterback is leadership. He has got to provide leadership."

Jim Plunkett: "The tough thing about being a rookie quarterback is that you don't have a backlog of successful plays to fall back on."

George Allen: "Terry Bradshaw has everything. He has size, strength, determination, leadership qualities and an unbelievable arm. In about five years he should be a hell of a quarterback."

Alex Karras: "I never met a quarterback I liked. They're all candy-asses."

Bill McPeak: "The quarterback of the seventies should be agile, possess leadership qualities, have poise and, above all, excellence in passing. If he can run, that's a plus. Speed at any position is a plus in pro ball."

Emlen Tunnell: "A great passer can make good receivers out of just ordinary ones . . . but I've never seen an end who was great enough to help

"The quarterback of the seventies should be agile, possess leadership qualities, have poise and, above all, excellence in passing. If he can run. . . ."

make a quarterback any better than he already is."

Al Davis: "When we decided to go to war, really go to war with the NFL, it was their quarterbacks we went after."

Dave Slattery, Washington Redskin executive assistant: "A great quarterback can lift an average team to championship heights. Look what Van Brocklin did for the Eagles."

Jerry Wynn, public relations director for the Chargers: "In John Hadl we have the greatest non-star quarterback in football. He leads the league in everything, and we have guards who are better known. Maybe I'm not doing my job."

Frank Gifford: "Everyone thinks of Joe Namath beating the Colts in the Super Bowl. No one remembers Matt Snell running off tackle for a hundred and twenty-one yards. That is what it means to be a quarterback."

John Brodie: "As long as you are enthusiastic and keep in shape, you can keep playing quarterback. There is nothing I could do at twenty-one that I can't do now . . . I couldn't run when I was twenty-one either."

Merlin Olsen: "The thing that makes John Unitas the greatest quarterback of all time isn't his arm or even his football sense . . . it's his courage."

Few, in any case, would disagree that the quarterback is the most conspicuous man in the game. It all starts with him. If he's good, his team has a chance against anyone. Guards don't pull off upsets, but quarterbacks sometimes do. Quarterbacks also lose games they shouldn't. That's the trouble with having quarterbacks who are nothing more than human beings. That is also the beauty of it.

"The most valuable thing I can say about playing quarterback and passing a football," says John Unitas, "is that these acts involve no deep, dark mysteries. The whole art, if I may call it that, is based on a few simple elements. The hard part comes when the quarterback must start making decisions: who to throw to, when to throw and why and how to read defenses. But even here, once certain principles are understood, the complexities unravel and the job becomes straightforward. Naturally, no two quarterbacks do everything alike. But we pretty much stick to the same set of fundamentals."

One of the most difficult tasks of a professional football quarterback is reading the defense. This is particularly true now that so many defenses are disguised and therefore difficult to read. Before a quarterback can successfully attack a zone, for instance, he must know what zone he is facing. Is it a double zone or a rotating zone or a combination? Or just what in the hell is it?

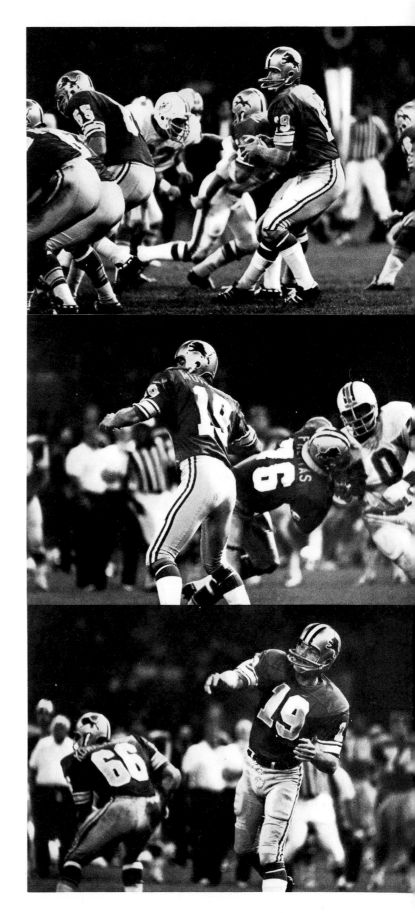

To do all that while dropping back and setting up,   105
the quarterback will usually be given three
and one-half seconds. On some plays he gets less.

One of the most difficult tasks of a professional football quarterback is reading the defense. This is particularly true now that so many defenses are disguised.

To figure out what he is facing, the quarterback must read the defense as the play starts by watching the move that the defensive players make.

Unitas has been reading zones every practice day of his pro career. His Colts have been playing the zone since he came up in 1956. "The first people you read," says Unitas, "are the safeties. If they're going to cover deep zones, they have to go right away. You should see the basic coverage as you step away from the center."

If the two safeties go to the right, it will be a rotating zone to the right. If they go left, the zone will rotate left. If the safeties split, it will be a double zone.

"After you check the safeties," Unitas says, "you watch the linebackers. If the deep backs are rotating to the right, the linebackers in the middle and on the left will have a long way to run to cover back on the left side. You can pick that up right away too. Usually, by the time you throw the pass, you've checked all seven guys back there."

To do all that while dropping back and setting

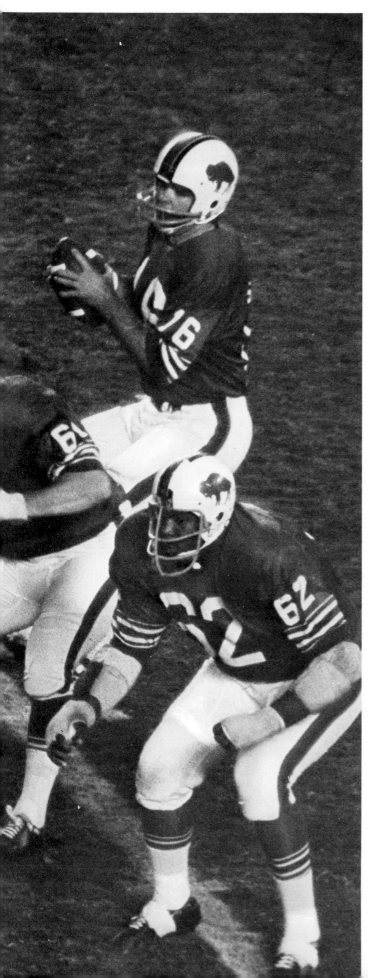

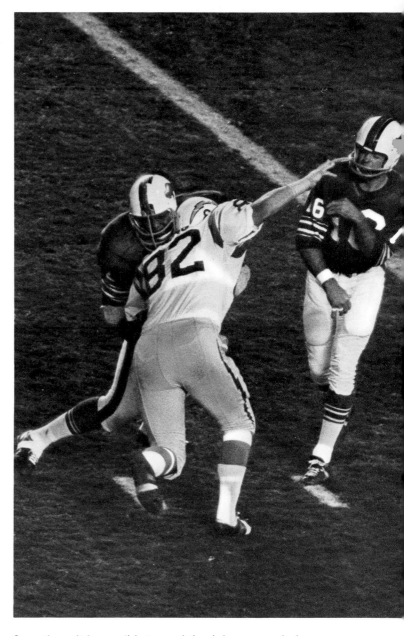

Sometimes it is possible to read the defense even before
the play begins. "The defense has to commit itself
by the way it lines up. You have to know what to look for."

up, the quarterback will usually be given three and one-half seconds by the opposition. On some plays he gets less.

Sometimes it is possible to read the defense even before the play begins. Virgil Carter, who completed 62 percent of his passes in 1971, says that he can do it. "The defense has to commit itself by the way it lines up," Carter says. "You just have to know what to look for. If the safety is going to have to run all the way to the deep outside zone, he'll show it by lining up closer to that direction than he would normally. He only has to cheat a foot or two for you to pick it up after studying him over and over on film."

Experienced zone teams like to think that they disguise their zones well, making it impossible to read them before the snap. But according to Carter, if a quarterback really does his homework, he'll be able to pick up some telltale keys.

Of course, diagnosing the defense is only part of the problem. As Unitas says, "After you read what they're doing, you just hope you have something going that will work. If you've called the wrong play, reading the safeties is of no more help at the moment than reading Sanskrit."

Not all quarterbacks see the zone as the shadow of doom. Bill Nelsen of Cleveland says that he likes to attack a zone, finding it a challenge. And New England's young passing wizard Jim Plunkett says, "If I have the time to throw, I have more success against the zone than I do against the man-to-man."

Time is very important, of course, to every quarterback. "There is not a quarterback in this league," says Kansas City's Buck Buchanan, "who can't eat you alive if he has time."

"My job," says Ram offensive tackle Charlie Cowan, "is to buy time for the quarterback. I sacrifice my body to buy him time."

Most coaches figure that a quarterback gets 3.5 seconds. That's not very long. And usually, against a strong front four or a blitz, that time shrinks. Many coaches break it down like this: 1.5 seconds to drop back, 2.0 seconds to release the ball.

It's not easy to be a professional football quarterback. You must have a strong and quick arm, durability, good vision and the ability to learn and retain. And you must be a leader. It's a tough job, tougher than most because of the enormous responsibility involved.

"I'll tell you, though," says Sammy Baugh, "I played quarterback for sixteen years, and I loved it. I wish I could have played all my life . . . or until I was sixty, like in most jobs. Being quarterback in the big league is the best job on earth."

Time is very important, of course, to every quarterback. "There is not a quarterback in this league who can't eat you alive if he has time."

4

THE

THIRD

TEAM

by Norm Schachter

As there are three seasons in every football year, there are three teams on the field during every football game—the offense, the defense and the six men in striped shirts. Norm Schachter, Ph.D., beginning his twentieth year as an official in the National Football League, explains why "an official is only as good as the last call he made."

Yankee Stadium exploded. Sixty-two thousand, eight hundred and ninety-two wide-eyed partisans were roaring and jumping up and down and pounding each other. "It's good!" they yelled. "What a play! Did you see that?"

I'd seen it. That's why I'd thrown my penalty flag. I had seen it and known it was wrong. But unlike the fans, I was impartial.

Then they spotted the flag. Imagine tens of thousands of people screaming "Kill that guy!" Can you imagine how you'd feel if you were "that guy"? Well, I was.

For the most part, I'm a pretty normal guy. I've had a father who was married to my mother, I have a wife and kids, I have a steady job. But then there's the other part: a certain extracurricular activity I perform every Sunday from August through January. I'm a professional football referee.

A football referee is really a very lucky person. During the game—and afterwards, too—you get nothing but help. It's the only job in the world that everyone wants to help you with. Everybody wants to correct your mistakes for you. And sometimes they're right. But if they'd been right about mine as often as they think they've been, I'd be long gone today as a referee. It's strange—people who would never think of telling a barber how to trim hair or a doctor how to prescribe pills or a butcher how to cut meat never hesitate to offer advice to a professional football referee.

Would it surprise you to learn that NFL referees have to take a physical and get their eyes checked once a year? During the half-time of a championship game a couple of seasons ago, we officials ran to the dressing room to get warm. The weather was pushing zero, and pushing hard. Finishing a second cup of hot coffee, I received a telegram from the eye doctor who had prescribed my contact lenses. It read "Saw the first half on television. It's time for a new prescription." Worse still, he charged me for the telegram the next time he checked my eyes. Only my eye doctor knows, and he promised not to tell.

There is a popular belief that only two teams are involved in a professional football game. Don't you believe it. The next time you watch a game, look the field over carefully. You will see a third team—six fellows in striped shirts and white pants, each with a whistle in his mouth.

But we—the third team—don't mind passing unnoticed. We live by the rule "If they don't know who's working the ball game, you've had a great day." The degree of anonymity an official achieves with the coaches, players and spectators is quite often the

A football referee is really a very lucky person. During the game—and afterwards, too—you get nothing but help. It's the only job in the world that everyone wants to help you with.

degree of his success. Of course, no official can go unnoticed forever. Sooner or later, he will be booed by the crowd. And worse yet, some people will learn his name.

I was once stopped for my autograph after a game in Baltimore. Two youngsters seemed quite grateful for my signature. As I turned to go, one kid whispered to the other, "Who is that old buzzard anyway?"

I turned back and told them I was the referee. The second kid ripped up the paper with my signature and told his friend, "If he has to tell you who he is, he ain't."

Unlike baseball umpiring, pro football officiating is an avocation, not a vocation. It is not a full-time job. We receive no regular salary, no pensions. We get paid by the game—anywhere from $250 (starting rate) to $500, depending on experience. Nevertheless, after a really tough game, an official feels as if he has worked a full week. And in a sense, he has. Most officials review their rules every weekday of every week of the season, and that's a lot of reviewing. Since there are six preseason games, fourteen league games and finally the play-offs, at least twenty weeks are involved.

The third team works as a six-man crew. The same crew members work together all season and generally, unless someone gets fired or retires, season after season. Crew-member and game assignments are received from the National Football League, our boss. After a Sunday game, each member of the crew returns to his home city. There, on Wednesday, he receives his game assignment for the weekend following his next game. That's about ten days' advance notice. He then returns a card to the League verifying his receipt of the weekend game assignment.

Most people don't seem to realize that we work for the league, not for the individual clubs. I'm sure that many coaches would like to carry their own crew of officials. But we're paid by the league and the league only. We have nothing to do with the clubs except to work their games as representatives of the league office.

We make our own plane reservations. I travel around 120,000 miles per season. I've flown almost two million miles, and am most fortunate in having never missed a game. We travel first class. Many of the airlines have sports representatives who get us reservations when we need help. I leave home on Saturday morning, as it takes most of a day to reach the city where I'll be working Sunday. My fellow crew members do likewise, and we all meet for dinner on Saturday night. Our contract states that on the night

before the game we must be in the city where we'll be working.

From November until the end of the season, we have to keep our fingers crossed and our eyes on airplane schedules. The weather during that time can present problems. But I can't recall an official's ever having missed his game because of bad weather. *Absenteeism* is just not a word in our vocabulary. Of course, I've had some close calls. I remember leaving my home in Los Angeles one Saturday for a game in Pittsburgh. We flew into some rough weather and had to land in Kansas City. I took the only flight that night to Chicago and stayed there until Sunday morning. At 6 A.M. I was at last able to get on a plane to Pittsburgh. We landed there at noon. I got to the stadium at 12:30 and gave the signal to start the game at 1:05. Fortunately for me, it turned out to be an easy game with few fouls.

Flying means other problems too: the people who sit near me. Occasionally they recognize me, and the conversation starts with three questions.

1. Can you get me some tickets?
2. Who's going to win?
3. Don't they have officials back there?

I considered having cards printed with answers:

1. No. I can't even get them for myself.
2. The team with the most points.
3. The officials back there are sent out West.

We don't mind passing unnoticed. We live by the rule "If they don't know who's working the game, you've had a great day."

117

Every week, one fellow is assigned to discuss a rule
in depth. Our rule book may not be too racy,
but we spend more time reading it than Playboy magazine.

Years ago, when someone on the plane, usually my seat partner, would ask me why I was going to whatever particular city, I would tell him I was a football referee. I would then have to listen to descriptions of all the poor calls that fellow had seen for the past 20 years. Then he would try to get me to second-guess someone else's call that he'd seen on television. No way!

In time I got smart. I never mentioned football. I said I was a school administrator—and caught hell for it. I was blamed for riots, nonreading ability, disrespect for elders and the drug problem.

I finally found the solution. Now when we're 30,000 feet above sea level and my seat partner asks me what I do for a living, I tell him I'm an undertaker. That ends all conversation immediately. The persons gets up after a decent interval, and the word spreads. I'm left alone, with all the room in the world. No one, and I mean no one, wants to hear about my profession. In fact, I'm thinking of printing some business cards, but I can't decide whether UNDERTAKER should be in caps, and whether the card should be rimmed with a black border.

All six members of our "third team" are good friends with one another. We have to be. After a tough game, no one else is going to step forward and say "Friend" to you. Our crew comes from all over the country. The umpire is from Pittsburgh; the field judge is from Akron, Ohio; the line judge is from Lee's Summit, Missouri; the back judge is from Redlands, California and the head linesman is from St. Louis. The referee (that's me) lives in Los Angeles.

The men arrive at different times on Saturday. The first man to arrive in the city that day (and it's usually Jack Fette, the line judge) rents a car and tries to meet the others. (We've told Fette that if he loses his driving license, we'll get another line judge.) If possible, the fellows wait for one another at the airport and come in as a group.

The league office makes hotel reservations for all the crews. Prior to the season, the officials select the hotels they prefer for each league city. The very best hotels are selected. It's first cabin all the way. We'll need our rest, especially if we'll have to make a run for it after the game.

No matter what else is planned, the six of us meet at our hotel at 5 o'clock Saturday afternoon for our first meeting. That's kickoff time for the crew that works the game the following day. There we review our last game. Every possible foul, no-foul and controversial call is rehashed. Everyone goes over what he heard, saw and read about our last game. When we've exhausted that topic, we review the calls we've heard or read about from the other games. With their inquiries about unusual calls from the previous Sunday, football fans keep the phones at the league office ringing all week long.

Saturday afternoon is also "book" time. Every week, one fellow is assigned a rule to discuss in depth at our Saturday afternoon meeting. One week, the field judge may go over all possible pass interference calls, trap plays and pick-off plays. He questions us on penalties, rules interpretations and the tough-call areas of pass interference. When he is through, another fellow is assigned a rule for the following week; it might, for example, be the umpire, who will discuss holding and illegal use of the hands. Everyone will get his chance to shine and be "head" man on a different Saturday. Our rule book may not be too racy, but we spend more time reading it than we do *Playboy* magazine.

That takes us up to seven or seven-thirty. Then it's time to eat, and meals, too, are a together thing. We seldom discuss football at them, for one of us might say something jokingly and be overheard and misunderstood. Politics and other sports are taken care of at this time, and for guys who hate to be second-guessed, we certainly do our share of it. Maybe second-guessing is a part of human nature.

After dinner it's back to work for "Saturday Night at the Movies." We watch the film of our last game. Throughout it, everybody comments freely. It's "Back it up, let's look at that shot again. There! What do you think?" and "Good thing I didn't call that a clip. Damn good block, right? Real close!" for two or three hours. How long depends on how difficult a game it was.

When I check into the hotel on Saturday, the bell captain has a film projector ready for me. The home team has sent it over for our use; the line judge will return it to them next day at the stadium. On Tuesday or Wednesday the league office air-freighted the game film, and that too is waiting at the hotel for me. Our umpire will return it to the league on Monday.

There are five reels in our game film. One is for kicks: field goals, kickoffs, punts and try-for-points. Two are on the offensive plays—one reel for each half. The remaining two reels are defensive ones— again, one for each half.

With each film package, we get a play-by-play resumé of the game. It's the same resumé reporters receive in the press box. It details every play, the yardage to be made, the spot of the snap and the position of the ball on the field. We also go over every-

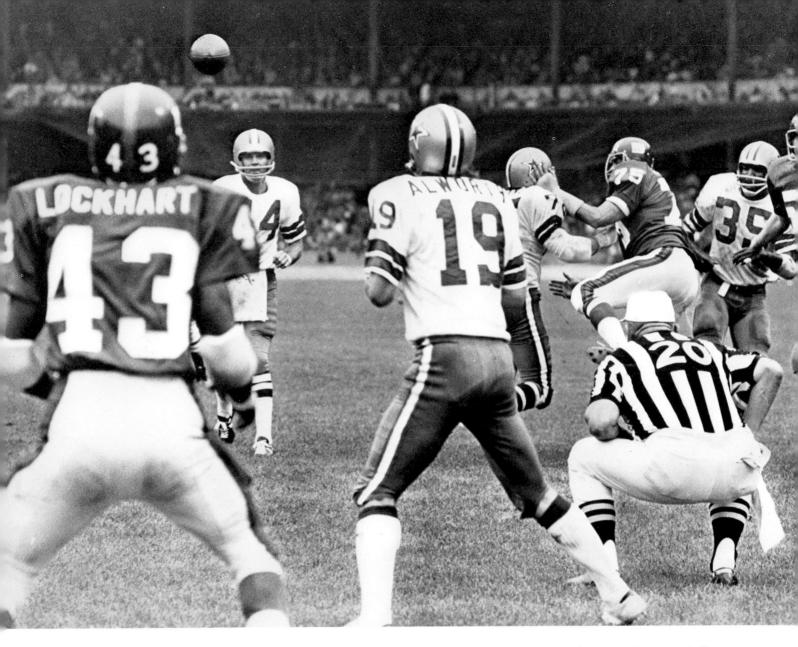

thing I heard on Monday from the league office when I called in my report. The league had heard from the Supervisors of Officials, the game observers, newspaper reporters and coaches. These comments were relayed to me, and I relay them to the crew along with the league's comments on the game film.

As we view the film, we try not to second-guess ourselves. We use the film as a teaching device. We're constantly trying to improve our positioning and mechanics. We stop the film, rerun it and dissect it thoroughly. When we are finished with it, we review what we're going to concentrate on the next day. By this time it is around 11 o'clock, and we are about ready to call it a night.

We meet again for breakfast at nine. Once again, we try not to discuss football, but occasionally people recognize us anyway. I remember Super Bowl V in Miami, a couple of years ago. It was the morning of the game, and we had just sat down for breakfast at the Doral Hotel. I had never stayed there before. When it came my turn to order, I hesitated and muttered, "I don't know whether to get ham and eggs or sausages and eggs."

The waitress didn't look up from her pad as she said, "That's probably the toughest call you'll have to make today."

I glanced up in surprise. "Ham and eggs, please," I said calmly.

"Well, you blew it," she said as she wrote it down on her pad.

I had never seen her before. And the game didn't start until one!

We arrive at the stadium an hour and a half before kickoff. Our contract requires us to be in our dressing room at this time for our pregame conference. No one is excepted; if someone isn't there, he had better have a good excuse. As referee, I conduct the conference. Its primary purpose is to review basic principles of officiating as they relate to the particular

*After any controversial call,
especially one that's against the
home team, people start
growling and questioning, "Where
the hell did they find him?"*

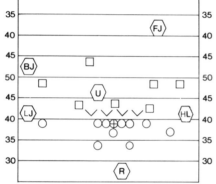

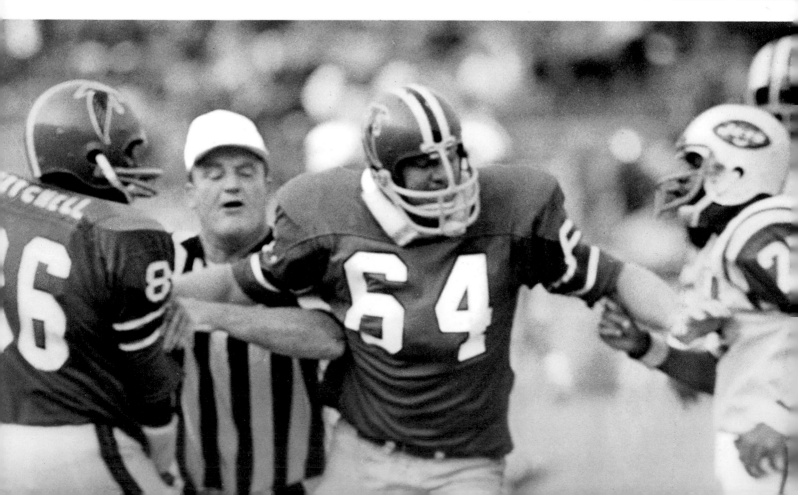

game. There isn't time for a complete review of the rules, and one wouldn't make sense anyway. All the crew members know the rules and their interpretations. This time is more profitably spent in going over items that might create problems on the field. A knowledge of teams' systems and individual-player habits is valuable in the pregame conference. Everyone on the crew contributes certain aspects of his respective position. We go over positioning, teamwork and potential trouble areas. It's our last shot to get ready.

Some of the items covered are:

1. Pregame duties—positions, television procedures.
2. Physical aspects of field—markings, player benches, personnel on sideline, press box phone, ball boys, chain men.
3. Timing and related functions—review of basic situations, last two minutes of each half, crowd noise procedures, extension of periods (and sudden death in postseason games).
4. Position and coverage—free kicks, fair catch, safety, on-side kicks, out-of-bounds, touchbacks, fumbles.
5. Running plays—coverage in side zones, forward progress, short yardage, measurements.
6. Pass plays—short ones, long ones, illegal passes, quarterback running, interceptions.
7. Punting situations—long kick, possible clips on run backs, short kick (in-bounds or out-of-bounds), blocked kicks.
8. Field-goal attempts—position of field judge and back judge, blocked attempts, touchback situations.
9. Time-outs—television time-outs, two-minute warning, team time-out, injury time-out.
10. Calling of penalties—when, where, who, communication to referee, signals.
11. Enforcement of penalties—spot of enforcement, yardage, down after penalty.
12. Miscellaneous—safety situations, fourth down fumble, shift rule, backward pass and fumble situations in last two minutes, substitutions, disqualifications, teamwork, unusual plays from previous games, game cards.

When we go out on the field, we're ready. The flip of the coin is a half-hour before kickoff. During that half-hour, all six officials have definite and different responsibilities which have to be performed.

The field judge checks to see that 12 balls are available. They're provided by the home team. The air pressure of the 12 balls is checked. The umpire checks all players whose hands are bandaged or taped as well as all players wearing special protective equipment; he has to be certain they will not injure other players. The head linesman locates the yardage chains, checks them out and reviews procedures with the chain crew. The chain crew (boxman, two rodmen and alternate) are not part of the officiating crew. They are appointed by the commissioner for each league city. They are local men.

The line judge contacts each coach and informs him of the official time, schedule of kickoff and any pretoss program. He also locates the field telephone operator and announcer.

The back judge and field judge check the field and the markings. They usually start on the fifty-yard line on opposite sides of the field and go to their left around the boundary lines.

Three minutes prior to kickoff, the referee and the two team captains meet in the center of the field, and the referee signals which team will receive and which will kick off. We're now ready for the game.

Perhaps a word or two on what the officials do prior to, during and after a play would give a better understanding of our job. Look at the diagram and locate the six officials.

The referee (R) has general oversight and control of the game. He is the final authority for the score. He stands behind the offensive team, eight to twelve yards to the right of the quarterback. He stays on the right (unless there is a left-handed quarterback), for one of his toughest calls is whether the pass is started or not. He must also assume a position that affords a clear view of all backfield players. He explains and enforces all penalties and gives the signals for television and the spectators.

The umpire (U) plays directly behind the defense, about three to five yards back of the ball. He watches the interior line play. He learns very quickly to move, for the smart quarterbacks will use him as a target or screen for forward passes. When an official gets hit, nine out of ten times he is the umpire. And nine out of ten times that will get the biggest laugh of the afternoon.

The head linesman (HL) takes a position at the end of the line. He handles the chain crew and all plays in his side zone, off sides, illegal motion and holding of the end and flanker.

The line judge (LJ) stands across from the head linesman; he has very basic responsibilities. He checks to see whether a pass thrown behind the line is a forward or backward one, whether a scrambling quarterback throws a pass behind or beyond the line of scrimmage, and whether or not there is illegal motion on line and shift plays.

The back judge (BJ) is responsible for picking up the runner in his side zone when he crosses the line of scrimmage. He spots the ball on runs which develop away from him. Pass interference is also one of his big calls. He plays from 12 to 15 yards off the ball downfield from the line judge.

The field judge (FJ) is the deep man. He keeps busy. You may think he is a spectator, but he's moving and thinking all sixty minutes of a ball game. As a general rule, he favors the side of the head linesman prior to snap. He stands about 20 to 25 yards downfield. He watches for pass interference, holding of the tight end, first touching of a kick and out-of-bounds plays. He is especially careful not to let the ball get between him and the sideline, goal line or end line. He checks the 30-second count. That's how much time a team is allowed to get the ball in play after the referee gives his signal to play.

Though the referee is in charge of the game and crew, he cannot overrule an official's judgment call. All six officials have equal responsibility. A rule interpretation can be discussed, but never a judgment call unless the official has been blocked out and must look for help.

A knowledge of the rules is very important. Judgment and common sense are even more important. Some NFL officials are more knowledgeable than others on rules, but all of them have tremendous judgment.

All the teams and all the players and coaches play by the rules. It's too expensive to foul. Yardage comes tough in the NFL. The individualized offenses of certain teams do not present any special problems to the officials. Mike Wilson, former Supervisor of Officials, once told me that there were only two questions I should ask myself about any play: "Is it right or wrong?" and "Is it five or fifteen?"

The second-best bit of advice I received was given me by Dutch Heintz, a retired referee and now an observer with the league. He stated time and time again, "Never blow the whistle unless you see the ball."

It saved my job once, I'm sure. Washington had a third-and-inches play on their 34-yard line. If ever there was a time to pick up the first down on a plunge, this was it. It started that way too. The quarterback—I think it was Snead—handed off to the fullback, who drove over the center for an apparent first down. I moved in quickly, too quickly. It was a fake hand-off and a dandy. I was about to blow my whistle to kill the play when I heard this tremendous roar from the crowd. I looked up to see Bobby Mitchell alone in the end zone, waiting for the long forward pass to reach him. I didn't blow the whistle, and therefore didn't blow the play. But it was a close one. Now I don't care how long it takes me to find the ball. I don't blow the whistle unless I see it.

The league office brass, Mark Duncan, Mel Hein and Art McNally, keep all the officials alerted to any new officiating wrinkles through phone calls and constant bulletins. During the summer, the officials meet for a four-day clinic in which they view and review movies of calls of previous years, mechanics and positioning. They also go over techniques. All possible types of offenses and defenses are reviewed for officiating positions and mechanics. Unusual situations from previous seasons are discussed thoroughly. It is not a second-guessing game. If there were mistakes made, they won't be made a second time. There is also a review-of-the-rules test. The league mails out a rules-review examination of 200 questions. The questions incorporate the various rules within play situations. It is an open-book exam; the officials have two months to complete the test and return it. Most officials who live within a reasonable distance of each other get together five to seven times over a period of six weeks to discuss the test questions. Our group —not to be confused with our crew—meets one afternoon a week in April and May from four until nine; then we all go out to dinner and talk football.

The obvious, run-of-the-mill fouls are no problem. It's the unusual and seldom seen ones that create conversation. Dialogue varies, but it's the same routine.

The officials who don't live near one another use the phone a great deal. Mark Duncan claims that he would work for a salary equal to just the phone bills the fellows run up (at their own expense) in getting the answers. It's high, I'm sure, for the officials are as conscientious in their approach to the game as are the players and coaches in theirs. It's an exacting profession.

By now I'm sure you understand why an official really "hurts" when someone believes he just drops by on a Sunday afternoon to work a couple of hours. It's *not* a couple of hours. It's years of experience, hours every week of reviewing the rule book and thinking football. It's the weekend of preparation. And it's a complete dedication to a job that makes sense and is enjoyable. It's like my Marine Corps experience. I wouldn't take a million dollars to do it again, but I wouldn't have missed it for the world.

What makes a good pro official? That's a difficult question. Even officials differ on what it takes. I have my own criteria. The items I list are sound and extensive experience, poise, a keen sense of humor, excellent physical condition, the ability to laugh at yourself and the "guts" to make the big call against the home team with the clock running out.

Physical condition is most important. Physical alertness is as important as mental alertness. It doesn't come easy, and it gets tougher to maintain as you gain valuable experience with age. Heavy men take a bad picture. Television shows every pound. I, as well as all other officials, have to be in shape to stay on top of every play. I ride my bike five miles three times a week, and the other two days I run and exercise an hour each day. Saturday is travel day, and Sunday I run my usual four to five miles in refereeing the game.

Besides his uniform, there are two things a pro official needs to have. One is a basic understanding of the rule book. The other is a thorough knowledge of the *Officials' Manual*. But neither book will teach you how to make instant decisions, adjust to emergencies, show poise and temper control, be courteous and considerate yet firm and decisive and be consistent in your calls. Proper preparation can eliminate potential problems. Competency and integrity are basic requirements. You can't learn those qualities from any book.

Sunday afternoon is not a play day. It's work. Hard work. Some fans think, "How lucky can a guy be? Here they not only pay those fellows, they get in free. And look how close they are to the game." It may look as if the men are merely watching. As a

referee, I have to make certain they aren't. When I look downfield, I may be fooled too. I remember working a Green Bay–Dallas televised game in the Cotton Bowl. It was a great game; things were going right. I looked downfield and observed that the back judge had been looking at the stands too often. He probably was checking the sidelines. In the last quarter came an announcement: "A new Cotton Bowl attendance record. Seventy-five thousand, four hundred and seventy-three."

I called time-out and signalled for the back judge to come over. He ran up, thinking he was going to hear some officiating advice. Instead, I asked him, "Is that the count you got?"

He knew what I meant.

After any controversial call, especially one against the home team, people start growling and asking one another, "Where the hell did they find that official?"

The league office has come a long way in selecting officials. They work at it the same way football teams do when they evaluate players. Fellows are scouted, evaluated and selected after years of having their work observed. Along with observers' verbal and written reports, the films of games officials have worked in college and high school are studied. There is no easy road to the top in any profession—least of all in pro officiating. When the time comes for a

*This is the only business in the world where a man
has to be perfect in his first game and then get
better every week. I'm tested every Sunday afternoon.*

man to get selected, he has worked hundreds of high
school games and a major college schedule before
large crowds. He has been tested. Quite often it
doesn't work out, and the man selected lasts only a
year or two. The turnover is not too high, but the total
number of officials is not too high either. We have 84
officials, and if 6 are released in a year, that's high—
especially if you are one of the 6.

When the league is interested in a prospective
official, things are not left to chance. One of the
league's observers, usually a former pro official who
has retired, watches the fellow work many times
throughout the season. Quite often, different observ-

ers will watch him work. The observers spot-check a
"potential" prospect on his judgment, reaction under
pressure, decisiveness, game control, positioning and
coverage.

If the reports are favorable and the observers
think the prospect can handle the job, then one of the
league supervising officials watches him work. Mark
Duncan, Mel Hein or Art McNally from the league
office will give him the once-over—and not very
lightly. They also check with the pro officials who
might be familiar with the man's ability and potential.
If everything comes up to their standards, he is offered a contract. Quite often, we officials tip the

league office about prospective qualified officials.

We're quite cautious in our evaluations. I learned to be careful the hard way. I received a call from the league office one day years ago. They were interested in some fellow from my section of the country. The usual questions were asked, and finally the big one:

"Norm, is he an official you think would make it?"

"Yes, I do," I replied. "He's worth a contract. He's a good man."

"Fine," answered Mike Wilson, who was then Supervisor of Officials. "We'll put him on your crew."

Without thinking, I shouted back, "Hey, wait a minute! I don't think he's that good yet!"

What I meant was, he has the potential to be a good official, but let him learn with someone else. The prospect joined our crew and is now one of the top officials in the country.

Once someone asked me, "When is a football official ready for the professional leagues?"

The answer I gave was "When he has worked five years in them."

I had a solid background in officiating before I reached the NFL. I had worked literally hundreds of games. I had done some high school officiating before joining the Marines. After I got out, I worked high school and college games on the West Coast for eight more years before I finally heard from Bert Bell in 1953. During his era as commissioner, there were no applications for becoming an NFL official as there are today. People were scouted, checked and offered a contract. Commissioner Bell asked me if I was interested in working the pros. I was. He sent me a contract and cautioned me, "Don't say anything to anyone. We'll release the publicity at the right time."

That was nineteen years ago. I wonder when the right time is going to come.

In March of 1971, a well-dressed man of about 35 came into my office. We shook hands and he came right to the point. (This happens often.)

"I've watched you work and seen others work," he said. "I'd like to become a National Football League referee. It looks like fun and not too tough, and I love to travel."

I looked at him. What the hell did he mean, he watched me work and thought he could handle the job!

"What you need to do is to drop Mark Duncan a letter telling him you're interested, and he'll mail you a letter with an application form," I said.

The man nodded. "I've done all that and have the letter. I'm having trouble filling it out."

"What do you mean trouble? Just list your answers and include your college schedule of games for this year and mention last year's schedule."

"Well, I've never worked any major college games."

"That's okay. List the small college games you've worked, or even the junior college games."

"I've never worked those either."

I didn't say anything for a few seconds. I wanted to be kind, and besides, it was a league affair. I finally said, "Send him your high school schedule then if you haven't done anything else."

"I've never worked any high school games either."

"Did you ever officiate anywhere?"

"Sure I did. I worked the bases in the Little League where my kid plays."

I suggested that he join the local Football Officials Association, start working high school games and come up from there. Perhaps in later years he could legitimately apply, I told him.

Mark Duncan, Director of Personnel, has told me that people are always writing in to become officials. The League sends them a letter that lists certain items necessary for consideration. Here is the letter:

The following are the requirements necessary to become an Official in the National Football League:

We expect our men to have a minimum of ten years' experience in officiating football, at least five of which has to be on a varsity collegiate level. Our candidates must be in excellent physical condition, belong to an accredited football officials association and have previous experience in football as a player or coach. Each applicant is requested to furnish us with a copy of his entire football officiating schedule for two previous seasons. In addition, he must supply statistics regarding his height, weight and age (officials are usually hired between the ages of thirty-two and forty-four).

Once the applicant has satisfied us that his credentials do meet the requirements, we send the application. We then place this man on an observation schedule and have members of our staff scout him while he works portions of his officiating schedule.

If the league feels that the applicant fulfills the basic requirements, he is mailed an application form. The form requests definite answers on questions such as:

1. Present employment—previous five years
2. Present position—duties
3. Height and weight
4. Wear glasses—correction
5. College attended—number of years

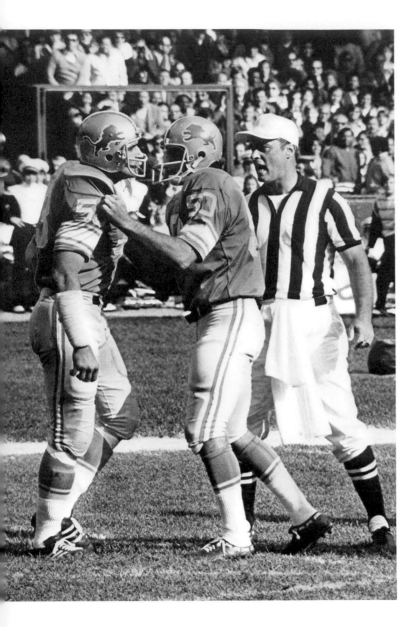

6. Sports in which you participated in college
7. Other sports now officiating
8. Have you had a civil judgment against you?
9. Ever been arrested?
10. Years in officiating football
    High School_____ College_____ Other_____
11. List number of varsity games worked
12. Personal references (three)
13. Bank references
14. Football officiating schedules
    Last year's _____   Next year's _____

Today's pro football officials come from all parts of the country and all walks of life. They are all successful men in their chosen professions. Their breadth of experience is varied, their one common interest football. Many of them had played college and pro football and coached on the different levels of competition; they became referees to stay in football. They are all college graduates, though this is not a league requirement.

We have officials who are lawyers, college professors, deans and registrars of universities, presidents of businesses, druggists, superintendents of schools, principals of large secondary schools, district managers of steel corporations, directors of sales, full-time public speakers, bank presidents, land developers, architects, sales counselors, directors of athletics, insurance executives, sales managers of sporting goods companies, mechanical engineers and a number of PhDs. One of them is even a state senator from Texas.

What bugs me is that just about every person who ever saw a pro game thinks he could be a pro official. They won't believe that it takes years of hard work and sweat, with lots of good bounces and luck, before you reach the big time. And as I've said before, it takes experience. Remember the story I began with, about Yankee Stadium exploding? If it hadn't been for my years of experience in hundreds and hundreds of games, I would have blown the call and the ball game.

It was the fourth quarter, with just a few minutes left. The Giants were playing Dallas in one of the crucials. (They're all crucials for the officials.) The ball was on the Dallas five; it was fourth down, the game on the line. Pete Gogolak, the Giants' soccer-type kicker, came in for the field goal that could win the game. The ball was snapped, placed down and kicked. Dallas's Bob Lilly broke through and blocked the attempt. The ball hit his chest and bounced back. With the swiftest reaction I've ever seen, Gogolak kicked the ball with his other foot as the ball came up off the ground on his left side. That's when the Stadium exploded. The kick went over the crossbar and out of the end zone. A dramatic win! Or was it?

That's when I threw my flag. The Giants rushed me, yelling, "What's the flag for? What's the penalty?"

I told them, "I don't know what it is, but I know it's wrong." It was an instinctive reaction.

Within a few seconds, I remembered. You can't kick a loose ball. And that's what a blocked kick is. The only ways the field goal would have counted were either for Gogolak to have recovered the ball and drop-kicked it himself or for his holder to have recovered it and held it for Gogolak to kick again. But possession was definitely necessary.

Since the Giants had put the ball out of the end zone, I gave it to the Cowboys on the twenty. I can still see Don Meredith coming out on the field and asking, "What happened, Norm?"

"Touchback, Don," I said. "Don't ask any questions. You came out smelling like a rose. Get the ball in play before they come after both of us."

That story illustrates what I mean by the value of experience. I had been around too long and worked too many games not to *sense* that the play was wrong, even though the *reason* it was did not immediately come to me.

Football is a game of bounces. A good official needs good bounces. Sometimes it's better to be lucky than good. Things may move along very nicely for 59 minutes of a ball game and then—bang. All hell breaks loose. It seems as if things that were bouncing right start to take that crazy bounce. It is then that experience and common sense make the pro official. Most people could learn the rule book even though it is over 100 pages of technical stuff. But—it is the instantaneous call that makes the difference. There are no committee meetings, no films to review and no second chances when the call has to be made. It's bang-bang! Right now! During an average game, an official will have to make 50 to 60 sudden decisions which could affect the outcome. There is no room for guesswork; there must be a decisive right call. Sometimes the decisive right call is a no call.

To be a good official, it helps to have a sense of humor. Besides, some very funny things are said out on the field. One official was telling me about his getting hit (accidentally) from his blind side by a player and knocked down. Another player ran over to help him up and asked, "What happened?"

The official had more than his pride hurt. "Got hit from the blind side," he muttered.

"You mean right between the eyes?" the player asked.

When Weeb Ewbank was coach of the Baltimore Colts, he once told me, "I don't want any breaks. Just give me my fair advantage."

That's what I'm paid for—to see that no one gets that "fair advantage."

I remember a funny remark made by Jim Lee Howell, former coach of the Giants. One game when the line play was a bit hectic, I penalized the Giants for a holding foul. It had happened right in front of Howell's bench. He bellowed, and his assistant coach yelled at me, "Let's use some sense out there!"

Howell looked at me and said, "If he had any sense, he wouldn't be out there."

Television and the instant replay have made it easy for the viewer to second-guess. But I don't get any instant replays to help me make the call. There's no second look. It's bang-bang! The instant replay

has also proved to the fans of the country how good the officials are. For this reason, I think it's a blessing. Now we don't have to defend the call. It's right there—over and over again. It doesn't ever change.

Fans don't realize that each official is assigned a certain area to cover. The officials don't watch the ball carrier; they watch the action in their zone of responsibility. A paying customer can watch only one thing, whether it's the ballcarrier, the end going deep or the guard pulling. He has one set of eyes. Our crew has six sets, and we cover the entire field.

It's interesting to note how the crew has grown over the years. Years ago, there were four officials. Then we went to five, and about five years ago, we went to six. The game required it. It is more open, faster and much more varied now. Players are quicker, smarter and faster. We needed that extra man, but I doubt that I'll be around when we'll have as many officials out there as players.

Actually, it did happen once. At the first Super Bowl game, which I refereed, we had six working officials and six alternates (just in case). That made 12 of us out on the field.

When the League added the sixth man and placed him opposite the head linesman and gave him definite responsibilities, they didn't know what to call him. It was finally decided to call him the line judge. I remember one of our officials saying, "It doesn't matter what name they give him. As soon as the whistle blows to start the game, they'll call him a blind bastard anyway."

We work very closely with television. The time-outs are so important. It pays for a lot of the traffic. The money helps the clubs, the players and even the officials. We try not to give a television time-out until

Watch the 'old-timer' offensive ends. If they're close to that sideline, they drag that second foot to get it in bounds. This confuses and brings on the noise.

both teams have had possession of the ball. We also won't stop a drive if it is within the other team's 20-yard line. Besides, the networks get a time-out for commercials after every score. Television gets three time-outs the first and third quarters and four the second and fourth quarters. The referee is required to give the coaches a two-minute warning before the end of the second and fourth quarters. We never forget that, as some of our rules are different the last two minutes of a half. When I'm walking or running over to tell the coaches that there are two minutes left, the broadcasters usually go with a television commercial.

Do you remember that bitter championship game between the Cowboys and the Packers in Green Bay in 1967? I blew my whistle to start the game just after they announced it was 22 below zero. That's cold! When you get hit, it smarts a bit. I blew my whistle to start the game, and that was the last time any official was able to blow his whistle. They all froze up. Joe Connell, the umpire that day, tried to blow his whistle on the second play. Nothing blew, and when he took the whistle out of his mouth, quite a bit of his lip came with the whistle. The game was worked by talking to the players, and no one ever knew the difference.

Late in the fourth quarter of that "freeze" bowl game, the television man signaled he needed his last time-out. By that time of the afternoon, they claimed it was 35 below. I called a referee's time-out, because I knew just how much money was riding on it— $150,000 or so.

Just as I signaled time-out and shouted it (since my whistle wouldn't whistle), Bob Skoronski, number 76, the offensive captain of the Packers, came running toward me. The captain is the only player who can legally request a time-out, and he knew he hadn't called it.

"Who the hell called that time-out?" he wanted to know.

"I did, Bob."

"Why?"

"For the players' pension fund," I chattered back.

"Great call! Great call!" he said.

Quite often the television fans and the stadium spectators see the players and referee talking. The dialogue varies, but basically it's the same routine. Players wonder "why" the penalty, since they honestly believe they didn't commit a foul. They're serious— and so am I. An official had better not laugh on the field. No one appreciates it. Big men are bashing one another, and it ain't funny, although sometimes something happens that we milk for a laugh to break the tension.

The obvious, run-of-the-mill fouls are no problem. It's the unusual and seldom seen ones that create conversation. Such a foul was called against the New York Giants a number of years ago. Andy Robustelli and Sam Huff were still doing their thing. They were both defensive captains. Andy and Sam didn't like the explanation and didn't like the penalty. Both of them are smart. They thought all the time on the field. Andy didn't hesitate to tell me how he felt about the call. As I was walking off the 15, he walked with me and kept complaining about it. Just as I finished my walk, I turned to him and said, "Andy, it's a rule."

"Well, then, it's a stinking rule," he yelled.

That should have ended the conversation. As he was walking away, I said, "Look, I didn't write the rule book."

Sam Huff had listened to the whole thing. He stopped, turned to me and said, "Yeah—but you could at least read it once in a while."

Norm Van Brocklin liked to help the officials. He was always keeping an official on his toes. When I worked a Vikings game during their first season in the league, there was a close call near the Minnesota bench. I heard the Dutchman's protesting voice loud and clear. The play had been close enough to the sidelines for me to hear him—and talk back. Without thinking and for no good reason, I answered (which is always a mistake) by saying, "Dutch, I call them as I see them."

Van Brocklin broke off a word and said, "I don't want you to call them as you see them. I want you to call them as they happened."

Flying back and forth across the country poses unique problems: time zones, irregular sleeping and eating habits, radical changes in climate. I often leave Los Angeles in short sleeves, no topcoat— summer apparel. When I arrive back East during November or December, the temperature is usually 40 to 50 degrees colder. I use a checklist so I won't forget my winter clothes. I don't mind forgetting the topcoat, but I would freeze if I forgot my thermal underwear, earmuffs and gloves.

For that "freeze bowl" game between Green Bay and Dallas, here's how I walked out on the field to referee the game. I had on my usual underwear, two pairs of thermal socks besides my football stockings, thermal underwear (tops and bottoms), turtleneck nylon ski sweater, plastic baggies on my feet, a large plastic covering that the cleaners use to return your suits under my football shirt, earmuffs, gloves and my football hat.

I still got cold. My extremities—fingertips, toes, nose—just never got warm. Officials go both ways,

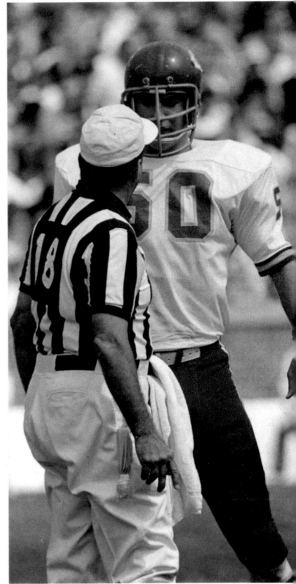

A quarterback can muff a play but be forgiven. But an official is only as good as the last call he made.

offensive and defensive, and never get a substitute. When the game ended, I hustled back to the West Coast, where the temperature was in the high 80s. My left heel had been frostbitten, and I had a lulu of a cold for eight days.

When I'm moving across country every week, I occasionally forget what teams are playing. But I'm always certain of the home town, since that's the city I'm ticketed to. One week runs into another, and it's difficult to convince people I've forgotten what game I worked last week, but I can always tell them where I'm going.

One weekend in Washington, I had checked into the hotel and was going up to my room. When the elevator had opened and I started to enter, I stopped to let someone out. It was Charlie Winner, at that time coach of the St. Louis Cardinals.

"Hello, Coach. What are you doing here?" I asked him.

"What am I doing here? My team plays here tomorrow. You're the referee."

As the door started to close, Charlie Winner turned around to look back at me. I didn't wonder what he was thinking. I knew.

One Sunday afternoon in Minneapolis, I was working a Vikings game. At half-time, Joe Connell (the umpire) and I were running to the dressing room. As I neared the tunnel, some fan in the stands yelled, "Hey, Norm! How are you? How's the family? Can I come down after the game to see you?"

He looked familiar. I turned to Connell and asked, "Where are we today, Joe?"

"Minnesota."

Then I remembered who the fellow was.

One inevitable question people ask when they find out I'm a pro football referee is "Say, what's the toughest call to make in professional football?" I'll list a few tough ones, just for a start.

A tough call for the referee becomes necessary when the quarterback, about to pass, is hit from the blind side and the ball pops out of his hand. Is it a fumble or an incomplete pass? It may sound simple here, but believe me, it's rough! You have to watch the quarterback's hand to see whether it is coming down as he is hit or whether the ball is knocked out of his hand. Remember that pro quarterbacks are smart and talented. As soon as any experienced one is hit from the blind side and the ball falls away, he immediately brings his hand down. A referee has to be watchful as hell. Otherwise, he'll be slickered. Last year in a Colt game, Unitas, a real pro, was hit—and the ball rolled out. His hand came down immediately. I ruled it a fumble. He charged over and said, "My hand was coming down—incomplete pass!"

I nodded and said, "You're right. Your hand was coming down, but you forgot to have the ball in it."

The play I'm about to describe is a controversial one, which means that someone is going to scream no matter what is called. It's often a delayed call and a tough one to make.

The flanker will go downfield, cut over and brush or block the linebacker or defensive back. The offensive end may come into the same territory, also to block. A run should materialize. But sometimes it doesn't. If the play is "busted," the quarterback may have to throw. And if he does, the tough part follows.

The rule states that it is offensive pass interference if any offensive player touches a defensive player beyond the line of scrimmage if there is a forward pass. This restriction begins with the snap from center. So it's perfectly legal for an offensive end or flanker to go downfield and block—as long as there is no pass. If one is thrown, however, his once-legal block becomes illegal, and a penalty must be assessed. It is a delayed call because the official has to remember where the block or brush took place before he can throw the flag there. By this time, no player is near the scene of the foul; the flanker or end may be 30 yards away. The crowd doesn't see why the foul is called, since no one is anywhere close by, and that's when the uproar starts.

As I said, quarterbacks can be tricky. When Y. A. Tittle was passing the New York Giants to a championship, he was trapped one day about eight yards in back of his line. He couldn't get the pass away. He ate the football. But there was defensive holding on the play. That meant that the penalty (the rule has since been changed) was enforced from the dead ball spot. That's where Y. A. was dropped. I picked up the ball and started to walk off the five-yard penalty for defensive holding.

Y. A. Tittle ran up and said, "Hey, Norm, wrong spot. It's a forward pass play. Enforce it from the previous spot."

I looked at Y. A. Forward pass? I thought. He must be joking. "That was no forward pass," I said. "The ball has to be thrown before it's a forward pass."

Y. A. Tittle was no fool. He knew. He just wasn't sure I knew or would remember. It was worth a try. Not to me, though.

That same year, during another Giants game, I called an intentional grounding of a forward pass. Tittle had thrown the ball away as he was being chased to the sidelines. No one was within thirty yards of the pass, but he would have been dumped for a big loss otherwise. Tittle rushed me even though he knew why I had thrown the flag.

"Hey, it was a busted play," he protested. "Shofner should have cut the other way, and the ball slipped."

I looked at him. "Y. A., if you don't throw any better than that, you'll be gone," I said.

Tittle won the Most Valuable Player award that year, but the play had cost him 15 yards and a down just the same.

Another tough call is a pass completion near the sideline. In pro football the receiver has to have both feet land in-bounds (on the field) for a completed pass.

Watch the "old-timer" offensive ends. If they're close to that sideline, they drag that second foot to get it in-bounds. Our rule differs from that of college and high school, in which receivers need to land with only one foot in-bounds. This fact confuses many spectators, and brings on the noise.

A very difficult call is deep pass interference when both the offensive and defensive men go for the ball. During a forward pass, defensive players have as much right to the ball as offensive eligible receivers. Any bodily interference, however severe, between players who are making a bona fide and simultaneous attempt to catch a ball is not interference. Quite often it's just a little push or shove that makes for that "fair advantage." The field judge who is down-field has to decide whether the attempt is a bona fide one or whether there has been contact prior to this attempt.

While we're on the subject of pass interference, let's talk about the trap on a forward pass. It happens when a ball is thrown to the tight end, who goes behind the umpire and in front of the field judge. The field judge has trouble looking past the tight end when the receiver turns his back to him and makes the play. The receiver could trap a low pass and the field judge not see it. That's where crew help comes in. The umpire turns as soon as the ball goes over his head. He has a clear shot at the play. The field judge looks for help. That's when the umpire makes the call.

It sounds simple—but it's not. It's the field judge's call, and he has to ask for the help. He will look at the umpire, who will then make the call. I've worked games where we didn't get our crew signals straight. The field judge would signal good, and the umpire would signal no good and incomplete. What do I do then? Well, I ask them both if either one wants to back off. Usually one does, the one who signalled too quickly. If both are sure, but another official also saw the play, he comes in to give us some help. Otherwise, I go with the man whose area the play happened in. And pray!

Many people wonder just how much protection a quarterback gets from the referee. The Rules Committee is definitely committed to the policy of protecting the passer. A passer who is standing still or fading backwards is obviously out of the play once the ball has left his hand. He is to be protected until the pass ends or until he starts to move into a distinctly defensive position. The referee, and this is a judgment call, must determine whether the defensive player had a reasonable chance to stop his momentum during his attempt to block the pass or tackle the passer while the passer was still in possession.

If you are close enough to the play, just after the pass is thrown, you will hear me yell, "Leave him alone!" or "Stay away from him!" If the defensive player continues on and knocks the passer down, it is a fifteen-yard penalty and an automatic first down. If the pass is completed, we still add fifteen to the end of the completion. And—if there is a touchdown, we penalize the fifteen on the next kickoff. It costs a team yardage to rough the opposing quarterback after the ball is thrown. The rule book specifically says that "care should be exercised by the referee to insure ample protection of the passer after the ball has left his hand. Watching or determining the flight of the pass by the referee is a secondary responsibility under these conditions."

Until the pass is thrown, the quarterback is the same as any other back and receives no additional protection. He can't be roughed, but then, neither can any other running back. Protection only starts after the pass is made.

I remember a big tackle on the 49ers who always came in hard after the quarterback. He would throw his forearm most of the time and miss the quarterback, but not by much. Once, I told him, "Watch yourself. It'll cost you fifteen if you touch him."

As he walked by me, he nodded. On the next play, his forearm came across the quarterback's helmet after the quarterback had released the ball. I threw my flag. "That'll cost you fifteen," I told him.

He looked at me and replied, "It was worth it."

But it wasn't. San Francisco had intercepted the pass and scored. I took the score away, but actually, it was he who took it away. I gave the ball back to the other team, tacked on 15 yards and signaled a first down. They went in for a score. That illustrates why the good players hate to foul.

A kicker has equal protection. The responsibility of avoiding contact with the kicker belongs to the defensive player if he doesn't touch the ball. I'm certain that experienced punters belong to the Screen Actors' Guild. If a defensive man gets close enough almost to block the kick, a dramatic punter twists and groans as he falls to the ground. It's quite theatrical, but the referee usually leaves him there with, "Get up, you weren't hit. You're making me look bad."

His bench sees the kicker fall and the familiar chant starts: "Roughing the kicker, roughing the kicker . . ."

Frequently the kicker's teammate will block a defensive man into the kicker. Though the defender bumps him, it is the result of the block. Roughing the kicker is not called. Some blockers get very cute at rolling an opponent into the kicker. They work on the percentages. They believe that sometime a foul will be called. It's wishful thinking on their part. The referee has no one else to watch at that particular time. He gets a good look at it.

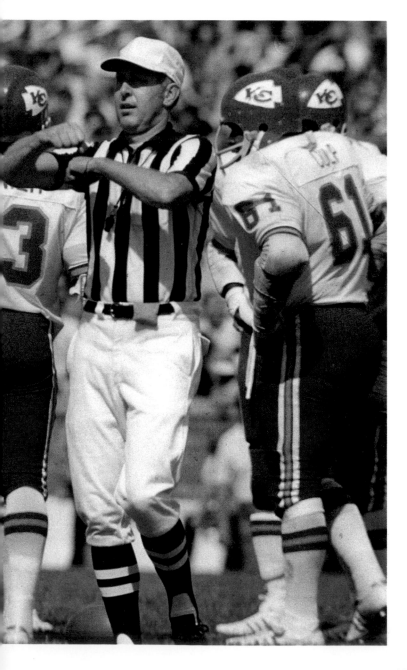

I speak to lots of groups throughout the year. One question always asked is, "Doesn't it bug you to hear the fans get after you?"

Not really. I know it isn't me. It's the uniform. And it doesn't matter who's wearing the uniform. If you have ever pulled on a striped shirt and walked across the white lines of a football field, you know what I mean.

I have to keep telling myself it's nothing personal. When the howling gets unreasonable, I think of the average fan. He's the quiet type. He never answers back to anyone. Everyone's on his back all day long. After a hard day of listening, he goes to the ball park and gives the referee hell. It's the only chance he ever gets.

When you're raising a family and your kids watch you work a game, things can get sticky. I remember a game in which a controversial call set the place off like a giant rocket. We had to hold up the game before the quarterback could make himself heard over the noise.

On the way home, I carefully delivered a planned routine on how crowds treat officials, how impersonal the booing was even though it sounded personal and how biased fans are. I carefully structured the routine to make my sons react to the boos impersonally, the way I do. Finally, I turned to the oldest one, who was nine, and said, "Well, Tom, it didn't bother you any, did it? You know what I'm trying to say?"

Tom didn't even think. He blurted out, "Yeah, I know what you're trying to say. And it is personal. I was booing louder than all of them put together. You booted that call."

Many spectators believe all the ills of poor officiating would disappear if the officials knew the rule book. That's wishful thinking. There is no magic like hard work, hustle, a sense for good position, a knowledge of your responsibility and a redoubling of the effort of the crew.

We have our rule book, our *Officials' Manual*, directives and guidelines. We read them. We study them. We practice them. With good luck and a good bounce, we'll do a great job.

This is the only business in the world where a man has to be perfect in his first game and then get better every week. I have to prove myself again and again in every game. I'm tested every single Sunday afternoon.

A quarterback can muff a play but be forgiven because he has also made great plays. A coach can be forgiven for losing a big game because the fans remember big games he has won. But an official is only as good as the last call he made. He'd better pray it was the right one.

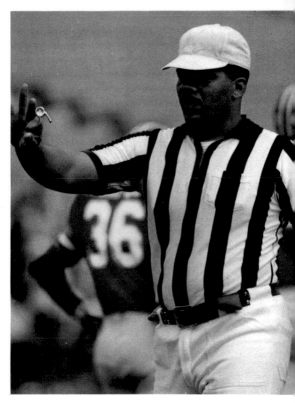

The turnover is not too high, but the total number of officials is not too high either. We have eighty-four officials, and if six are released in a year, that's high.

133

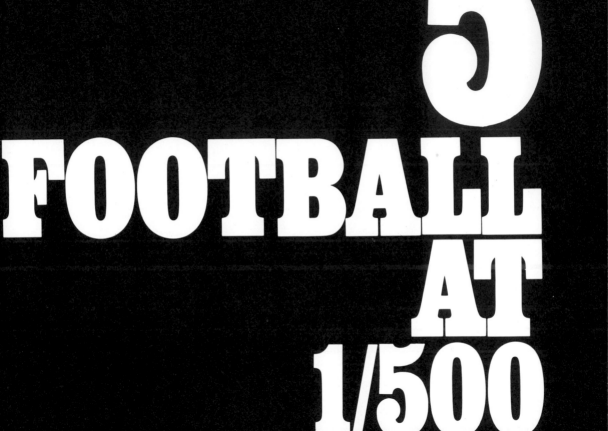

FOOTBALL AT 1/500

It is the photographer's sensitivity and awareness that determine the graphic meaning of an experience. Chosen and created subjectively, his pictures become for other people objectively what happened.

"Looking through a camera's viewfinder is an experience of creativity. The essence of photography is to show the familiar in terms of newness and meaningfulness."
—Dave Boss

"The toughest football shots for me are
pass receivers catching the ball."
—Fred Kaplan

"I don't like artificial turf.
I like dirt and mud."
—Tony Tomsic

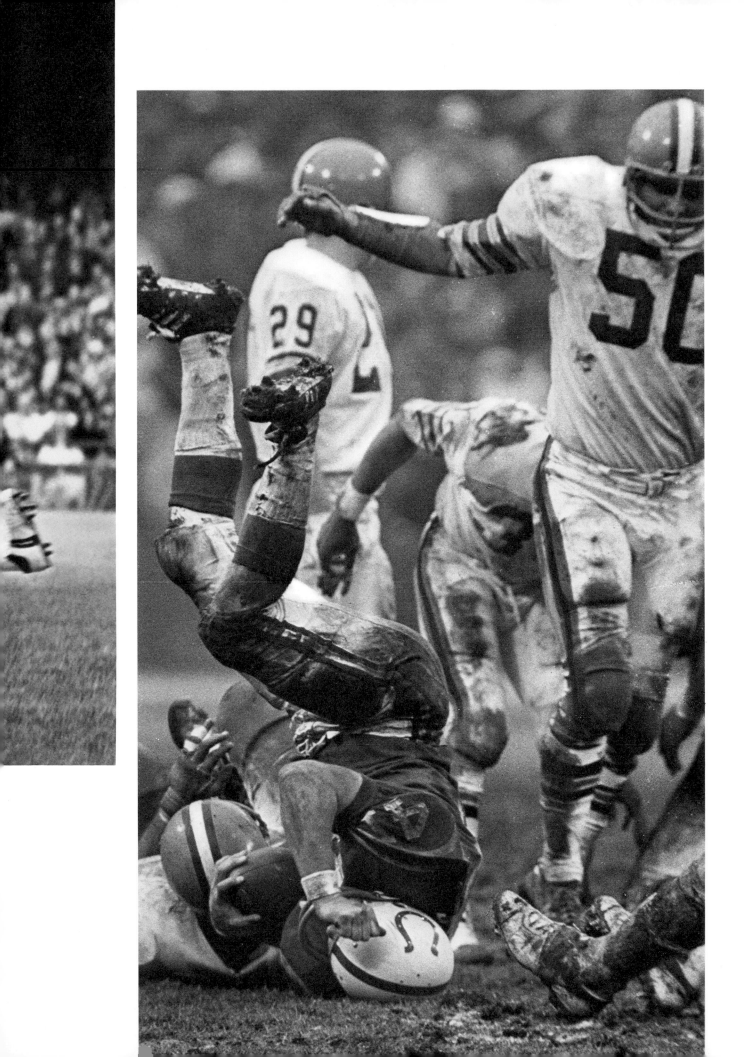

"Many photographers prefer a 50mm lens or a 200mm lens, but I like the 600. It's harder to use, but it brings the action up tight and, hopefully, shows some expression."
—Melchior DiGiacomo

"Shooting at high shutter speeds, the camera allows us to understand what the eye often misses."
—Dave Boss

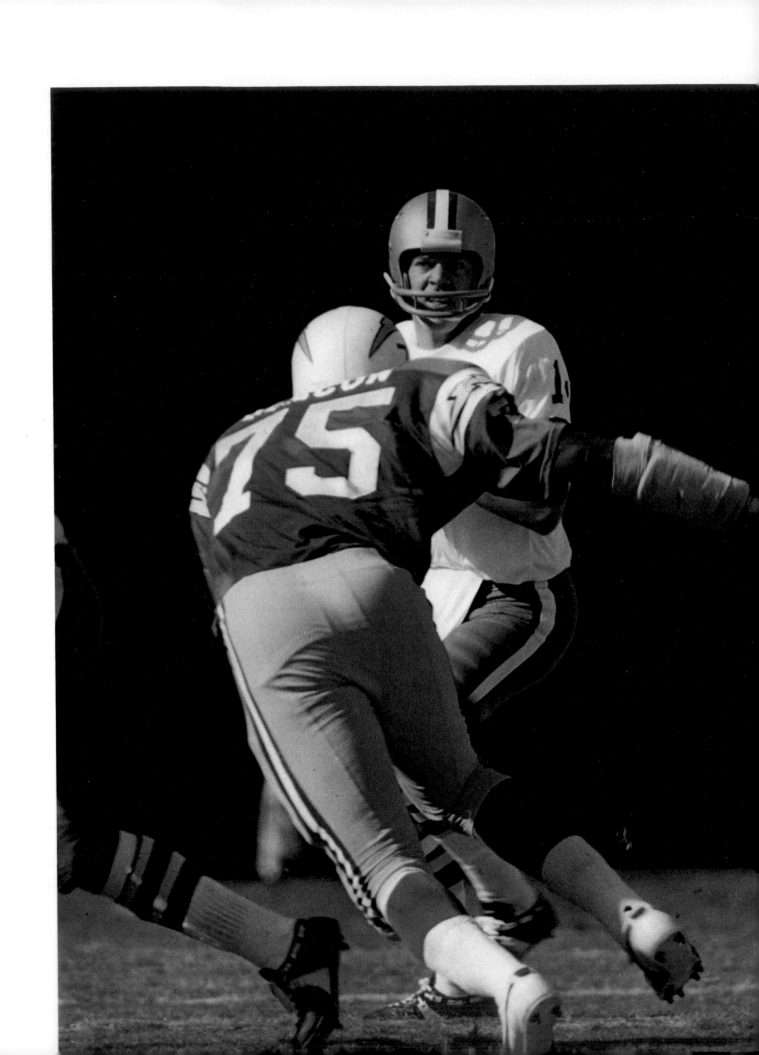

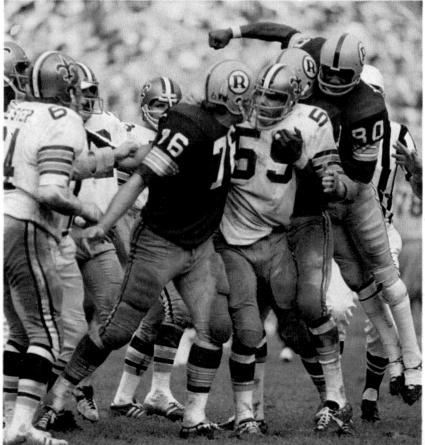

"To catch the action, you've got to try to read the plays. If you know the coach or the quarterback, you'll have a good idea of where the play will go."
—Tony Tomsic

"I try to shoot in the style of a photo-
journalist. During a game, there
are a lot of bombs thrown, a lot of tackling
done, but for me, the story is over
at the sidelines."
—Melchior DiGiacomo

"The key is knowing the sport, knowing what is going on on the field."
—Richard Raphael

"When it's obvious that it's a pass, I try to see who
the quarterback intends throwing to, then as
quickly as possible pick up that player with the
600mm, focus and shoot. Luck plays a part."
—Fred Kaplan

150

"By isolating his camera with a telephoto lens upon one figure in a game of twenty-two men, the photographer can make that one figure more important than his teammates or opponents."
—Dave Boss

"The one place I don't like to shoot from is the end zone. I like the sidelines where it's harder to follow the action but where the real action takes place."
—*Richard Raphael*

"One of the remarkable qualities of photography
is its ability to render fresh and exciting
the commonplace occurrences. The most appealing
pictures are usually those that instantly
clarify familiar objects or experiences."
—Dave Boss

"Some players have unique qualities,
which I try to capture. Sometimes
a player is known for his meanness, but
meanness on the field is a
difficult thing to get."
—Tony Tomsic

*"Sport breeds involvement
and intensity. The
moods of the players often
tell as much about their
game as does their
action on the field."*
—Dave Boss

"It all depends on what
you're shooting for.
It might be an essay on
football—what happens
after the play, for instance—
but a newspaper is looking
for action."
—Richard Raphael

"I guess if I could photograph only one position,
it would be the quarterback. He runs,
passes, holds and gets hit. Everything revolves
around him. If I'm shooting coaches, I'm
using a long lens. They can be kind of touchy."
——Fred Kaplan

"The essence of photography is to show the familiar
in terms of newness. Creativity means
challenging the familiar, the established and ordered
forms of our lives, and finding freshness
and originality in these forms."
                                            —Dave Boss

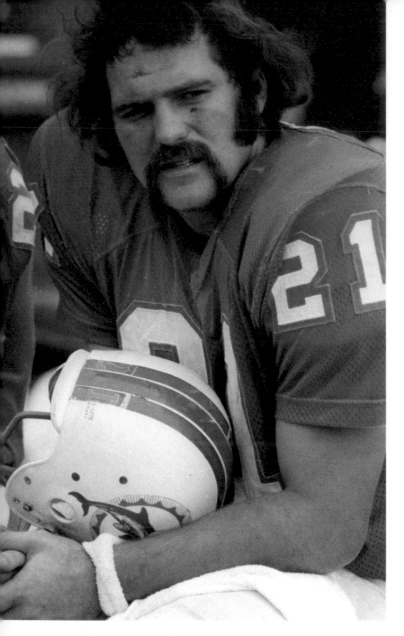

"By understanding his environment and using his creative processes, man explores and discovers himself. The camera is the perfect medium to transfer personal experience to graphic documentation. It is the reflecting mirror not only of the subject it records but of the man who records it. His pictures convey his own experience while portraying his taste, sensibility and self-expression."
———Dave Boss

"The reason for choosing one lens over another is,
simply, that one lens is equipped for shooting
a certain scene while another is not. If you want
to show a lot of things happening, you use a
wider-angle lens. For one man, you use telephoto."
—Melchior DiGiacomo

"I especially like the 80–200mm zoom lens. It is versatile and as sharp all the way through its zoom range as any prime lens. If the play turns out to be a sweep to my side, I can switch from one range to another and pick up the runner before he gets too close for comfort."
—Fred Kaplan

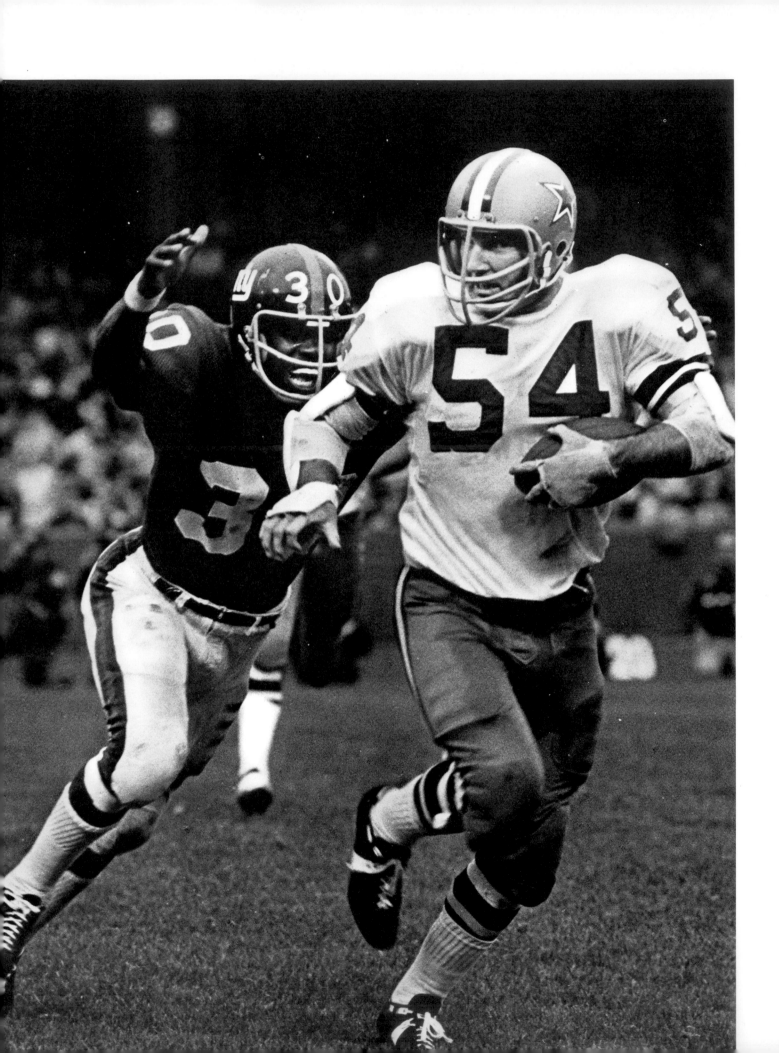

"The real trick is knowing the game you're photographing. Does the situation call for a short pass? Be ready to swing over the middle for a possible interception. Does the quarterback like to run?
Keep the camera trained on him."
—Tony Tomsic

"When you're isolating on a player or on an incident, often the best time to shoot is just prior to, or just after, the point of interest. This is true on kicks, for example, and especially true for focusing on quarterbacks when you know the greatest impact will come after the ball has been thrown."
—Tony Tomsic

"The photographer has the prerogative of rendering parts of our world more visible through his ability to interpret it through graphic forms."
—Dave Boss

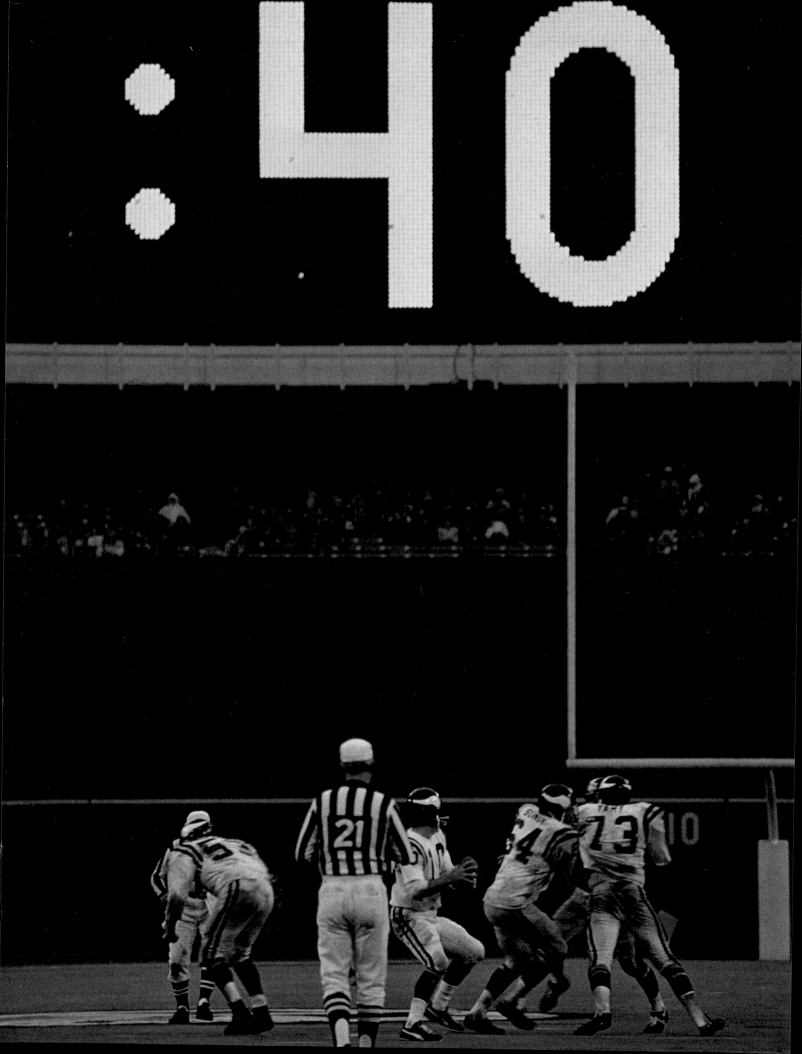

"There is no time for
decision and, unlike
television, no
instant replay. In
the cascade of tumbling
bodies,
there unfolds human
experience. The
photographer must determine
which he wants and then
shoot it—instantly—
before it dissolves into
new forms and actions."
—Dave Boss

*"There are human emotions to be photographed
and details of the participant's involvement with
his game to be understood. The camera often
searches out and communicates the expression
of those moments better than words do."*
　　　　　　　　　　　　　　　　—Dave Boss

6
THE BETTER WAY

by Skip Myslenski

I seek through
comprehensively
anticipatory design science
and its reduction
to physical practice to
reform the environment....

—R. BUCKMINSTER FULLER
I Seem To Be A Verb

It used to be
a yardstick. If you
had your teeth, then you weren't
much of a ballplayer.
It was damn near a badge
of honor. I won't
say they knocked their own
teeth out. But
they were happy if they
didn't have them.

—BILL GRANHOLM
Equipment Manager
Chicago Hornets 1946-1949
L.A. Rams 1950-1967

Football's efforts to reform its environment began as far back as 1905. It was at the time that Penn University, preparing for its annual game against Swarthmore, decided that its best chances rested in neutralizing Swarthmore's star lineman, a 250-pound tackle named Bob Maxwell. That Saturday, they pummeled him mercilessly until, finally, he was helped from the field. The next morning, a photograph of Maxwell's bloodied and swollen face appeared in newspapers across the country. President Teddy Roosevelt reacted with outrage. "Improve the game," the president declared, "or I will abolish it by executive edict."

The campaign was on, and through the years football—especially professional football—has moved with, adapted to and borrowed from the knowledge provided by our technological age. The game has become refined in pace with science, evolving as no less fierce than before (indeed, probably even more so), yet much more precise. Adaptation has spawned brutality flavored with elegance; the field now showcases finesse as well as strength. The overt macho-hero is today a rarity. No longer are there teams like the aptly nicknamed "Monsters of the Midway," the 1940 Chicago Bears. (On the team's way to the field for that year's championship game against the Redskins, each Bear stopped at the trunk containing the team valuables and defiantly deposited his bridgework.) Instead, football today is customized and computerized.

The changes have not always been fast. "I look at some of the equipment today," says Bill Granholm, "and I think, 'Hell, I did that fifteen years ago for a guy,' and wonder why we knew about it and only did it special." Nor have they always been welcome. "I remember when face masks first came in," says ex-New England Patriot general manager Upton Bell, thinking back to the early fifties. "A lot of the guys were reluctant to wear them. They thought it was against their masculinity."

Improvements followed the times, their roots often to be found on the pad of a Rawlings designer or in the test tube of a DuPont chemist. Explains Bill Nall, one of four researchers at Rawlings, "When we find a new product we like, we work with the labs at DuPont or Monsanto or General Electric. We get two or three people from our company busy on a particular item, and at the same time they might have three or four people in their labs working on the material for this particular application. We might need special paint, so we work with a company in New York that will put four of their people on it. We work with both Rubitex and Uniroyal; they usually work on energy-absorbing padding."

The consequences have been widespread, resulting in expanded nomenclature (you no longer speak of plastic when you are actually talking about acrylonitrile butadiene styrene), the refinement of products (whether the cotton webbing in a helmet should now be replaced by polypropylene) and new creations (the hydraulic-pneumatic helmet). Equipment is now custom-made; uniforms, custom-styled; shoes, customed for the field. Even the peripheral material has changed, modernized by science. The St. Louis Cardinals divorced an antiquated 200-pound tackling dummy nicknamed Mona and acquired an 11-foot 1-inch, 800-pound Tack-L-Matic training machine, promptly nicknamed the Killer. Not all the team has adjusted; muses guard Irv Goode, "My heart still belongs to Mona." Nearly half the teams have chosen artificial turf over the real thing. Isometrics double-dated weight lifting. Gatorade, Quick Kick and Olympade replaced water. Knee operations reached new sophistication; says Chicago Bears' team physician Dr. Theodore Fox, "Ten years ago we would have put a brace on a player's leg and he would have been finished." A psychology test has determined a high draft choice: Atlanta said that its selection of George Kunz over Ron Sellers and Leroy Keyes in the 1969 draft was finalized by Kunz's score on an exam given by Assessment Systems Inc. And the IBM 360 helped ferret out both Calvin Hill and Duane Thomas for the Dallas Cowboys.

Bill Granholm, now a special assistant to the NFL, does not allow himself nostalgia when he talks of these sophistications. Still, he can think back—often with a seemingly wistful smile—to his past. "A lot of the things they do today were then a reflection of some gamesmanship," he recalls. "I remember in 1950–51, we had a set of helmets on the Rams with face masks on them. We kept them in a bag next to the bench. We wouldn't use them unless the other team started throwing elbows and fists. Then the captain would come off the field and tell the coach, and we'd pull those helmets out. Then our guys'd go back in, and it was no holds barred. Today, that's the way a game starts."

"It's all part of the times," adds Upton Bell. "I think that not only has football become more distinctive, but the uniforms and everything else as well. Before, you were in the days when football was three yards and a cloud of dust. It was inhabited by drab people. I'm not trying to knock it. I'm just saying the uniforms were drab, the plays were drab, *everything* was that way.

"In my mind football is a game that's gone from being very tough, eat-'em-up, to being refined. Sometimes it is like a ballet."

Face masks are forged from steel wire, aluminum or plastic; the aesthetic tastes of players have demanded some seven different styles.

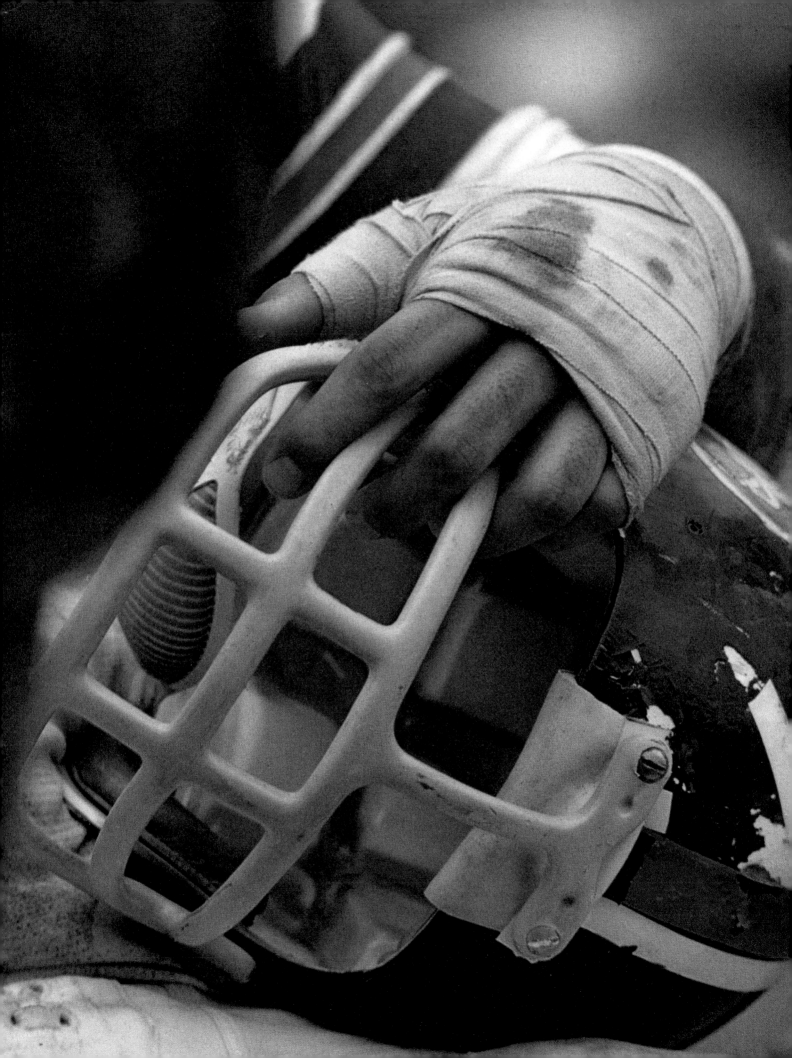

If you catered to the whims of a pro ballplayer, the equipment manager would go crazy. They're a bunch of prima donnas.

—*Sporting goods manufacturer*

Pretty soon they'll be wearing Hawaiian blue and pineapple brown.

—*Bill Granholm*

Some of the following facts will help illustrate the special relationships that exist between a player and his equipment:

Bobby Layne's favorite shoulder pads lasted for 15 years.

Bill Bradley brought the shoulder pads and helmet he wore at the University of Texas with him to the Philadelphia Eagles.

The Buffalo Bills asked USC for O. J. Simpson's college helmet when they found that none of theirs fit him properly.

Dallas Cowboy linebacker Chuck Howley has worn the same shoulder pads since 1959, the year he entered the league.

Former Minnesota Viking wide receiver Red Phillips had to be fitted with new equipment just before a game with the Lions; his bag had been lost by the airlines. The shoulder pads he finally wore were not a perfect fit. Phillips dislocated his shoulder that same afternoon.

A test showed that former Detroit Lion linebacker Joe Schmidt dealt with blows carrying the force of 5,780 g—5,780 times the force of gravity. By comparison, an astronaut on takeoff feels the pressure of around 10 g; an airplane pilot tends to black out at about 20 g.

After Miami Dolphin running back Larry Csonka suffered a ruptured blood vessel in his head, a doctor told him that he could never play football again. Csonka was fitted with a special helmet and is now one of the league's best backs.

Professional football's advancement in technology has resulted in coming up with a battle dress as personalized as a scarf designed and autographed by Peter Max. Not only has the equipment itself become more carefully styled, but even the necklines of jerseys are often specially sewn, stockings specially cut, sleeve lengths specially measured.

"Before, it was putting some protection on without regard for conformity to the human body," says Bill Fredericks, whose company has outfitted the Rams since their move to Los Angeles in 1946. "But now we make pads that fit the contours."

Changes came, though players balked. "You find superstitions," says Bill Nall of Rawlings. "Sometimes you're afraid to try out something new on someone who is hesitant. It just might be the time he is going to get that injury and BOOM!" "Some of it's psychological," says Bill Granholm. "Some of the players claimed that the face mask limited their intake of oxygen."

Disparate forces provided the motivation for change. Scientists, of course, discovered ways to improve the game and simply perfected their ideas and presented them to teams; players suggested alterations, hoping to improve their performances; equipment managers tinkered; manufacturers became more competitive as the sport grew into big business; and more and more, everyone became safety-conscious. "Things they wear now for protection," claims Granholm, "they didn't use to wear until they were hurt. They used them to cover a sensitive area."

The greatest safety concern has focused on the head and, by extension, the helmet—with good reason. George Sullivan, trainer at the University of Nebraska, says, "Ninety percent of the deaths that occur in competitive sports results from head injuries." Materials used on the outer shell have progressed from the old leather to cellulosic material to acrylonitrile butadiene styrene to polycarbonates, all derivative forms of thermoplastics. Cotton webbing has been replaced by the more durable polypropylene; vinyl foam has supplanted foam rubber. And the helmet gut—the source of most protection—now features suspension, pneumatic, pneumatic-hydraulic and hydraulic linings. Face masks are forged from steel wire, aluminum or plastic; the aesthetic tastes of players have demanded some seven different styles. Even mouthpieces, which were once mass-produced and shipped in boxes, are now specially fitted to each individual.

Construction improvement has been made here as well. Originally, the face mask was screwed right into the helmet, so that if a man were hit on the mask, he would absorb the full blow. Today the mask is screwed into a small piece of rubber, which absorbs some of the force.

The research necessary to make these improvements has been slow, complex and continual. "We've done research in helmets and shoes equivalent to what DuPont does in chemicals," says Gerry Morgan, president and board chairman at Riddell. Their most spectacular result was the pneumatic-hydraulic helmet, a major innovation in this line of protection. "Moneys expended on it?" Morgan continues. "I'd have to say hundreds of thousands of dollars over a period of years." The probes involved tests for acceleration with accelerometers; experiments carried on in Houston with rocket sleds, and they included results of a 25-year-long (and still continuing) study at Wayne State University. They attempted to determine the amount of force the brain mass could take and the degree to which the head can protect itself. Explains Morgan: "We have to try to understand what it takes to move the brain mass within the skull, to move it in such a way that it creates injury to the blood supply to the brain."

Riddell's contribution—for the present—is the aforementioned pneumatic-hydraulic helmet, brought out before the 1968 season, which it claimed would improve safety conditions between 100 and 300 percent. The change was in the gut, where the traditional foam padding was replaced by 12 fluid (hydraulic) cells, 12 air (pneumatic) cells and 10 "fail-safe" closed vinyl crushable foam cells. The air pockets absorbed light blows and provided the fit. The shell came in only two sizes; in just 30 seconds these cells could be blown up by a hand pump and fitted to the individual player's head. The fluid cells, filled with methyl alcohol because it has a low freezing point, absorbed the major portion of the heavy blows. The 10 foam cells were the last resort, the margin of safety in case any of the fluid cells broke.

Yet despite the new helmet's claims for greater protection, players and teams have been reluctant to change. O. J. Simpson wears one; Larry Csonka was fitted specially after his injury, and it allowed him to play. But players are still in many ways creatures of habit, beset by superstitions, changing only after injury or when questioning their equipment. "I suggest the ones who wear it now are the ones who have bad heads," says Morgan. "When they become skeptical of the equipment they are wearing, then they seek help."

Certainly that may be some of it. But the newest helmet (the Gladiator, brought out in 1972 by the Gladiator Company) *is* a modification of the pneumatic-hydraulic, *is* in fact itself hydraulic and *is* already used by some of the Dallas Cowboys.

"The thing is, you don't have the problem of blowing it [the Gladiator] up every time," says Jack Eskridge, the Cowboys' equipment manager. "They size it by insert rather than by depending on valves. See, the biggest problem with the other helmet right now is that you have a malfunction of the valves. When you take the helmet and put it in a nonpressurized bin on a plane, it'll vary back and forth. You never know what's going to happen. You have to blow it up before every game. And it's a psychological thing with the players. They think maybe it's loose here, tight there. It's a real headache. But this new one fits

very comfortably. It's like a Texas cowboy down here. He takes a brand new saddle and rides out in the lake with it, you know, and gets it all wet and it forms to his body. The purpose of the hydraulic area in this new helmet is that if a player's got a knob on the back of his head or a funny forehead, you know the helmet will conform to it."

Though inner protection and comfort have been the main concerns, they have certainly not been the only areas studied. Over the years, coaches have pleaded for a softer outer shell, some padding to protect the man being hit. At the beginning of the 1971 season, New York Jet coach Weeb Ewbank bemoaned the plastic's lethal nature. "We've had more injuries on the Jets related to helmets this season than to the field," he claimed. Then he enumerated: Joe Namath's pinched nerve in the back of his knee, the result of a helmet blow; Matt Snell's bruised knee; John Riggins's injured hand. "Just rap your helmet with your knuckles and you'll bruise them," Ewbank said.

Yet here change is not likely. Riddell tested with thicknesses up to three-quarters of an inch before it found any appreciable increase in protection. But the more significant—and overriding—factor was proof showing that the added pads adhered to a jersey during a tackle. "This is a situation where the head is supposed to slip one way or the other," explains Riddell's Morgan. "With the soft outer surface, it won't slip. It'll hang up. . . . So we save this poor chap out there from a bruise to the ribs, a broken finger, a broken arm or whatever. But we did indeed subject the wearer to a possible slipping of the cervical vertebrae and the extreme possibility of rendering him paraplegic. What the hell would you prefer—a broken hand or being paralyzed from the neck down?"

Examination continues, however, with the adaptation of improved testing devices and new digital readouts of the severity input. Modifications and refinements in the helmet will continue. "Oh, Lord, yes," says Morgan. "To think not is like saying, 'Now that we have the carburetor and the wheels, this is going to be the ultimate.' There's no such thing. Everyone will try the road beyond that. As the helmet approaches the need or indeed surpasses it, then it is used beyond that."

It was the better recognition of the shoulder pad's uses, more than any great concern for safety, that prompted its initial alteration. There followed almost immediately players' complaints of new shortcomings, which resulted finally in even further modifications. "The linemen and the backs would all wear these *huge* cumbersome-type pads," Upton Bell recalls. "In fact, they couldn't see in some cases."

191

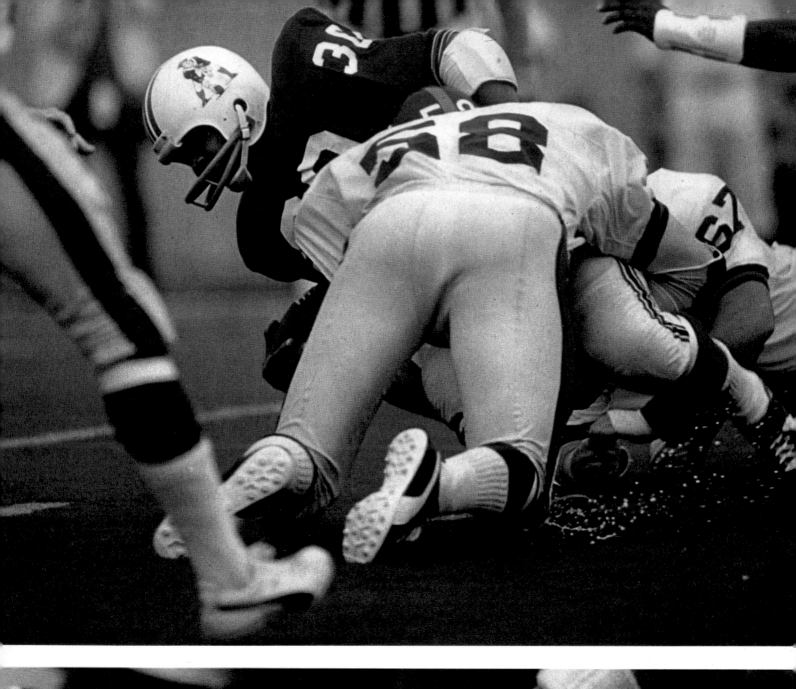
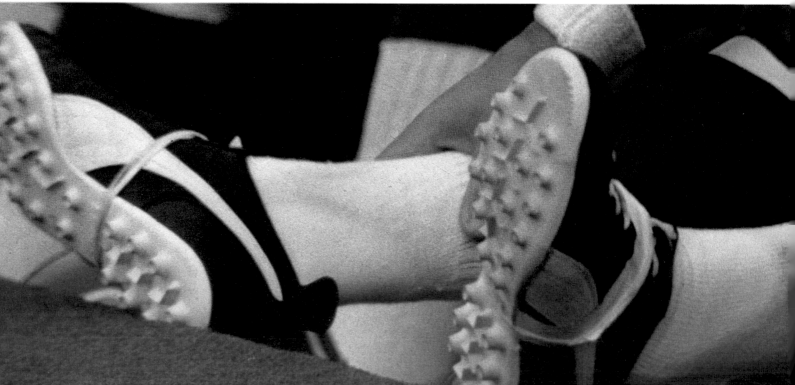

The biggest problem rested in the original construction when the pad fit dead-center over the shoulders, protecting equal amounts of a player's front and back. "It was set on top and came down to about here," explains Bill Granholm, leveling his hand across a nipple. "Then someone realized you had to be an arrow to block like that."

Designers made the natural move, shifting the pads off-center and bringing the frontal protection down over the sternum, where much of the blocking is done. But the change left the back of the pad sticking out, an open invitation to clever defensive linemen, who immediately started using the cleft as a handle. Offensive players screamed, and the understrap was added, fitting the pad snugly to the back.

The shoulder pad itself has become, more than any other, the most personalized piece of equipment, designed for size, for position, often for the individual. Love affairs arise. Besides Layne, Bradley and Howley, there was Bob Waterfield, who wore the same pair throughout the whole of his eight-year career, and Norm Snead, who actually pleaded not to have his thrown away. "Some of our players have been here since the early sixties," says the Cowboys' Jack Eskridge, "and all I do is take their shoulder pads and get them cleaned and reconditioned for them each year. They're like creatures of habit. Take Chuck Howley's. I've rebuilt it so much that while basically it's the same pad, all the parts are different."

Even the minor, less-regarded equipment has not been free from subtle refining. The knee pad is now made of better foam and contoured more exactly to the joint. The thigh pad, once placed in the middle of the leg, has been shifted to the outside, where there is more and harder contact. Hip pads (or girdle pads) have become less cumbersome and lighter. Neck braces, rib pads, forearm pads and wrist pads all are available, and each is used to varying degrees, depending only on the player's position and his individual flair.

Yet, despite the equipment's newly fashioned look, the greater regard for style is nowhere better seen than in the uniform itself:

Upton Bell: "Oh, they're more style-conscious now than before. I don't hear them complain, 'Gee, I don't like this color jersey.' I think they've become more style-conscious in their shoes. That's an absolute. One year, half the team wanted to wear black, half the team wanted to wear white. I told them, 'Look, wear one or the other, I don't care if they're green. But, Christ, we can't look like a carnival out there.'"

Bill Granholm: "Even linemen have wristlets on. Now what the hell's a lineman doing with a wristlet? It makes him look good. . . . And I can remember when a coach thought a guy who wore white *shoelaces* was a hot dog."

Bill Fredericks: "Oh-h-h, are they style-conscious. It's part of the selling. We've had some criticism with the Rams' color combinations, that they look like milkmen and all. There've been attempts to doll them up a bit. Oh, yes. They're conscious of it."

A little bit of society, a little bit of practicality, a large dose of science and just a dash of television were combined to provide the impetus for the change in uniform style.

Science contributed the material, progressing from the heavy, nonstretchable canvas to coarse canvas, through cotton, through durene, finally to nylon and stretch nylon. "Until something else comes along, nylon is it," says Fredericks. "*Nylon is it!* That's the name of the game."

The canvas was also used to make World War II army duffel bags; nylon was first used to make women's stockings. These alternate applications symbolically prefigured the changed appearance of the professional football player from an ill-fitted, uncomfortable-looking ragamuffin to a sleek and, in some cases, sexy model. "The attractiveness of the uniform today is much more important than it was years ago," says Fredericks.

Color television prompted some of that; the new freedom in men's clothing nudged it a bit more. Regardless, new techniques were found to satisfy the demands. Fast dyes and a fast-dyeing process allowed greater and more permanent color. The advent of nylon introduced a colorfast material that wouldn't run or fade, displacing cotton, which loses color after exposure to the sun and/or repeated washing. The numbers were made larger. "We used to have numbers no bigger than four inches," says Bill Granholm. "Now, some of the numbers they wear on their shoulders are bigger than that." And names were added to the back of the jerseys. A new process was even discovered for attaching names and numbers to the players' jerseys.

"The number that was always considered the Cadillac," says Bill Fredericks, "was the nylon cloth number sewn on the jersey. That's nylon combat cloth. It must be cut out, then zigzag sewed. In the last two or three years, though, the tendency has been to get away from that and toward impressing under heat, to the impressing of vinyl, rubber-type numbers right into the jersey.

"But remember," he adds, "that this also has a

Everything but track spikes seems to have flooded the market in an interminable number of styles, ranging from the traditional seven-cleat shoe to the multicleated soccer shoe. . . .

practical advantage. The vinyl number is lighter in weight and becomes part of the jersey. It stretches with the jersey, whereas the sewed nylon combat cloth did not stretch. Generally, any tearing point is right at the edge of the number, because the jersey is made out of knitted nylon material, and the sewed number is made of nonelastic material."

This happy combination of both practical and artistic benefits solidified the romance between football and nylon. It proved lighter than anything used before; it proved more flexible; it allowed for cool-weather jerseys of nylon with durene back and warm-weather jerseys of nylon mesh; it fit more snugly and kept the protective equipment in place. "It's like a rubber band," Fredericks explains. "It comes into the player and holds the pads. At the same time it gives him complete mobility."

Throughout this apparently strange yet harmonious and flourishing relationship of football and

technology, the principles have continued to refine themselves in just such ways, first through science as the supplier, then in the game as the "satisfied customer." The steps have not necessarily been big or small but rather subtle refinements, and as they move together through the seventies, expectations are for more of the same.

"I doubt .that the basic configurations will change," says Bill Nail of Rawlings. "But in the materials involved is where the major changes will come."

Adds Bill Granholm, "I can't see anyone's coming up with anything revolutionary, unless you change the game. Everyone knows you can change the equipment and rules and cut injuries down near zero. But it wouldn't be football. And I don't think it'd be worth watching."

What exists now is a game streamlined not only by its adaptation to new ideas, but also by its very people. Indeed, though the equipment today is more

"I have a feeling they do things today they wouldn't do without so much confidence in their equipment. They do things that border on the suicidal."

expensive (it costs some $250 to dress a player for a game) and more flexible, its total poundage equals and perhaps surpasses that of the past. What has changed is the relationship of the player—now bigger and faster—to that equipment. Claims Gerry Morgan of Riddell, "The equipment has to be lighter by 60 to 80 percent with reference to the player's ability to deliver a hard-telling blow."

Then he explains the resultant situation mathematically: "The weight size of the player and his speed ability—there's the difference. Consider the kinetic energy formula: what hits you and how fast it's moving. $E = \frac{1}{2}mv^2$. Now squaring anything is a dangerous thing. And going from 10 flat to a 9.5, 9.4, whatever, you're developing a tremendous potential energy. Thank God, it can't be developed into one compact small ball. If it could, there'd be no football."

Or, more simply, from Bill Granholm: "I have a feeling they do things today they wouldn't do without so much confidence in their equipment. They do things that border on the suicidal."

"Plastics. [pause] Plastics."
—Businessman's advice
The Graduate

The best-laid schemes o' mice and men
gang aft a-gley;
An' lea'e us nought but grief and pain,
for promis'd joy.

—Robert Burns
"To a Mouse"

I'd rather play on grass. It just smells good.
—Steve Zabel
Philadelphia Eagles

Puppy love!

Perhaps that's what it was. But that frenetic romance between football and artificial turf has now reached middle age, and after those initial throes of infatuation, it has suddenly found itself beset with the problems of an unsettled marriage. Like the poet who thought the new face so radiant only to find that constant attention rendered it no different from a thousand other faces, almost everyone now recognizes ersatz grass as mortal.

Players complain; owners and manufacturers resist; studies are made, researchers ponder, shoes are tested, accepted or rejected with fervor matched only at a Gimbel's sale. And over it all a certain Brucean humor pervades. The result has been more one-liners than Bob Hope uses on a trip to the war zone. The usually volatile managing general partner of the Oakland Raiders, Al Davis, probably best explained the situation when he calmly said, "We're in the

Astroturf revolution now. And, as with all revolutions, everybody doesn't go along at first. So some games are on synthetics and some on nature's carpet."

Revolution was expected; but no one, certainly, foresaw its complications. The movement started quietly enough. In the late fifties, scientists at Monsanto, makers of Astroturf, were already investigating the practicality of artificial surfaces and in 1964, spurred by a grant from the Ford Foundation, they installed a field house floor in Providence, Rhode Island. At nearly the same time Bill McKnight, then president and board chairman at Minnesota Mining and Manufacturing, makers of Tartan Turf, visited the Garden City Race Track with horse trainer John Nerud. After rain had ruined the day's festivities, Nerud said to McKnight, "The greatest thing that could happen to horseracing would be a synthetic track." McKnight was struck with the idea and promised to have his researchers look into it—and in 1961, Minnesota Mining poured a batch of semiviscous polyurethane resin over some Belmont Park asphalt and created an eighth-of-a-mile artificial walking oval.

But the chemist's answer to Concord's shot heard round the world was to come a bit later, in 1966, when Monsanto unrolled its rug under the Astrodome in Houston and renamed it Astroturf. The clamor surrounding this unveiling matched that usually reserved for a new head of state. Astroturf's claims were extravagant indeed. Artificial turf, its proponents insisted, would cut down on knee injuries; it would insure perfect footing in any weather; it would keep uniforms clean; it would eliminate bad bounces; it would cut down on maintenance costs. And while there were dissenters, they were dismissed as hopeles traditionalists. Mother Nature's children. Romanticists.

Artificial turf is not grass. That is one of the few declarative sentences on which all concerned will agree. Even the various turfs themselves bear little resemblance to one another. Astroturf is constructed in three parts: a top, grasslike portion, made of nylon fibers; a second layer of polyester fiber and nylon tire cord; and a shock-absorbing underpad of synthetic rubber and vinyl material. Within this framework there are nuances. The surface at the Astrodome is woven nylon ribbon; at Soldier Field, tufted ribbon; at Comiskey Park, knitted ribbon.

Tartan Turf is a two-piece unit, an outer surface of half-inch finely woven nylon over a half-inch underpadding, best described as a softer version of the rubbery surface its makers used on their racetracks. Tartan people claim that their nylon is less coarse than that of Astroturf.

Poly Turf, the latest addition, is a polypropylene

and polyvinylchloride (plastic derivatives) combination, tufted somewhat like carpeting and, its supporters say, able to withstand adverse conditions better than the others.

And those may well be the only givens in the whole of the artificial-turf question. For what these chemical creations have brought with them breeds nothing but contention. While supporters have re-affirmed their original claims (and had some justified) that injuries—and particularly knee injuries—would be reduced, the dissenters have pointed to skin abrasions, uncomfortably hot feet, swollen joints and any variety of even more serious problems. Shoe manufacturers have not found the perfect model, one which would, if not eliminate, at least reduce the abnormal number of slips and slides across glazed artificial surfaces.

There are less controversial problems which have produced interesting solutions. John Connor, the head of the Orange Bowl's maintenance crew, must prowl the sidelines with an assistant during each game, both men alert for any smoker who might try to extinguish his cigarette on the carpet. After a two-year period, they found only 50 burns. They couldn't paint lines for a midweek NCAA soccer tournament, since a football game would follow that weekend. They laid, instead, 722 yards of adhesive tape. And a study found the surface contained 40 percent nitrogen and associated elements and 60 percent organic elements. This prompted an American Biltrite (the makers of Poly Turf) vice-president to say, "Nitrogen is not part of our synthetic surface system," and to blame the problems on air pollution and on the area's dense airplane traffic.

The reactions and solutions to both these and the more substantial problems fluctuate from the scientific to the homemade. One study pointed out that normal ground temperature is 95 degrees or less and that normal foot temperature is between 96 and 97 degrees. Hence, an athlete on grass loses heat through his feet; but on hotter surfaces, he not only retains heat but gains some. Another research team devised a test in 1970 (then revised it four times in the next two years) to determine the shock-absorbing properties of playing surface systems: "The g value at each millisecond is read and raised to the 2.5 power and divided by 1,000. The resulting quantities are added to give the severity index in seconds."

Simpler and better understood remedies were introduced. The Astrodome turf was shampooed with 40 barrels of Schlitz beer; Monsanto developed an Astro Zambori water-removal machine; and American Biltrite introduced the Love Machine, a vacuum cleaner that stood the fibers up instead of matting them down.

Now shoes are changed like underwear with careful regard to both that Sunday's surface and the weather report.

Whatever the final outcome from the use of artificial turf, it might be interesting to remember that whenever a major change is introduced abruptly, whether good or bad, people complain. What would have happened had players grown up on artificial turf and then suddenly been introduced to real grass and dirt? Would there have been the outcry, "Hey, what happens when I get cut? It'll become infected!"

Shoot, some players have 25–30 pairs of shoes sitting in their lockers.

> —Jack Eskridge
> *Equipment manager*
> *Dallas Cowboys*

No one really knows the criteria for developing a safe football shoe.

> —Gerry Morgan
> *President, Riddell*

Lenny Moore and his synthetic spats may have started it, this search for a different shoe, and Joe Namath may have rekindled it—but artificial turf is now the vortex, the whirlpool around which all new ideas eddy. In the past a player owned one pair of shoes and two sets of cleats, the standard three-eighths-inch spike and the mud cleat. "And way back then," says Bill Granholm, "they had to buy them. They made sure they lasted for the full year, sometimes two."

Now shoes are changed like underwear, with careful regard to both that Sunday's surface and the weather report. "If somebody rains on a field, or urinates, well, it changes the whole damn thing," says Gerry Morgan. "And if you have an Orange Bowl-type polypropylene field, one hundred degrees ambient, where the field may be a hundred and forty degrees, where we now have a grease field, there's nothing I know of that will work except track spikes. And those are very hard on the opposing players."

Everything but track spikes seems to have flooded the shoe market in an interminable tide of styles, ranging from the traditional seven-cleat shoe to the multicleated soccer shoe to a tennis shoe to a Canadian broom shoe with suction cups. Both the back heel and the front instep have been varied, alternately and together, with such devices as torsion bars and circular plates. A member of the Cleveland Browns bought eight pairs of different shoes at his own expense. Brown running back Leroy Kelly adopted ripple soles, modified but still similar to those used by nurses. Even Puma and Adidas, two German companies better known for their contributions to track, joined the hunt, passing out both samples and money, yet remain unable to find the perfect formula. And through it all a Houston orthopedic surgeon, Dr. Bruce Cameron, watched and then had perhaps the

final word. "Mother Nature gave you smooth soles to slide over the ground," he said. "If she wanted you to be cleated, maybe she would have given you warts."

Coaches, of course, have little time for such philosophical ruminations. Still, they've taken an equally askance, if not quite so pedantic, view of all the experiments. "The players are being given shoes free," noted Bud Grant of the Minnesota Vikings. "They're endorsing shoes and trying all different kinds. Most of the shoes are lightweight, thin-soled and badly supported. Many of the injuries to the feet are a result of the bad shoes they are wearing."

Weeb Ewbank talked some of his Jets into wearing high tops and promised a campaign for even more disciples. "Did you ever hear of an Achilles tendon when we had high-top shoes?" he asked. Then he answered his own question. "Of course you didn't. They protected the ankles and gave them support. The oxfords the kids wear today don't do that. I've convinced some of our players the high tops are best, and I'm going to try to convert more of them."

The multifarious turfs have certainly demanded some changes in footwear, though not necessarily back to the past. In fact, one study identified the conventional seven-cleat shoe as a major factor in knee injuries; it recommended a multicleated soccer shoe, which, the study said, had a greater weight-bearing surface area and lessened foot fixation (the primary cause of knee injuries). Another, more revolutionary concept has been applied by Wolverine Products. The basic principle is torque, and the result is a shoe with a tension bar on the heel and a unit able to swivel through a full 360 degrees on the instep. Dr. Cameron, who claims the shoe could cut knee injury by 70 percent, explained logically, "As man becomes a swiveler, he will have moves he can't make when he has to have cleats in the ground. Any time you work in science and want an answer, go back to nature. She already has the answer. Simulate it and usually you are right."

Even in the seventies, Mother Nature is still a much talked-about woman.

The interesting thing about computers and football is this. Our programmer doesn't know whether a football is filled with air or feathers. But mathematically he can help us. We tell him what we want. And he ends up getting it for us.

> —Gil Brandt
> *Head scout*
> *Dallas Cowboys*

I'll tell you, using a computer is kinda like getting hooked on marijuana. You know, you start with something and you want to go more and more and more, it's so interesting what comes out of it.

> —Ibid.

Football's joint venture with technology in search of the better way has not limited itself to merely refining the weapons. Indeed, it has refined the man and the game he plays as well. The lasting and generally enthusiastic acceptance of computers as valuable aids is in stark contrast to the controversy surrounding many of the other technological intrusions. Initially conceived as scouting adjuncts, computers have since been utilized to help prepare game plans, to assess a team's own tendencies and, in the highly sophisticated Dallas Cowboy system, to measure the scouts themselves. Though by no means finally realized or fully perfected, the IBM 360s and the Univac 1108s have become as important to football as silk sheets and quadraphonic sound are to the *bon vivant*. No good man is without them—or, at least, without access to them.

Says the Patriots' Upton Bell quite simply, "I love computers and I use them all the time." He pauses for a moment, then adds, "And I'll tell you one thing it's done. It's created a lot of thought in a lot of people's minds. It's made people, whether they like the computer or not, a lot more aware of what they can do. It's brought a lot more thinking to the game itself."

The most publicized and the most recognized application has been to scouting—and to the subsequent scouting syndicates. Yet the more recent and, eventually perhaps, the more far-reaching adaption has concerned itself with play analysis or, simply, with team tendencies and the game plan.

First attempted by a Maryland-based organization at the behest of the Washington Redskins, the use of computers has since been endorsed by a majority of the National Football League. Indeed, Nick Skorich, the head coach of the Cleveland Browns, once cited the computer as an important factor in a victory. The team had used it for the first time that previous week, he admitted in the locker room after the win, and "it helped considerably." Virgil Carter, the technologically inclined quarterback of the Cincinnati Bengals, has published a paper entitled "Operations Research on Football," a study to determine the basic strategies in the game. And ex-Cleveland Brown quarterback Frank Ryan created Pro Probe while playing under Vince Lombardi in Washington. (Lombardi appointed himself executive consultant, then later credited the computer service with a big part in the Redskins' surprisingly successful season.) "Football possesses a great number of easily identifiable characteristics . . . related directly to the game's decision-making process," Ryan explained. "And as sports rivals become more evenly matched, the plays evolve into more complicated

maneuvers. Thus coaches and players are required to grow more knowledgeable, and this is where the computer must step in."

The worth lies not so much in what new information the computer can offer ("It's no better than the information you put in it," says Brandt. "You put garbage in, you get garbage out"), but in the speed and efficiency with which it organizes the material. Ryan, for example, claimed he could receive data on 298 plays within two-tenths of a second. The Cowboys have the next week's game plan by dinnertime on Monday—a somewhat impressive feat, since they do not receive the final films of their opponent until Monday noon. The Los Angeles Rams get their information back a mere three hours after it's sent crosstown to be processed. Says Ram coach Tommy Prothro: "It gets information back to you in a hurry. But I don't think it can do a better job than you could if you had time to do it yourself."

Despite his mild protestation, the Rams, like most other teams, still use the service. The knowledge it feeds a team is familiar—play analysis by down and distance, field position and formation—but processed by means now so refined that the output often is mainly pictorial, including field diagrams and graphs. The Cowboy system even draws in formations. "Our book comes back, and I mean to tell you it's so comprehensive it's unbelievable," says Brandt. "I mean, it tells you which plays they run inside the twenty, which plays they run in two-minute drills. It's just very, very comprehensive." The final offering is the detailed summation. Before a game with the 49ers, the Rams, for example, could find out that in a given situation "there are no real tendencies to play. You have a 62 percent chance of running a zipped defense based on the formation used. Red equals zip weak. Brown equals zip strong. . . ."

"The computer presents *such* a better picture than you've ever had before," muses Upton Bell. "And . . . it can tell you some interesting things."

For years professional football and college football have acknowledged each other with mutual forbearance, colleges claiming the innovators, branding professionals as mere debtors receiving credit because of greater publicity. Yet Woody Hayes, the redoubtable old coach of Ohio State, once saw fit to borrow an idea from the pros. "For the first time we're using computers to help us recruit," he admitted.

Then he explained. "We've got it broken down into five levels of potential—superstar, star, starter, substitute and no prospect," he said. "Each individual is then graded and rated in five categories—jumping ability, speed and quickness, strength, leadership, communications and character stability.

"In jumping ability the superstar is able to leap tall buildings with a single bound, the star must take a running start, the starter leaps short buildings only, the substitute crashes into buildings and the no-prospect doesn't recognize buildings.

"In speed and quickness the superstar is faster than a speeding bullet, the star is as fast as a speeding bullet, the starter not quite as fast as a speeding bullet, the substitute is not quite as fast as a slow bullet. The no-prospect? He wounds himself while firing the gun."

He moved to communications and character stability. "Here," he said, "we expect our superstars to be able to talk with God. The star should be able to speak with angels. The starter talks to himself. The substitute argues with himself. And the no-prospect loses those arguments."

The computer's most valued application thus far has been, of course, in scouting. And though Woody Hayes's banter is obviously hyperbolic, it is not wholly inaccurate. Reasons for the utilization of computers in scouting are obvious enough: a greater amount of competition, a greater number of players to see, a greater number of schools to visit. "And a computer can accomplish in twenty minutes what a man would accomplish in a month," says Gil Brandt.

Over any one college season, as many as 2,000 players may be watched, graded, processed and considered. The scouting syndicates have certainly helped: CEPO (Giants, Browns, Packers, Falcons, Redskins, Cardinals, Saints, Patriots); BLESTO VIII (Bears, Lions, Eagles, Steelers, Vikings, Colts, Dolphins, Bills); and Quadra (Cowboys, Rams, 49ers, Chargers). The computer has merely made the job that much easier. "A lot of people have animosity towards computers," explains Brandt. "They feel eventually it's going to take their job. They say, 'A man is better than a computer' and so forth. But really, you're not trying to replace a man. You're just trying to help him."

There is particular reason for listening to Gil Brandt's opinion of computers, for it was the Cowboy organization that first adapted them to football, and Gil Brandt was there when the first program ran through. Today, the general consensus is that the Cowboys have the most sophisticated system in foot-

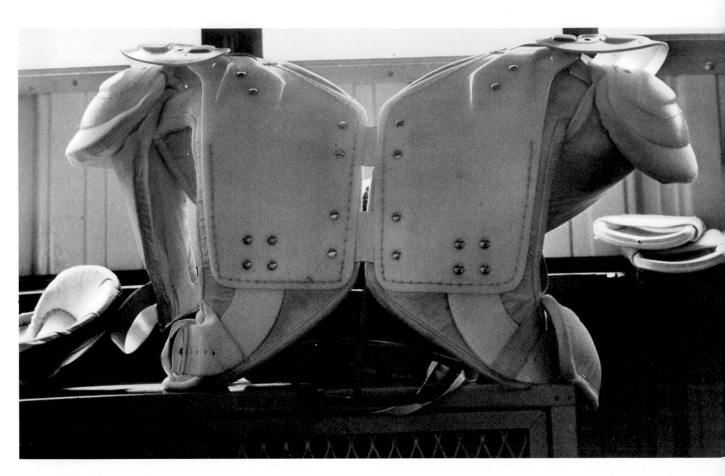

Football's joint venture with technology in search of the better way has not limited itself to merely refining the weapons. Indeed, it has refined the man and the game he plays as well.

ball, with Brandt its guiding force. He expounds:

"First of all, let me tell you why we got into the use of computers. Originally there were twelve teams in the National Football League, which meant you were drafting two hundred and eighty players, I believe it was. All of a sudden, the American Football League came into existence. It was general knowledge that certain players had been signed before the draft, so you'd have to pass those up, and consequently more than two hundred and eighty names were needed for the draft. Also, everyone started to realize that the Ohio States and Notre Dames were not the only ones who produced football players, that they were coming out of Elizabeth City State Teachers College and San Angelo State and places like that. Consequently, instead of processing three hundred and fifty players, we were processing fifteen hundred players. And just to read about fifteen hundred players was a full-time, year-round job. We just found that we were having too many players to process and not enough time to do it.

"The other thing that came into it is that computers played no personalities. For example, certain people have a chance to visit Nebraska, and they see a tackle there who's an exceptionally nice fella, and he'd like to play for the Cowboys, and you just happen to talk to one of the coaches who recruited him, and *he's* very high on him. We found out that subconsciously you were rating this guy a little bit higher than maybe the guy at Minnesota who didn't care who he was drafted by; if he was drafted by the Cowboys it was okay, he'd play with them, but it really didn't make any difference. I think a lot of this happened, and it influenced your manual rating. But when you turned around and put him in a computer, you were putting in numbers, and there was no human factor involved.

"To help us, we even rate our scout. We rate his rating. For example, we know that scout A's sixes are comparable to scout B's fives. And what we do every year is to go back and analyze the draft of three years ago. We break it into four categories: players that scout rated correctly; rated too high; rated too low; and the ones he missed completely. Let's say Alan Page was in the draft, and let's say our scout gave Alan Page a low grade. Obviously, that's as bad as giving a failure a high grade.

"We also found out in going back over things that at certain positions there are certain traits that are very, very important to those positions; so we reprogram every year. Now just for example: In 1965, using tight end as a position, we gave speed 14.64 percent of the total grade; in 1966 we dropped that speed down to 11 percent. We kept character the same. In 1965 we had competitiveness as 7 percent of the total grade; in 1966 we raised it to 10.5 percent. So every year, we keep going back and back over these things, trying to better ourselves all the time, and also to establish a guide for our scouts to follow—to find what it takes for a player to be successful at tight end or linebacker or whatever position.

"There are always players that for some reason or other everyone misses on. I think probably what that comes down to is the one thing you can't measure: the desire to excel. There are only four things you *can* measure in a football player. You can measure height, you can measure speed, you can measure weight, you can measure intelligence. The rest is just a visual thing, and you rely on the scout's good judgment in assigning a number for that particular category. In other words, there's no way you can test agility. There's no foolproof method of doing it. The same with desire. If you could somehow draw blood, stick a needle in a guy's arm and say he has great desire, he has medium desire, whatever it may be, then you'd have a chance.

"Now, there are five characteristics in every football player. Character is one; quickness is one; competitiveness is one; mental alertness is one; strength and explosion are one. In other words, those five characteristics are found in every football player, but they're weighted differently. Then there are *position* specifics for every football player. Mental alertness, for example, is the most important thing for a quarterback. So let's say you get seven in mental alertness and two in strength. Then turn it around and say Gil Brandt gets a seven in strength and a two in mental alertness, and I'm also a quarterback. Well, we both have nine points. But because mental alertness is so much more important in a quarterback than strength, you're going to be ranked way ahead of me.

"Now, let's turn it around again. We have a table we use for each position. Let's say a five-foot ten-inch quarterback who weighs a hundred and sixty pounds gets minus three points, and a six-foot three-inch quarterback who weighs two hundred and fifteen pounds gets six or seven points. Again, we go back to our previous draft and find out how important height is in a quarterback. Or how important strength is in a defensive lineman, or how important quickness is in a back. So when the tall quarterback is up against the short quarterback and just height is used as a criterion, the short guy is going to be penalized. But if he's got enough plus points in other categories, that builds him back up.

"What I'm saying is, the computer tells you what to look for in a football player. And it tells you by past history. Let's take the 1965–66–67 draft. Out of that

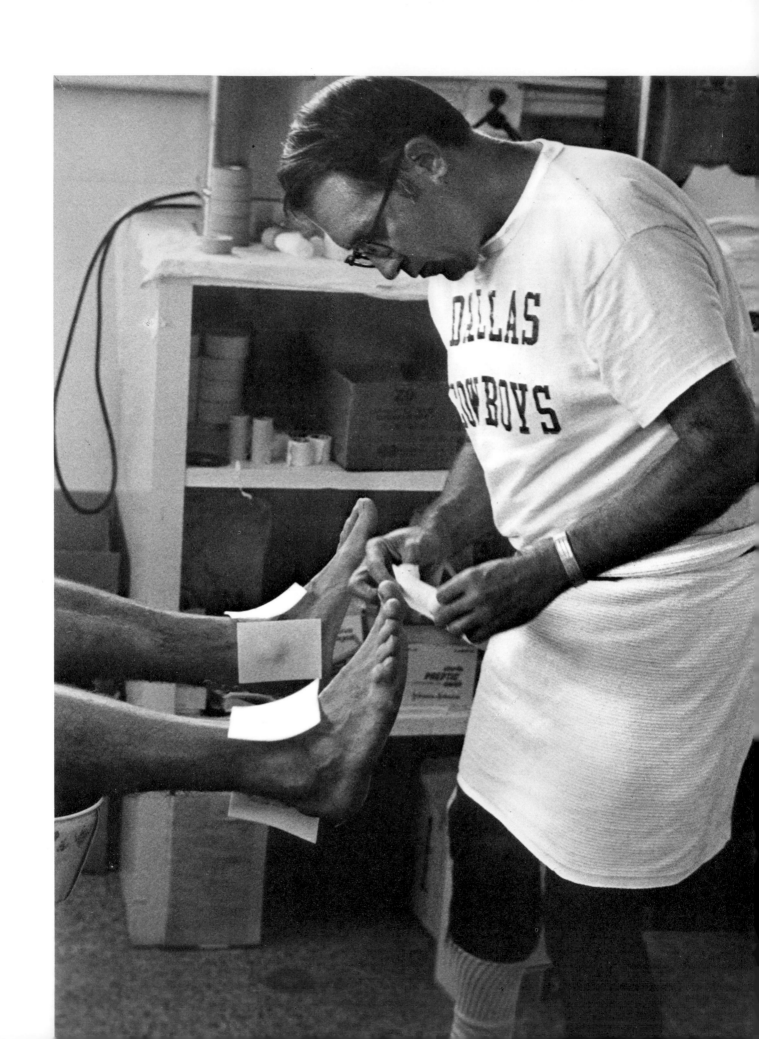

draft came one defensive tackle who is a superstar and four defensive tackles who are little stars (by that I mean they play in the Pro Bowl). Now you go back and find out what the characteristics are that showed in those players. From this you adjust your scale. What you end up with is a proven theory. A lot of people have a lot of theories. And the one that sounds the most convincing is the one that you usually listen to. You hear people with theories on the Vietnam war. The one that sounds the most convincing is the one you'll respond to. But a proven theory is a fact, and you can't argue against cold, hard facts. When you get your information from the computer, you can say, 'Hey, factor X is the most important factor in a running back. Here's the past data, and that's that.' This is what indirectly helps you find a Calvin Hill or a Duane Thomas.

"I get the first list on who the best college players are at the end of their spring practice. But then during the year, say on October 25, I can get another list; on October 30 I can tell you who the best are from a new list; on November 15, as more information keeps coming in, we update it; and so forth. Sometimes a player will drop or rise suddenly. A good example of this was Earl McCullough a few years ago. He went into his senior year way down the list. All of a sudden he jumps up to eighteenth or twentieth. Boy, when this happens, you send someone back out there to check if what we're seeing here is really correct.

"What you'd really like to know, but can't, is what style of football they'll be playing three years from now, because that's when a player starts producing for you. If you could tell me that everyone was going to be using as much zone in three years as now, or if everyone's going to start using the Wishbone, then you have to rate a [Jack] Mildren or a [Rex] Kern higher and you're going to have to rate defensive halfbacks without great speed higher, because you'll be playing zone or Wishbone.

"See, there are so many factors involved. And that's why it's so hard, even with computers, to come up with the perfect football player."

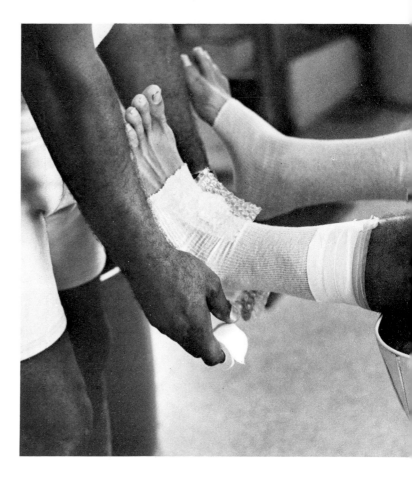

Football is his job. If an injury can be taped or frozen, he will play, and if it can't, he will summon reserve strength and trust the pain to tell him whether to give in. He plays because he is good. . . .

The name of the game, in psychological terms, is killing your opponent without insulting your own pride. When expert football players, with maximal experience as performers and magnificent all-around physical equipment, use their keen minds to dedicate themselves intensively to contest, the wonder is that there is not serious injury on every play.

—Dr. Chester Pierce
Psychiatrist

203

A doctor used to be regarded as a necessary evil, if that. But now he's the coach's best friend.

—Dr. Theodore A. Fox
Team physician
Chicago Bears

The seemingly limitless flexibility of football has, beyond any doubt, redefined the game itself. "In the old days," say Dr. James Nicholas, team physician of the New York Jets, "when you just sat there and plodded your way through and you could see everything in front of you, you weren't deceived, and there probably was less injury unless they fell on top of you. But today, if you're distracted, you'll be hit much harder. When you see a man coming at full speed, you are set to meet him, and you distribute the impact. But when a man is coming and you don't see him, you're relaxed, and you're going to get hurt. The more you deceive a man, the more apt he is to be hit at an unguarded moment."

So with this new game of the seventies—a game defined by deception as well as by strength—has come greater concern for safety. And, as with equipment, football has allied itself with the newest advances in medicine. "In the past, when someone hurt their knees, they just never played again," continues Dr. Nicholas. "But professional football has created the demand for injured players to return to play."

Teams themselves have shown this heightened awareness, and their physical examinations may now include such refinements as electrocardiograms, blood studies, orthopedic exams and case-history studies. Recurrent knee injuries have besieged the surgeons and led to more detailed analyses and more sophisticated operations. "The watchword is diagnose early and operate early," says the Bears' Dr. Fox.

Dr. Nicholas, for one, has adopted the "five-one" operation, a method he perfected while treating Joe Namath's tender knees. The technique is similar to one used some 50 years ago on cancer patients but recently rendered obsolete for that purpose by the massive use of vaccine. Its bases are tendon transfers, ligament reconstruction and extensive re-

habilitation. Another innovator has been Dr. Mark B. Coventry at the Mayo Clinic in Rochester, Minnesota, who has attempted replacement of the entire kneecap or the entire knee structure with an artificial unit.

Apart from the knee, there has been experimentation in mending broken bones. Ten micro-amps of current are applied through a fine stainless-steel wire already inserted into the cracks between segments of the broken bone and hooked up to a battery-transistor device secured in the cast. According to two doctors at the University of Pennsylvania Hospital, this treatment could reduce mending time by 30 to 50 percent. Says Dr. Fox quite simply, "Professional athletes get the best care—it's part and parcel of big business."

This care has even been extended to include psychological treatment. Though most teams still use such studies merely to aid scouts and coaches, Dr. Chester M. Pierce, himself once a player and now Professor of Education and Psychiatry at Harvard University, has projected further utilization. "Suppose that a professional football player," he says,

"whether veteran or rookie, begins to worry about making the cut. His anguish interferes with his sleep. More specifically, he alters his amounts of deep sleep [the most restful] and dreaming sleep. Soon, both the quantity and the quality of his sleep are very different, and in fact his biologic rhythm is put out of kilter. These physiologic alterations manifest themselves in ways that jeopardize football success.

"The rookie quarterback cannot read blitz patterns—not because of lack of comprehension, but because his thinking speed is reduced as a result of loss of slow-wave [deep] sleep. The veteran guard misses a blocking assignment because of an error of omission in his thinking process. The cornerback's reactions, only a critical second slower than usual, might be due to a lack of sustained attention, which is a manifestation of a chronic, subclinical sleep disturbance.

"After a physiologically wretched night in bed, occasioned by worries over mistakes in practice, a giant defensive tackle becomes much more susceptible to pain. Despite even valid protest that subjectively he has had a good night's sleep, the altered sleep cycle could be the reason for this man's crumbling under a relatively innocuous blow."

Relating this theory to possible preventative applications, he continues, "Whenever a person is injured, an interview could be conducted to elicit the immediately preceding events in the person's psychosociocultural life. These data could be computed with other information gleaned from that player and others. Soon, thematic patterns might emerge that could have much preventative value."

Complex, certainly, and refined is this eclectic panorama presented by football, now far removed in so many ways from its original, one-dimensional production. Where baseball holds audiences by its measured pace and logical (and identifiable) order, football beckons with a series of momentary confrontations, seemingly chaotic, yet inherently (and often unidentifiably) structured. While many are awed at the sight of a rocket's lift-off, few understand the intricacies of the preparation. So it is with football.

Like the Beatles' progression from the simple beat of "She Loves You" to the discriminating nuances of "A Day in the Life," the game has evolved from a predictable and worn tune to one of delightful and surprising diversity, often complete with its own light show. As new equipment was offered, new uses followed it: first the face mask, then blocking and tackling with the head. "It was," said one old coach, "like giving a safety belt to a wild driver and telling him he can race."

With new uses, a new tone: "The use of syn-

Science contributed the material, progressing from the heavy, nonstretchable canvas to coarse canvas, through cotton, through durene, finally to nylon and the latest stretch nylon.

thetics has made equipment lighter and stronger," says Bill Granholm. "And that makes the players faster and gives them more confidence . . . sometimes to the point of a false sense of security."

And with the new tone, the new player: "I think football's a game that can't be significantly changed much more," says Upton Bell. "But I think the players will continue to get bigger, stronger, quicker, faster and more intelligent. And in the end, the whole thing is the player."

Gerry Morgan of Riddell: "If you want revolutionary ideas in some of the fields of research, one that we've been searching in for the past fifteen, maybe eighteen, years has to do with the use of electromagnetism. We do indeed create more and better and smaller and lighter magnets. I have on my desk here a piece I've been looking at for the last three years. It's a flat piece, about twenty-five thousandths of an inch thick, and it's flexible. You can bend it like linoleum. Add another piece the same size, and they stick together. They use it now for door closures on cabinets and whatnot. This is a very beautiful thing to work with, because you don't have a straight-line curve, you have a differential curve. And using a differential curve means you have the ability to soften out immediate impact.

"It's like a fighter. If he were to accept all the jabs directly, the guy would be punchy within a short time. But a jab comes into your span of attention, and you start to move with it or slide from it. You create a tangential curve. A parabolic curve, actually. The electromagnetic change is the same thing, inversely proportional as the distance, and it behaves as a parabolic curve. If this were made available to us with sufficient lines of flux or strength, hell, this would be the paramount thing to use on a football field. Actually, if you want to expand your imagination to something unbelievable, we could induce a polarity thing for the player, so that as one guy comes slamming into the other guy, he's slowed down—not enough to stop his tackling, but enough to keep him from injury. . . .

"Now, you asked for way-out things. And that's way out."

The promises of future-plus, perhaps. But the meaning is clear: Experimentation continues, and with it the perpetual reformation of football's environment. The technology of the seventies manifests itself already, in the better way; thinking of tomorrows only recalls the old paradox that wisdom should reckon on the unforeseen.

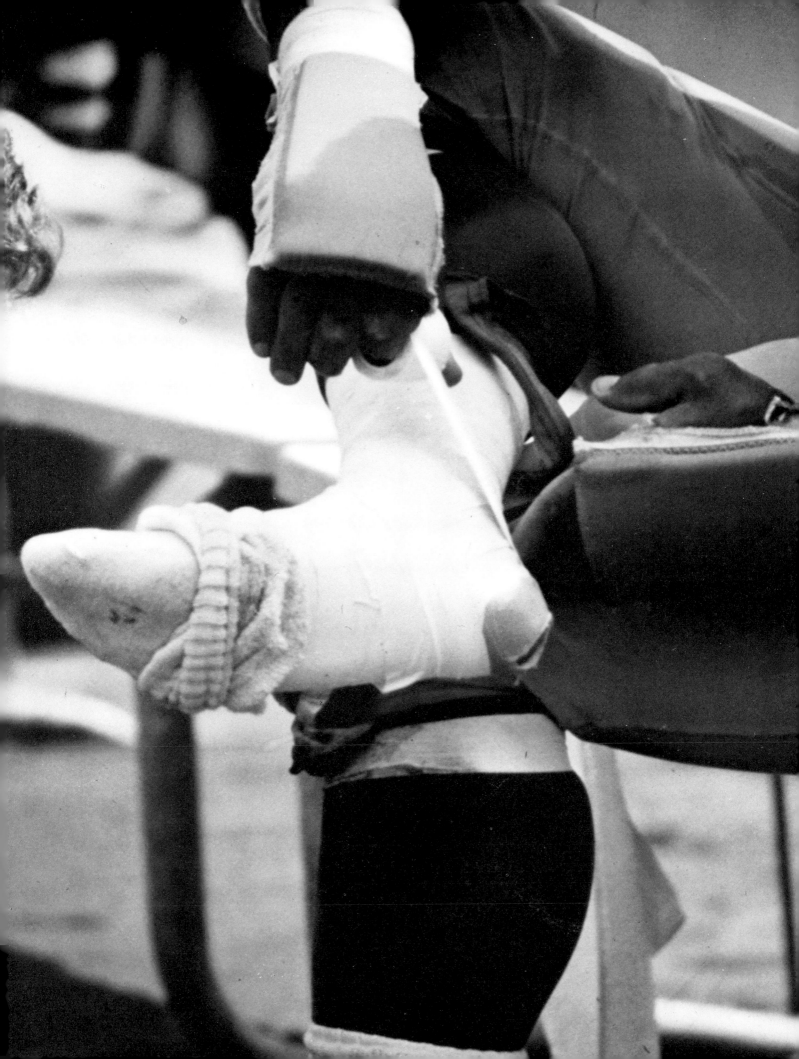

7

THRESHOLDS

by Steve Taylor
and Mercer Field

In the beginning was the Kickoff.
The ball flew spiralling true into the end zone where it was snagged, neatly hugged by a swivel-hipped back who ran up the field and was smeared.

"You are in jeopardy. You are willing to take chances and to fail. You accept the suffering that goes along with the elation of making it."

Sunday after Sunday, special kinds of men meet on America's football fields. They force their bodies and minds to an ultimate point, and sometimes beyond; they tax their bodies and minds in the frost-bitten air of the north—in snow, sleet, drizzle, mud —or under the heat of southern winter suns, more oppressive because it is alien. What seems at first glance to be a wild heaping disorder of battered bodies becomes the Game. These men are members of professional football teams. Their individuality becomes merged, until they are two identities striving to outwit and outmaneuver each other in intricate patterns. The competition is savage; it is gut combat. No man can expect to compete in this arena and survive unscarred.

The rookie dreads his first big injury, unsure of his capacity to recover, fearing the pain, hoping he will overcome it. But football is his job. If an injury can be taped or frozen, he will play, and if it can't, he will summon reserve strength and trust the pain to tell him whether to give in. He plays because he is good, better than good.

MAXIE BAUGHAN, RETIRED LINEBACKER, WASHINGTON REDSKINS: You couldn't take a man off the street and break his hand and then say, "All right, get out there and play." Not without offering him a lot of money.

Money can be a powerful incentive. If, however, a player is motivated only by money, he does not belong on a professional football field. The football pro has a deep love for his game; he is proud of his teammates' respect; he endures the hardships of training camps and travel, knowing his career may be cut short by injury. When he sprains his ankle, he has it taped and returns to the game. Football is more than his job; it is his mistress.

JIM MARSHALL, DEFENSIVE END, MINNESOTA VIKINGS: A professional has to play with a great deal of pain at one time or another. It helps him feel that he is a strong specimen, that he can tolerate hardships the ordinary man can't.

WAYNE WALKER, LINEBACKER, DETROIT LIONS: One of the great satisfactions of this life occurs when an important game is coming up. You are hurt, you know the guys need you, and you think, "I'm going to get in there and see if I can't gut it out for them." You do. Sure, you shouldn't be out there, but you get the job done. They don't have to come out and tell you they are grateful for what you did. You can feel it.

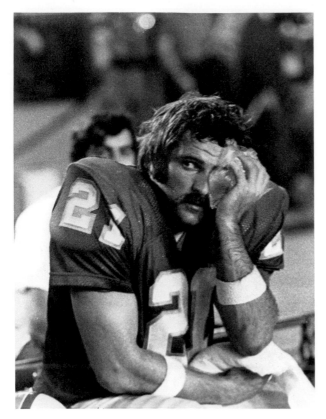

"I think each man needs pain, because if he hasn't the discipline to endure pain and continue, he knows something is lacking in his emotional makeup."

BUCK BUCHANAN, DEFENSIVE TACKLE, KANSAS CITY CHIEFS: I like to be out on the field. You are a part of something when you are directly participating. Whatever the consequences, you want to be there. I don't think about getting hurt. I try not to think about it at all. Of course, you do when you get blocked and one of your legs goes. The first thing that comes to your mind then is that you've had it. You have to get up and shake it off.

JOE NAMATH, QUARTERBACK, NEW YORK JETS: Going up and down stairs is a problem for me once the season is under way. Even walking bothers me. But it's something you accept; that's the way it is. You're lucky if you have legs at all, and if they hurt, they hurt. I know that by the time I'm fifty, I'm really going to have problems walking, but there isn't anything I can do about it. Of course, I have a definite weakness—if I were to get hit with a direct shot to the knee, then I would be out for good. I love the game. Basically it's my whole life. So I end up playing again. I realize how much football means to me.[1]

There are nearly as many theories about what drives men to accept the painful challenge that is football as there are theories of human behavior. Charley Johnson played most of the 1970 season with a broken left collarbone. Billy Van Heusen holds the Denver Bronco record for knee operations—seven. Johnny Robinson, recently retired safety for the Kansas City Chiefs and named to the all-time AFL all-star team, recovered a fumble and intercepted a pass in Super Bowl IV while playing with three broken ribs.

CHARLEY JOHNSON, QUARTERBACK, DENVER BRONCOS: Why do they do it? I think there are two or three reasons. Number one, basic human nature has you physically testing yourself against other people. Another is that it's very pleasing to be able totally to put yourself into something and immediately know the results—instant gratification or instant evaluation. The other is that you are in jeopardy. You are willing to take chances and to fail. You accept the suffering that goes along with the elation of making it. All three reasons explain why you play football for twenty-five years of your life.

BILLY VAN HEUSEN, PUNTER, WIDE RECEIVER, DENVER BRONCOS: You put up with the pain because football is such a tremendous challenge. It's a great feeling to play pro ball. You're in front of the people, and it's a thrill to be able to perform. I guess everyone is a glory hound basically. You can be running a pass pattern and be hurting, but if you beat the guy,

[1] Mike Rathet, "Joe Namath, Crises Quarterback," *The Sports Immortals*, p. 295.

you really don't think about the pain. You are happy that you beat him. The satisfaction overrides the pain. Getting off a fifty-yard punt with good height: that's what it's all about. I'll suffer to do it.

JOHNNY ROBINSON, RETIRED SAFETY, KANSAS CITY CHIEFS: It's a business and you've got to treat it as a business, because you've got to support your family. It's like asking a guy who is president of General Motors whether he would work without pay. Ask a bricklayer with a broken hand if he would object to having a doctor stick a needle in there to kill the pain so he could make sixty or seventy bucks to take home to his family. He'd tell you, "Hell, no."

You take tremendous pride in the fact that your ability to play could make a key difference in the outcome of the game. Once a player feels that it makes no difference whether or not he's in the game, it's time he got out.

I like to play tennis, but if I sprain my wrist, I'm not going to go out on the courts. I'd take six weeks to heal, soaking the wrist in hot water every day and complaining about it. If somebody asked me to play, I'd say sorry. But when football comes around, for the next fourteen or sixteen weeks I play—sprain or no sprain. That's what I'm paid to do. It's something I have great pride in. Once it's over, I'll take aspirin instead of having my hand injected, and I'll put my arm in a sling and protect it as well as I can.

Many elements go into any one player's ability to cope with pain. How vital does he consider his performance on a particular day? How strong is his personal motivation? How sensitive is he to pressure from his trainer or teammates? Is he young and in top condition? Has he recovered from a similar injury in the past? Does he believe in mind over matter? How does he react when other men are injured? Most important, does he have a high or low pain threshold?

BERNIE CASEY, RETIRED WIDE RECEIVER, LOS ANGELES RAMS: I believe that through discipline and mental conditioning a man can learn to accept pain as part of his endeavor. In fact, I think each

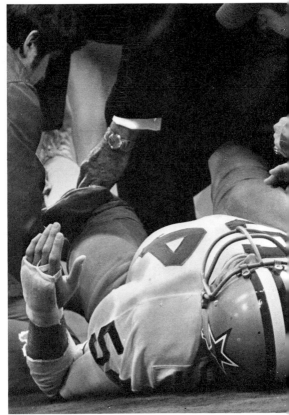

"Every time you hit, there is pain, but you learn to take it. You know you're going to have it, but not forever."

215

"You go with pain because you know you have a job to do. It's going to hurt, but you know that by playing, you can help the team."

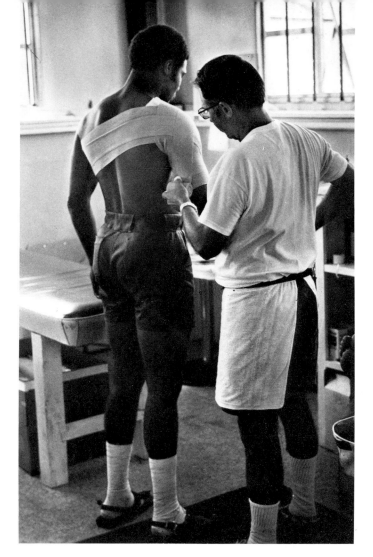

man needs pain, because if he hasn't the discipline to endure pain and continue, he knows something is lacking in his emotional makeup. That's not to say you should go out and get hit by a car. But every man must find his own way to operate with pain.

CARL LOCKHART, SAFETY, NEW YORK GIANTS: You go with pain because you know you have a job to do. It's going to hurt, but you know that by playing, you can help the team, and you find yourself in there doing what you are supposed to do.

BUCK BUCHANAN: Usually, when the time comes to play, regardless of how you might feel or how painful it might be, you play.

The coach knows whether a guy will play for him when the time rolls around. If it's not a crippling injury, I don't see why you can't play. When my knees were hurt, my performance was not what I would have liked it to have been, but I went out and did my best. I had both knees taped. This restricts your movement quite a bit and the least little thing really hurts. If your finger is hurt bad, you can usually play eighty-five or ninety percent. I have played with a broken outside toe. I had a piece of steel in my shoe to protect it.

But Johnny Robinson played with something that to me was unbelievable: fractured ribs. I don't know if I would have played with that kind of pain. Any time he got hit, you knew he'd probably have gotten it in that area. In one respect, you've got to say, "This guy is crazy." In another respect, you feel that he is going to help your team. And, of course, we won a championship game that way. That meant a hell of a lot to our team.

The toughest guy we ever had, to me, was Shel Hendrick. One time we were playing and he got his thumb torn almost off. He ran back to the sidelines between plays and said, "Hey! Straighten this son of a bitch out and tape it up so I can get back in this game." Afterwards, I took him to the hospital. Once he had an operation on his rectum in the middle of the week and played that weekend. Time would come to play and he would play. He was a wild man. He played middle linebacker before Willie Lanier came along.

I remember the time Lanier passed out. I thought, "This guy is dead." That's the first thing that came into my mind. He just dropped. The play was over and we were in the huddle. He was calling signals. He just went down like a big old god damn tank. Bam. He was standing and talking and looking around, and all of a sudden he just went down.

I don't remember the shot he took. Sometimes you've got to stick your head in there and sometimes you shouldn't. If you've got a shot on a guy, especially if you're as strong as Lanier is, you can tackle with your chest. But to stick your head in there and really take those bangs—man, that's crap.

Everybody has his own level of pain. You see a guy trying to dodge it at times. I'm going to say something to him then. We put the needle to him. We might say, "Well, god damn, you know you played that one in the tank?" or, "God damn, you haven't played all week. We're working our asses off and you're cooling it." It's best to stay on the sidelines if you're going to hurt the team.

We were playing at Buffalo, and Otis Taylor caught a ball against the Bills. As he went to go into the end zone, Butch Byrd hit him with a forearm, up the side of the jaw. Otis fell into the end zone for a touchdown and he jumped up and ran to the sideline holding his jaw. One of our scouts, Lloyd Wells, saw him coming and said, "Don't you come holding your jaw like that. I've known you since high school. I know there's nothing wrong with you." Otis wanted to kill him. He was cussing and screaming. Once in Baltimore I was making a play, and Bill Curry fell across my leg and I hollered and screamed. After Curry found out that the leg wasn't hurt that bad, he said, "Why don't you get your old ass out of the way?"

KEN BURROUGH, WIDE RECEIVER, ATLANTA FALCONS: When I fractured my wrist, rolling over after making a sixty-six-yard catch against the Lions, I got the same feeling I had when I sprained both ankles at once at San Diego State. In that first moment I thought my career was finished. Something had happened to me that was just going to end everything. I got up and the wrist was dangling. Then I got some composure coming off the field, and they cinched the wrist with tape and I went back in. Tape does wondrous things. They can lock the wrist or cinch it up without knowing whether it's broken or a torn ligament or whatever. So they cinched it up, which gave me play in my fingers. I could still run and I caught a touchdown after that, about a thirty-four-yarder, and three more passes later. It all made me feel great—until after the game. I was in bad shape then.

They put a cast on, and I didn't know what to think about playing again. The man made up my mind for me, I guess. At a news conference they asked the coach if I was going to play, and he said, "Well, he played half of the game with a broken wrist, so I don't see why he can't continue."

I played the rest of the season.

I feel proud every time I go home and look up on the wall and there's an Atlanta Falcon helmet. I come from a foster home in Berkeley, California, and I've risen to this. I think of all the people who said I'd never make it. I don't believe I have to prove my masculinity by playing in pain.

TOMMY NOBIS, LINEBACKER, ATLANTA FALCONS: You've got to learn to play with sprains. I've had sprained ankles that, taped, weren't bad enough to keep me out of the game. I remember playing with what seemed like three rolls of tape on my ankle, and I've played with broken fingers. You have to wear some kind of protection, and that's uncomfortable. Every time you hit, there is pain, but you learn to take it. You know you're going to have it, but you know it's not forever.

In my freshman year I had to play with both knees taped, but you see other people do it, so you decide you can. Of course, it's going to hurt your play anytime you're not able to go one hundred percent. I've had pretty good luck—only two knee operations so far. I went back and tried to play after one of the knee injuries, but I just knew I couldn't do the job. Say you have a torn cartilage. You can get a tape job and hold that cartilage and it's not going to lop on you. You may be able to get out there and

''Older players seem to take pride in playing with injuries.
You're hurt, you play. . . . The newer athlete has different
values. He doesn't feel there's constant pressure on him.''

avoid some of the pain, but you're not going to be able to do the job.

You can protect yourself from certain injuries with pads and tape, but even if the pain is gone, can you operate well enough? You have a functional problem linked to pain. As long as I can do well enough to help our team, I'm going to play. If you're hurt and not doing your job, you should get out of the game until the thing is fixed.

To be truthful, my pain tolerance is not that high. My first knee injury was hell. I knew it was serious the moment it was hurt. As far as having a knee drained, some guys can have that big horse needle stuck in and it doesn't even bother them. Every time one of those damn things gets stuck in me, I'm gonna yell just looking at it.

BOBBY GUNN, TRAINER, HOUSTON OILERS: I really think for a guy to come back fully he needs to take another shot very similar to the first, so he can say, "It happened before. I can come back."

RANDY JOHNSON, QUARTERBACK, NEW YORK GIANTS: I'm a firm believer that it's mind over anything for a quarterback. My first serious injury was a pulled inner abdominal muscle. They had to shave part of my bottom, and right above the penis they inserted Novocain. It was hard to set up, but not so serious that I couldn't play. I missed just one game.

I worry some, but not during play. I don't go into a game thinking about whether the play I call is one I'm likely to get hit on.

I've seen guys who couldn't make it during practice but were out there on Sunday. Sundays are completely different. Bob Griese was hospitalized with intestinal flu one Saturday night before a game. He didn't start the game; he was too sick. Then, when the score got to 21–0, he came in and threw four touchdown passes.

Older players seem to take pride in playing with injuries. You're hurt, you play. Take a real big tough old-school lineman like our center, Greg Larson. He's had maybe ten knee operations, and he's got this wrong and that wrong, and he's got a bad heart; but he plays every Sunday regardless.

The newer athlete has different values. He doesn't feel there's constant pressure on him to prove that he can go out and run with a pulled muscle. Sometimes this causes friction. The older player, a tough gritty guy with high pain tolerance, will get down on a younger player who comes in and says, "Hey, you know, I'm not going to play. And I don't care what you say. If I run on the muscle, it's going to get worse instead of better." The older guy will call

"I think of all the people who said I'd never make it. I don't believe I have to prove my masculinity by playing in pain. It's just personal motivation."

him a pussy. I guess it all depends on how much it means to you.

Pain and football go together. When the thought of pain becomes anything more than a subconscious worry on Sundays, when you go out there thinking "I'm going to get hurt," you might as well get out. That's when you stop being a competitive athlete.

ALLEN HURST, TRAINER, DENVER BRONCOS: A person's reaction to pain, his threshold, will become higher as he plays. Motivation to get the job done will cover over the discomfort. A football player can perform with pain better than the layman. The pain is there for both and it is equal, but the player's tolerance level is higher and this allows him to perform. In addition, football produces a situation of optimum medical care in the event of injury.

There isn't any ball club that is completely healthy. This keeps an injured man from feeling sorry for himself. He seems to have what other guys have had, and others have come back. A superbly conditioned athlete who has youth on his side can be pushed a little faster toward recovery.

LARRY GARDNER, TRAINER, DALLAS COWBOYS: Different players have different pain thresholds. Some have a more sensitive nervous system as far as the pain receptors are concerned. There's not much they can do when those pain stimulants are flowing into the brain. It's not a question of dogging it. Some people can take pain better than others.

When I first came to the Cowboys, one of the things I heard was that Mel Renfro had a real low pain threshold. In a preseason game against Los Angeles he fractured his nose. At half-time we got the bleeding down and iced it. He asked me to have the equipment manager put a full cage on his helmet so he could play the second half. I have no doubts that Renfro would play with a broken hand or shoulder separation and do the job. So much for a low pain threshold.

In San Francisco in the NFC championship game, we thought Walt Garrison had reinjured his knee. After we talked to him, we found out that on the same play he had sprained his ankle and cracked a clavicle. Coach Landry said he was out, but Walt said, "No, sir, I'll play." He did, and well. Other players wouldn't have kept going with any one of those three injuries.

JERRY RHEA, TRAINER, ATLANTA FALCONS: You've got to know the personality that goes with the pain. There are guys who are tough and guys who are real softies, and you have to know whom you are

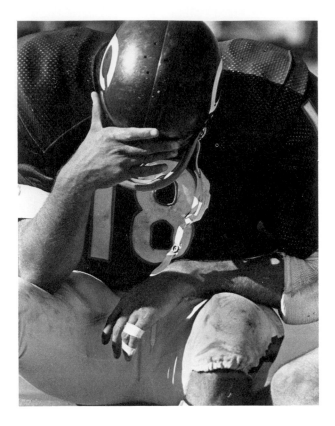

Failure is in direct conflict with confidence. It is the worst pain.

Most pros agree that the battle to recuperate from injury is as difficult mentally as it is physically.

MATT SNELL, RUNNING BACK, NEW YORK JETS: I got a spot on my knee about the size of a half dollar. It hurt me for sixteen weeks straight, night and day. What happened was that when I got tackled, the guy's helmet hit me right at the top of this big bone and it dented the bone and chipped a little piece off it. Sixteen weeks, night and day—what can they give you? It doesn't help that much. I found out from the doctor that barometric pressure affects a knee joint, or any joint, because the joint expands and contracts with the rise and fall in the pressure. It drove me crazy. I couldn't sleep.

I've separated my ribs four times. Our doctor is very reluctant to give you a shot in any moving joint, but my rib was sliding a little bit. So he gave me a shot and I could stand it.

RANDY JOHNSON: Many times before a game I've

dealing with before you can evaluate what they tell you. Some guy has a hangnail and wants to come out, and another guy has a fracture and won't even tell you because he's afraid we'll pull him.

John Zook has been with us three years and has never been in for treatment. And he's in there where people are doubling him and are going to take cheap shots at him. Is he just strong and immune to injury or is he immune to pain? George Kunz is a superhuman. He had a knee operated on almost immediately after it was locked. Within five weeks, he had returned to the lineup and played the whole game for us.

Malcolm Snider will come in for treatment maybe three or four days and then say, "Forget it. I've got to play Sunday. I'm wasting my time here." We've got one who is a bleeder and bruises easily. He'll be hurt on Sunday and all week you'll think he'll die. But Sunday he gets well.

CHARLEY JOHNSON: When I get hurt, I miss the game so much that I ignore my problem just so I can play. If you stay in when you have no business playing, it's frightening. You won't accept the loss of your effectiveness, and nobody is going to tell you you're not doing the job.

In order to keep from facing failure, some guys say they must have been hurt when they blow a play.

"Here you are, thousands of miles from home, and all you've got to look forward to is the knife. What do you say?"

had my knee drained. They draw out the fluid and put in a mixture of cortisone and Novocain. If they didn't drain it, there wouldn't be any flexibility in the knee.

BOBBY GUNN: It's one of the duties of the physician and the trainer to try to make the players understand that a pain killer taken just so a man can perform is a highly artificial tool. It is pain itself that tells a player to what degree he can perform.

BILLY VAN HEUSEN: I know some guys will hurt a finger and want Novocain until after the game, but I don't because if I get numb in the spot and then get hurt and don't feel it, I can be in trouble. I just like to feel and know in my mind what is wrong.

ALLEN HURST: There is no way that we will give a shot of Zylocaine to a ballplayer who sprains an ankle, because we know if he gets whacked there again he could tear it or completely break it and wouldn't even know. But we have given pills to keep a player in a ball game because of a bruise. A small

pain pill isn't going to hurt him, but we try to cut down the use of medication as much as we can.

CHARLEY JOHNSON: I can put up with pain better now. I'm not so concerned about what is going to happen to my body. I know I'm going to get hit. Most of the time the excitement of playing will block out concern. You won't remember getting hit hard until you see it in the films. The mental awareness of what's going on overshadows and outweighs everything. When you really get a good hit, the pain is enough to block out everything else. But that only lasts a while.

The responsibility of keeping up morale falls to the trainers, who must be sensitive enough to pick up from the slightest hints any mental or physical problems that develop among the squad.

JERRY RHEA: The veterans are hard on rookies. Sometimes a rookie doesn't understand. He may have to come in an hour earlier than the vets to get taped, because there is no way we can tape eighty people in

*"We aren't waving a magic wand in order to heal.
All we're trying to do is put this injury
to rest so that the body gets over the initial shock."*

one hour. During the season we have a 12:00 meeting and the rookies have to be taped and out by 11:00 —even outstanding rookies who are starters. They just don't understand and keep asking, "Why do I have to come in so early?" You can be a heel all your life, but you can be a rookie only once.

We try to encourage them to do well. They've got to realize that unless they're seriously hurt, they've got to be ready to play on Sunday. That's what they're paid for. It doesn't hurt quite so bad on Sunday. The adrenalin flows and the band is playing and the crowd is yelling and it's a money day.

Our doctors are very conservative with drugs. I don't give anything on my own. Ten years ago, doctors just weren't consulted that much. Things have changed now.

We chart the players daily when they're in for treatment. We do all the routine tests: EKG, chest X ray, urinalysis, blood study. In training camp we have one doctor who checks the upper body—respiratory, heart, abdomen, ears, throat—and a general surgeon who checks the lower body. We have three orthopedic people to check all the joints, and we have a dentist, too.

These guys want to play. Players push themselves far more than they admit, for the simple reason that they want to stay in the game. It's a short life. Ten years is a terribly long time in pro football.

MATT SNELL: I was a gung-ho rookie. Over the first couple of years, I was moving the ball twenty-five or thirty times a game and I felt kind of weary. My third year I was at a plateau. I didn't think I was playing very well, so I tried a couple amphetamines. I don't know if I was playing any better, but I was sure more excited. Then I decided, "Am I crazy?" That's when I sat down and said, "If I have to do this, I should get out of the game." The competition should be enough. I haven't had any since. You can psych yourself into the same excitement.

RANDY JOHNSON: The percentage of players who use amphetamines is small. It varies with the pressure. I think ninety-five percent of the players who use them don't take them for pain. I think it's just psychological. Pain is secondary.

CHARLEY JOHNSON: My impression is that a guy plays differently if he's taken stimulants. His priorities are changed slightly. The most critical thing to me as a passer is how the receiver is going to respond to a certain picture he gets as he is going down the field. I can't think of anything more scary than to have all my receivers on stimulants.

BOBBY GUNN: A player's not going to perform at his best when he stimulates himself artificially. There haven't been enough tests run, in my opinion, but it has been proven to my satisfaction that the advantage the player on amphetamines thinks he's got is small.

Amphetamines don't help performance. There's a supposed masking of fatigue, but just plain conditioning is much more desirable than artificial efficiency. Americans seem to go to extremes to find the easy way and to avoid the best way, which in this case is hard work and proper rest.

We try to get authorities in the field of drugs to talk to the players, but until you've been in the trenches with them, you can't fully understand their needs, their desires. Watch them going down the field on the kickoff or under a punt. It's the ultimate in desire and desire is just one of the many positive, valuable aspects of this violent sport.

Just as players have various ways of coping with pain and injury, so they react individually to a teammate's disability or an opponent's weakness. Cheap shots are rare; nevertheless, if a man is injured and

still chooses to play, he must do so without expecting sympathy. Quarterbacks aren't the only ones to take advantage of an opponent's impaired ability.

BILLY VAN HEUSEN: Out on the field you don't really feel bad for anyone. You can't, because nobody feels bad for you. When you beat the cornerback but drop a touchdown pass, he's not feeling sorry for you. When you beat him, you don't know whether his ankle is bad or not. You just beat him the best way you can, and if you score, that's great.

I respect injuries because I know how crippling they can be. Even while watching college or professional football on TV, when a guy goes down, I find myself trying to guess what the injury is and hoping it's something the guy will come back from. You see a knee buckle or a guy get hit from the side and you know there's no question he's hurt.

If it's a teammate, you find yourself thinking, "who's going to play for him?" You evaluate his worth to your team.

I wish football could be played without injuries.

KEN BURROUGH: Strangely enough, when I had my broken wrist, quarterbacks never seemed to do anything to aggravate it. I think they had other things on their minds, but I'm sure if they'd had the chance they'd have done something or tried.

If I know a guy's got a sprained ankle, I might do a few things a little more quickly than I would otherwise to try to take advantage: make a quicker cut, make him come harder in the play, use his leg harder. And if the play is not in my direction, I might make him run longer. I think you have to take advantage. That's what the game is all about.

RANDY JOHNSON: As a quarterback I'd be naive if I said I wouldn't take advantage if Herb Adderley with a bad knee is on one side of Dallas's defense and Mel Renfro with two good knees is on the other side. You know I'm going to throw on Adderley.

The National Football League has a rule that teams have to report all injuries to the league office when they happen, so we can get reports on any player if we're suspicious he's hurt. But it works both ways. If they know I've got a bad knee, they're going to blitz their linebackers and try to get me quicker, because they know I'll be slower.

BOBBY GUNN: If you know an opponent's right ankle is injured and he can't drive off to his left side, you try to exploit that weakness. If you see a defensive back limping out there and he hasn't been taken out, you send somebody deep on that side. If he can't cover you, that's tough.

MATT SNELL: When Joe Namath got his knee torn up in preseason against Detroit we didn't know what had happened to him until half-time. You could feel the reaction going through the room: I couldn't believe it. You know what the guy is facing, especially if like myself you've been through it. Here you are, thousands of miles from home, and all you've got to look forward to is the knife. What do you say? Surgery doesn't mean anything? If he's been through it and you've been through it, you know that whenever they've got to put you on the table, it's not minor. Afterwards, you've got four or five days of tremendous pain and then, of course, the hard work to come back. You wonder whether it's worth it.

Pain is an inescapable companion of injury. As such, players don't find it particularly frightening. What is formidable for them is the difference between injury and incapacity. While the quality and quantity of pain can be anticipated with reasonable certainty, the extent of the resultant disability cannot be so easily determined and is therefore alarming. Anxiety is greatest in the face of the unknown.

ANDY RUSSELL, LINEBACKER, PITTSBURGH STEELERS: The fear football players have is not the fear of pain, but the fear that an injury will keep them from doing their job. In most businesses, you can be dedicated, work hard and prepare yourself physically and mentally; you will likely succeed because of your attitude. In football your career can be wiped out in one second, no matter what your attitude is. If you can't do your job, you're through.

ALLEN HURST: To be successful in football you've got to be able to perform. Vince Lombardi did a lot to emphasize the male ego and the Spartan way of life. It's a tough business and only the tough, proud ones survive. What is pride, really? People who are big are expected to be tough, too. You are playing with the best. To be the best of the best satisfies goals. By nature ballplayers just don't want to be frustrated.

BILLY VAN HEUSEN: Your biggest fear on any play is not pain but failure. People ask, "Don't you hear footsteps?" I really don't. I think any receiver knows exactly where the defensive backs are. As you play you learn to watch guys and get to know their reactions exactly. Your personal vision comes into play. You see guys come into the side on a play and things like that. You don't worry about getting hurt because you know where everybody is and you know how to protect yourself. But you worry about dropping a

"When you go out there thinking 'I'm going to get hurt,' you might as well get out. That's when you stop being a competitive athlete."

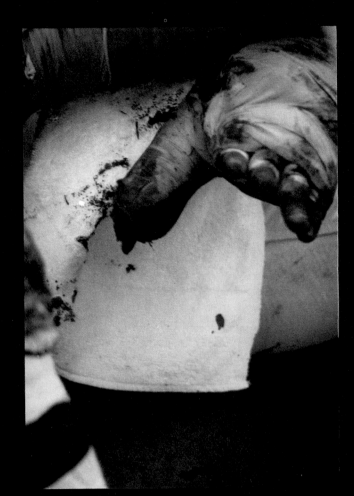

"A football player can perform with pain better than
the layman. The pain is there for both and
it is equal, but the player's tolerance is higher."

pass, you worry about fumbling, or as a punter you worry about a bad kick.

You know even before the ball crosses the line of scrimmage when you have shanked it. A strong feeling of depression comes over you. You just slump. You know everything you're going to get from the coaches, players and fans.

JIMMY BROWN, RETIRED RUNNING BACK, CLEVE-LAND BROWNS: I always made it a practice to use my head before my body. I looked upon playing football as a businessman might. The game was my business; my body and my mind were my assets and injuries were my liabilities. The first basic was to be in absolutely top-notch physical condition. I always tried to train harder than anyone else. I even developed my own set of calisthenics, things I could do in my hotel room if I had to. And over the years, I made a study of what things usually cause injuries, and, as much as I could, I avoided those things.[2]

I got out in my prime and without injuries. I got out before I ever had to be like I've seen so many guys—sitting hunched over on the bench, all scarred and banged up, watching some hot young kid out there in their place.[3]

WILLIE LANIER, MIDDLE LINEBACKER, KANSAS CITY CHIEFS: You can't play recklessly in this league. You can't annihilate these people. Everybody is as big as you are. They're all good athletes. Over a period of time if you attack everyone all out, you wind up doing more damage to yourself than to anybody else. I tried to do it that way my first year, but one play taught me my lesson. Now I get in several good hits in every game—but I select the hits. I make sure everything is set up the way I want it. If I'm off balance or at a bad angle, I make the play without excessive force. My style is of such a violent nature that if I slack off sometimes, I'm back to what everybody else is doing normally. Whoever said injuries happen when you start to be careful couldn't have had the well-being of the players in mind. I have a wife and family. I have to be concerned with my well-being. I know that if I play recklessly on every play, I'm exposing myself to serious injury. I know. I've been there.

I attacked somebody head first and I took the punishment. I was out cold on the field and didn't wake up for forty-five minutes. I had double vision and spent a week at the Mayo Clinic being tested and a lot longer than that worrying if I would ever be right again. I've been there, and if I can control it, I'm never going to be there again.

There's no way I'll ever try to hit anybody head on again. A good hit is beautiful. I enjoy it. But that

"In order to keep from facing failure, some guys say they must have been hurt when they blow a play. Failure is in direct conflict with confidence. It is the worst pain."

doesn't mean I'm going to risk my life. Trying to hurt somebody doesn't turn me on.

Trainers and coaches are as concerned about team injuries as players are. It is their job to see that the squad is in maximum physical condition, which will minimize the chances of injury. Off-season and preseason conditioning and workouts, as well as the speed and quality of recovery during the season, may mean the difference between being number one and missing the play-offs. An athlete in superior condition is less likely to be hurt and will recover from injury more rapidly.

SID GILLMAN, COACH, RESEARCH AND DEVELOP-MENT DEPARTMENT, DALLAS COWBOYS: When injuries hit the top teams, there is no leveling off of performance. A lower-division team won't sustain injuries so well.

[2] Mike Rathet, "Jimmy Brown: Brain and Body," *The Sports Immortals,* p. 136.
[3] Ibid., p. 139.

The day is gone when guys can come to training camp with big beer bellies and say they are going to use the preseason to get in shape. You've got to start to get in shape no later than April 1. The older you get, the harder you have to work. There's a decided correlation between the amount of weight lifting and running and stretching a guy does in the off-season and the extent to which he avoids injury during the season. A guy who's in shape will recover faster than one who isn't.

The problem in this day and age is that some of the players have so much going for them during the off-season that they're inclined to forget injuries they've suffered during the season. You've got to motivate these guys to come out for off-season physical programs.

The players are conditioned by degrees to live and work and play with injuries. Some guys heal in a hurry. Some guys never heal. Doctors don't know the answer.

If a guy's not prepared mentally to approach a season, then physically he's not there. If the mind is geared properly, then everything else falls in line. You can't win a championship with talented people if they haven't intelligence. You can't win unless you've got a forty-man squad that is high in pain tolerance. Pain tolerance is a physical thing. A guy decides he's got to play and there's something about the chemistry of his body that permits him to play.

BOBBY GUNN: All we are trying to do as trainers, physicians or surgeons is to provide optimum conditions under which healing may take place. That can make all the difference. If a player steps in a hole and rolls his ankle so that the sprain is on the outside—a common sprain for an athlete—you assume there has been tearing and/or stretching of ligaments, nerves and blood vessels—all types of tissue on the side where the sprain is. Initially, the body receives this shock, this trauma, caused by leakage of fluid into spaces where it is not normally supposed to be. To help the body immediately, we put cold on it. That sedates the area.

We also put pressure on to try to stop the hemorrhage. We elevate the injured part, which lets gravity help us by allowing the fluid that has leaked out to move properly. We use those three things—cold, pres-

"I can put up with pain better now. I'm not so concerned about what is going to happen to my body. I know I'm going to get hit."

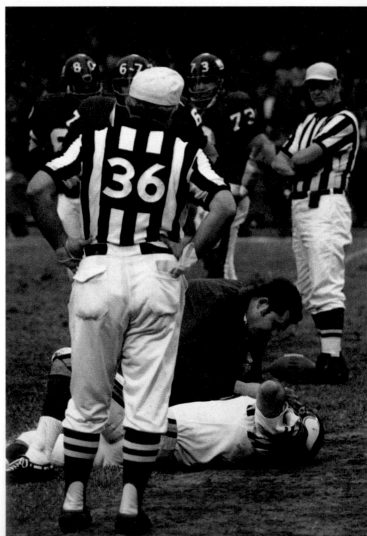

232

sure and elevation. We wave no magic wand in order to heal. All we're trying to do is put this injury to rest, so that the body gets over the initial shock. Many times when a guy is in apparent pain, we can calm down this initial shock in just a little time. He's still in one piece and feels ready to go.

Larry Brown is one of the toughest football men I've seen. The injury that got to him was the contusion on his forehead. It was a superficial hemorrhage just under the skin, but as it leaked out into a noticeable knot, it was a spectacular sight. We felt it wasn't serious, did the needed things at the time, put a bandage on it, and he went back in. He had a sore leg to start with and was wearing a thin vinyl covering over it for protection.

ALLEN HURST: Training camp is tougher mentally than it is physically. The guys are away from their families and housed in an armylike situation for two months. The routine is not so strenuous that it will ever allow the guys to get to the point of absolute fatigue, but physical and mental weariness go hand in hand. Mental staleness is what you have to worry about. We give them everything we possibly can to eliminate the fatigue mechanism: salt water replacement; fluid replacement before, during and after practice. We have ice available for them, but even someone like Bob Lilly considers retiring rather than go through another training camp.

You've got to treat players psychologically as well as physically. If a guy says he's not going to come back, you have to encourage him. Then he sees a little improvement. If a guy doesn't have a good rehab program after knee surgery, somebody to push him, somebody to work with him, you might as well forget it.

The athlete with superior physical conditioning is able to maintain his performance level longer. He's less likely to receive injury, probably won't be so severely injured and will recover faster.

Charley Johnson was working out in training camp after a knee injury. He went out on a bootleg and one of the safeties hit him when he was out of bounds. It was the same play, the same type of thing that had happened when he got hit in New York. He got up for a second, worked his leg, then jogged back into the huddle. "That's what I needed," he said. "For a year it's been in the back of my mind, would my knee stand up to something like this? And it did."

LARRY GARDNER: In the last few years, we have used the probability of decreasing injuries as motivation to get our guys to participate in our off-season physical strength program. We think the close to one

"A lot of people say it's a cruel game.
I accept it as a challenge." "It's a tough business
and only the tough, proud ones survive."

hundred percent participation of our players in this off-season program has had a large bearing on how injury-free we've been. We had four or five knee surgeries in the last two years. Before we were having four or five a year. More important, although we've had cartilage damage, not one of these injuries has required ligament repair.

The people we get in pro football are the great athletes. Actually, they haven't worked that much in high school and college and are further from their potential optimum strength than almost any other athletes. It's harder to get these people to work in an off-season program, because they've never had to and are stars anyhow.

Bob Lilly is one of the better athletes in pro ball. It was a little harder to convince him than most, but since he has gotten into the program and worked hard, he's become one of its biggest advocates. He feels this program can add two or three years to a player's career. Mike Ditka feels the same way. For the first time since college, he can dunk a basketball. He hadn't been able to do this for eight or nine years. The only injury that caused Ditka to miss time in the 1971 season was a broken hand. This program isn't going to strengthen bones, but it does help with a muscular injury. It makes a guy stronger and therefore better able to protect himself.

Calvin Hill got his knee hit in the New York game and had a heck of a hyperextension injury. He missed five or six weeks, played in the San Francisco game and got hit again; but he was still able to be pretty darned effective in the Super Bowl. If he hadn't been on our program, he would have had to have surgery the morning after the New York game.

MATT SNELL: I've had a broken nose, shoulder separation, rib separations. Those didn't bother me. I also have had serious injuries. I tore my knee up in Buffalo, and that affects you psychologically because your knee is unstable the following year. It takes a certain amount of confidence to come back. Lee White, our former fullback, came in as a rookie, got hurt in Kansas City and never recovered. He always ran like he was loping, trying to keep that leg back. I tore my Achilles tendon and that blew my mind. It's a weird sensation. You try to walk and your foot just sort of flaps along. I thought, "I'll never walk right again." It was a long hard struggle. Muscle in your leg is tough to build up.

I was in a cast for thirteen weeks and of course all the muscles were shot when I came out. The doctor said, "Get up on your toes." I couldn't. My doctor suggested weight lifting, whirlpool, massage, and he said, "You have to do a minimum of two

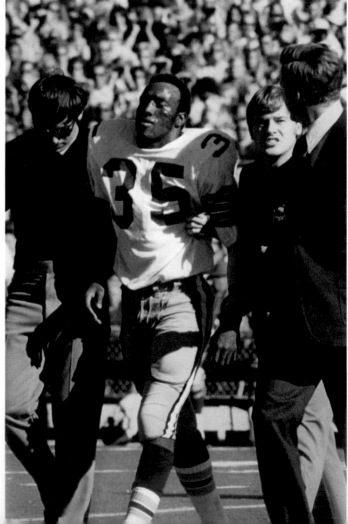

"We try to encourage them to do well. They've got to realize that unless they're seriously hurt, they've got to be ready to play. That's what they're paid for."

thousand toe rises a day." I said, "You're crazy!" He said, "Do you want to play again?"

So we started, and I went along, but I didn't see anything happen. Later on I got on a two-by-four and stretched against the wall. Then spring came and I was out there every morning by myself. And I didn't see any progress.

Pretty soon it started to come, but then I went to Kansas City and got hit straight on by Lanier so that the two bones separated in my leg and I tore a muscle in my back.

I've had almost three years of injuries. I don't know if I want any more. You get beat up to the extent they have to roll you out of bed, and on Thursday you're still sore from the past Sunday.

I think the day of the workhorse running back is gone, because injuries occur too often. If you've got a superstar, you can't afford to have him on the sidelines. You don't let him get tired. Every time I got hurt, it was in the fourth quarter. Apparently, injury comes with fatigue.

Bruised ribs are worse for a running back than for anyone else. Every time you take the ball, you put it in your stomach, and whenever you get hit, you fall on it. They teach you to protect the ball at all times. Bruised ribs are not a serious injury, but they're very touchy. I wear a long-sleeved shirt all the time to prevent cuts and burns, because I can't wear elbow pads. If I do, my arms tend to bounce and I fumble.

"These guys want to play. If they get the reputation of not being durable, they'll be gone.
Players push themselves far more than they admit."

BILLY VAN HEUSEN: I've learned to cope with pain to the extent that I'll play until I know I'm really hurting. Our trainer, Allen Hurst, has helped me tremendously in recovering from surgery. August 26, I had a cartilage removed, and I made a vow to myself. I felt I could help the team by at least punting and I said I'd be ready to play in two weeks. And I was. I'm not trying to say I'm a superhealer. It was just realizing my situation and trying to make the best of it.

In Oakland, I tore two ligaments completely, partially tore a third and both cartilages, and the leg has come back. It's the right one, my kicking leg. I was scared of the pain in the beginning and started to hit real lightly. After the first ball went eight yards, I thought twenty yards was awfully long. Slowly it came and the pain started to leave, and I thought I was just going to have to hit one time and that was it. I took a good shot at the ball, and it hurt. But it didn't hurt any more than the ones I was kicking twenty yards. I got over that hurdle, and finally the pain went away.

Who are these men who have conquered pain? These men who pass, block, blitz, punt with broken hands and separated shoulders, with bandaged ribs, sprained ankles, fractured wrists, taped and stitched, frozen and numbed.

They are the football professionals, brazen, bold, proud, stronger than oxen, bigger than life—invincible, invulnerable, inviolate. . . .

What makes such a man subject himself to football's agonies? What makes such a man live for and love this complex sport above nearly all else? There are many answers, each as explicit and incomplete as the next. Perhaps Walt Mason has given the best:

The Game was ended, and the noise at last had died away, and now they gathered up the boys where they in pieces lay. And one was hammered in the ground by many a jolt and jar; some fragments never have been found, they flew away so far. They found a stack of tawny hair, some fourteen cubits high; it was the half-back, lying there, where he had crawled to die. They placed the pieces on a door, and from the crimson field, that hero then they gently bore, like soldier on his shield. The surgeon toiled the livelong night above the gory wreck; he got the ribs adjusted right, the wishbone and the neck. He soldered on the ears and toes, and got the spine in place, and fixed a gutta-percha nose upon the mangled face. And then he washed his hands and said: "I'm glad that task is done!" The half-back raised his fractured head, and cried: "I call this fun!" [4]

[4] Walt Mason, "Football," *Sprints and Distances* (originally published in *Walt Mason, His Book* © 1916 by Barse and Hopkins, with permission of Grosset and Dunlap), p. 26.

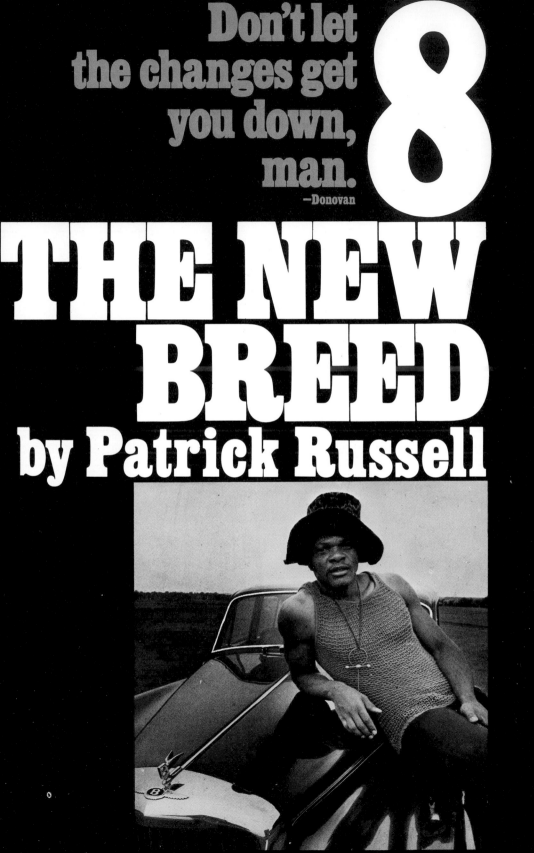

Don't let
the changes get
you down,
man.
—Donovan

8

THE NEW BREED

by Patrick Russell

The one-dimensional football player is dead. Today's pro is a new breed. He may also be an actor, editor, ecologist; abhor violence and strive to help his fellow man; wear his hair long, brag about his talent, knock his coach. He doesn't want to be just the great athlete he is—he wants to be himself, too.

For Bronko Nagurski the glory is a long time past. "I remember what it was like," he says.

"Was it rough?" you ask.

"Depends on what you mean by rough," he answers. "It was as rough as you wanted to make it, I guess."

"And you made it rough."

"I didn't give people any quarter out there. I ran into people hard, and I hit hard. But, then, that's what football's all about—hitting hard, getting in your licks. Still is."

"You see pro football on television now. Is it the same game?"

"Oh, well, the crowds you see now, we never saw then, and neither did we have the paydays these guys have. But I don't think that football player out there is much different—'cept maybe a little bigger and faster on the overall. I see them go at each other. They still like to hit."

"As hard as Bronko Nagurski?"

He chuckles. "Some maybe harder."

For Willie Lanier the glory is now.

"I'm a pretty well-behaved guy all week," he says, "but something happens out there on Sunday. I put on a helmet and become a little schizoid. I go out to fight the war."

"Is it more a war than a game?" you ask.

"It's both," he says. "It's both at different times. It's the war part of it that bothers me . . . the hitting."

"Willie Lanier is bothered by the hitting?"

"I am. And I've been trying to find the reason why. I'm a grown man with a family, yet I make my living hitting people as hard as I can. I can't help wondering whether that kind of conduct is necessary in the framework of life. I wonder how long a physical being can take that kind of punishment. As a result, I don't go all-out on every play anymore. I don't always hit hard."

"Isn't that almost heresy for a middle linebacker?"

"Maybe so. But I play this game aggressively enough that even if I don't punish people on every play, it won't be noticed."

"You may not enjoy punishing people, but your style suggests that there must be some gratification for you in hitting people."

"In a competitive way, I suppose, there is," he says. "It's the idea of matching body against body, as in boxing. And after the fighters have had at each other for ten rounds, they can still throw their arms around each other and say, 'You're a helluva man.' That's the best part of this game."

242

"Winning is still important; when that changes, this game will be in trouble. But there should be other enjoyments. . . . You can't measure life by its successes."

"Better than winning?"
"At least equal to it."

In the jungle of pro football Willie Edward Lanier is supposed to be a primitive. Maybe he doesn't swing from trees, but he could certainly scare hell out of you if you ran into him on a dark night. He is the Kansas City Chiefs' middle linebacker. Today's middle linebackers carry an image much like that attributed 30 years ago to running backs such as Bronko Nagurski—the intimidator, the hunter, the man with a killer instinct.

But while the images of Nagurski and Lanier may be similar, their philosophies are not, for the image disturbs the latter. "There are violent people in this sport," Lanier says, "but there are violent people in the world too. It takes all kinds." He pauses for a moment, then nods. "Yeah, things are changing out there. The people, the values, everything seems to be changing."

Lanier's philosophy about the game may be indicative of a trend. Since players today think of themselves as individuals, images are difficult to define. Asked whether Vince Lombardi was right when he said that winning was the "only thing," Lanier answers, "Winning is still important; when that changes, this game will be in trouble. But there should be other enjoyments. It's like, you just can't measure life by its successes. You've got to measure it by how you live and what you do."

The one-dimensional football player is dead. There are lots of things to do and lots of money to be made now. Winning is not the only thing anymore— and neither is the game itself.

Depending on your own philosophy, you may consider this attitude good, bad or a little of both. Where does devotion to duty begin and end? Or does it end? Or should it end? How do you separate the *I* from the *we?*

Jim Plunkett is a 25-year-old quarterback for the New England Patriots. He says, "It seems to me that today's pro football player is more sensitive to other people because he knows himself better. When you know yourself, you become a better member of the team. You understand better."

Walt Patulski is a 23-year-old defensive end for the Buffalo Bills. He says, "I like to think that I don't care about money. I like to think that moderate security is better than immoderate greed. But money is really what it all comes down to in the end. So you can't help but think about it."

Steve Tannen is a 25-year-old cornerback for the New York Jets.

He writes:

*Differences they come and go
Some more than the rest.
This game of ours has changed a bit
For worse and for the best.
But one change that
We also find
Increasing every day:
It's not so much the love of it
As the pension plans and pay.*

"Money enables you to do things," says Willie Lanier. "It's a means to an end. But money isn't everything either. It just gives you a new freedom."

"Emote," pleads the man with the clipboard. "You must emote. You must *feel* it." The other, bigger man on the stage moves to his left, and when he speaks, you know that he *does* feel it. Later he says, "Acting is in my blood. I love it."

He is (pick one): (a) Robert Redford, (b) Ryan O'Neal, (c) Carl Eller.

The sound of printing presses comes from another part of the building. The man behind the desk raises his voice. He wields a red copy pencil as if to emphasize his point as he says, "We're encouraged. Our circulation figures get a little better with each issue. When you grow like that, you just have to be encouraged."

He is (pick one): (a) Hugh Hefner, (b) Arnold Gingrich, (c) Ernie McMillan.

The man looks up at the furrowed bluff and shakes his head slowly. It is the work of wind and rain, and if it is allowed to continue, there will soon be no bluff and no furrows and no house on top. He says, "I'm concerned about our environment," and then he yells to two men down below, "Let's get those sandbags up here."

He is (pick one): (a) Ralph Nader, (b) Stewart Udall, (c) Merlin Olsen.

The man wears a tie that looks like an impossible dream of Peter Max. His pants are flared, and his shirt is tapered. He says, "Men's fashions are what's happening, and no one should be left behind."

He is (pick one): (a) Oleg Cassini, (b) Norman Hilton, (c) Garo Yepremian.

The speaker has force and presence. He has the young heads nodding when he raps the back of his right hand onto the palm of his left and says, "I have never been ashamed to witness my faith. I have never once been ashamed to say that God is my Number One."

He is (pick one): (a) Billy Graham, (b) Norman Vincent Peale, (c) Terry Bradshaw.

Not only are the answers obvious, they are also conclusive proof of today's maxim that a football player's work is never done.

Carl Eller is the destructive force on the right flank of the Minnesota Vikings' defensive line, which is called the Purple Gang. Mixing black and blue produces purple. It is a color that suits what Carl Eller does.

"Theater," he says. "What football really is, is competitive theater. It's just a different method." It is the method of Bud Grant in the fall after that of Stanislavsky in the winter and spring.

At a certain acting class in Hollywood, all eyes are on Eller. When he has finished, he flops into a

It is time people started noticing people.

244

theater seat and says, "I want to be in the movies, but I do not want to be there because they want Carl Eller, the football player." He looks at his watch and smiles. "I've got to be all the way across town in twenty minutes," he says. "But I haven't been on time for a ballet lesson yet."

Ernie McMillan is the man-mountain offensive tackle for the St. Louis Cardinals, a protector of quarterbacks and more than just another anonymous face. He feels that it is time people started noticing offensive linemen. He also feels that it is time people started noticing people. He had felt that way for quite a while when, three years ago, he did something about it. He started a St. Louis-based magazine called *Proud.* Ernie McMillan is black. The circulation figures have risen steadily. He says, "When you consider the mortality rate among magazines, you have to think we're pretty lucky. We have plans for regional magazines in other cities too."

Merlin Olsen, defensive tackle for the Los Angeles Rams, is a creature who would startle Gulliver. He is 6 feet 5 inches and 275 pounds. He has been an all-pro in each of his seasons in pro football.

You recognize Merlin Olsen on a football field by his alertness. He's always on top of the situation (usually a quarterback). You recognize him away from a football field too. He has been in the movies. He has co-hosted a television show. He has been (and still is) involved with a multitude of businesses, among them Erosion Control West, a company that specializes in saving receding beaches and houses endangered by slides. "The elements can do some pretty horrible things," he says. "Maybe we can't control nature, but we can work on what it does. The beaches are among our most precious natural resources."

Garo Yepremian, place-kicker for the Miami Dolphins, used to make ties in his basement but now sells them in a Miami Beach boutique.

He speaks with an accent that is a reminder of his background in Cyprus (he lived there until he fled to America a decade ago). He flashes an easy smile and says, "It's exciting, what's happened in men's fashions. The breakaway from the old, uniform styles was one of the big innovations of the sixties. Now the freedom is wonderful. It doesn't matter what you wear, and that is the way it should be."

Terry Bradshaw is the golden arm of the Pittsburgh Steelers, a brash quarterback who puts his ability where his mouth is. Away from the field, he is an active member of the Fellowship of Christian Athletes. He talks about the good life and lives it too. "Life is building from a good foundation," he says. "For me that's my faith in Jesus Christ. I don't pray to win, but I do pray to do my very best every time I go out there."

The bonds connecting these five men—other than athletic ability—are their independence and their search for identity.

"There have to be islands for me to visit away from the football field," Merlin Olsen says. "And if those islands happen to include helping people and helping yourself, well, that's all I can ask." He smiles and nods, as if to remind himself of the origin of it all. "But don't forget: Football is still the most important thing in my life, because when it's not . . . well, nothing else works either."

"Life is building from a good foundation."

245

The sentiment is the same when the speaker is Carl Eller. He talks from a seat in the back of the theater. On the stage a girl reads from Strindberg. "It's not that football is any less important to us," he says. "Our other activities are merely a branching out, a search for one's inner self. And it's nice to move with the times, to be able to be independent and do it all. That's what most people are searching for, I think."

Ernie McMillan says it another way when he talks about publishing: "Being an athlete really puts you out of touch with the community. Like an ivory tower. This magazine and its public contact has put me back in the mainstream."

These are all signs of the times in a world where hip-huggers no longer means snug-fitting hip pads, where a rehearsal is something more than a synonym for practice, where caring means doing.

Gene Upshaw cares. He is a guard for the Oakland Raiders, a 265-pounder who throws his off-field weight around at something more imposing than monster defensive ends and snarling linebackers. He works with the White House Special Action Office for Drug Abuse Information. But mostly he works on his own. "I've talked to the youngsters at the Boys Clubs in the Bay area," he says. "I've talked to them at their schools, and I've talked to them in their homes. They tell me about loneliness and ugliness, their family problems and their problems in school. A lack of things we take for granted—like love—can destroy a youngster when he can't find it in his own home. Then he goes out on the street and begins to hunt for a substitute.

"Not too long ago I talked to a boy who had done exactly that. He had found a drug pusher and gotten hooked. When he saw me talking to a bunch of kids, he came over and asked me to help him. I called this place I know and got him an appointment. They talked to him. They helped him. Through them he's going to be all right."

Upshaw has direct contact with the ghetto young. "Basically, they're good kids," he says. "They aren't any different than kids like me who grew up during the fifties. They have the same problems, the same frustrations . . . and they admire the same kinds of people."

He is asked whether or not that includes football players.

"Oh, my, yes," he says. "There are still a lot of kids—including teen-agers—who look up to football players. They want to model their lives after ours. I go to these youth meetings, and you'd be surprised at the questions I'm asked. These kids are interested in

the kind of life I lead, what I eat, the kind of car I drive, whether I smoke or drink, what I intend to do right after I leave them.

"They do know we're not saviors. They admire us. But they don't hero-worship us. They want to know everything about us. They want to know if things have been tough for us like they've been for them.

"Once when I visited the drug clinic, I met a guy who worked there. He said he had been on heroin, and he just wanted to chat with me. He wanted to find out if I had had a hard life and if I had ever gone off the deep end the way he had. He told me what he'd done and why he'd done it. He said he'd been a failure, that he'd never been able to do anything successfully. In school he got bad grades. When he went out for football, he couldn't make the team. He felt things were closing in on him. He was from New York, and he had lived in the ghetto. Drugs were as easy to get there as a can of beans. He was born and raised with junk. He had just turned to drugs as a natural course. But he'd fought it, and he told me he was beating it.

"And when he opened his soul to me, I knew one thing: Even adults want someone to listen to them. You see, when people ask that of you, there's just no way you can say no. No way.

"You know, once some reporter asked me what I wanted to do most in my life, and my answer had nothing to do with championships or the Super Bowl. I said, 'I want to be able to help people . . . especially those struggling kids I keep meeting. Playing in the Super Bowl is sixty minutes. But some of these kids have sixty years left to live.'

"They are begging for help . . . and I want to help them."

Helping others.

Jim Plunkett's mother was blind. She saw only total darkness.

His father was blind. He could tell night from day, but that was all.

They ran a newsstand at the San Jose post office, and together they raised two children, a girl and a boy.

For Jim Plunkett, growing up was different. He was not the one who is looked after, but rather the one who does the looking after. He worked in a grocery store, and also in construction, and the family put its money in the middle of the kitchen table.

"It wasn't as bad as it sounds," he says now, and you think, no, probably it was worse. And then he says, "We got along. And I don't think we missed out on anything really important. We had enough money and enough things . . . and we really didn't want for too much."

His father encouraged him to play football, but his mother was dubious about it. "Please don't get hurt," she said, finally giving her permission. Fate turned a deaf ear to her. Jim was a guard when, playing football in the fifth grade, he suffered a severely sprained ankle that sidelined him for most of the next season. In the seventh grade the malady was a mysterious bone disease. Out of football for nearly two years, he returned as a 5-foot 11-inch, 150-pound eighth-grade quarterback. The acclaim began then, but the injuries did not stop. Before he left high school, there had been two knee operations. But his most serious surgery had nothing to do with a knee.

In the summer before Jim Plunkett's freshman year at Stanford, a tumor was discovered on his neck. Doctors said definitely that he would not be able to play football that season and suggested that his career was over. The surgery was performed in August. In September, the irrepressible young man was playing football with the Stanford Frosh. Said Al Cementina, his coach at James Lick High School, "I'm not surprised. This is one tough Chicano."

It had been said of Plunkett that he was too reticent to be a good leader, and reticent he was. But he made himself a good leader by example.

Jim Plunkett could have named his college, but he narrowed his choices to Stanford and California (and finally chose Stanford) for one reason: He wanted to remain close to his parents. He felt that it was his duty.

In three seasons with Stanford, Jim Plunkett

eclipsed nearly every NCAA passing and total offense record. He passed up a chance to sign a pro contract after his junior year as a hardship case ("How could I advise kids not to drop out," he says, "if I had dropped out myself?") and climaxed his last collegiate season by leading his team to a Rose Bowl victory and winning the Heisman trophy. After that came his number-one selection in the pro draft by New England, and a six-figure bonus.

The story only begins there. His intensity and drive increased, and in his first year with the Patriots he was the quarterback for every offensive play—a remarkable achievement for a veteran, much less a first-year player.

It is natural to wonder whether Plunkett's drive is stronger than that of a player with an affluent background. Asked this, he pauses for a moment before answering. "I don't think so," he says. "When I started out playing football and baseball and other sports, I played them because I enjoyed playing them, not because I thought I was going to become a pro football player and make a lot of money. That never entered my mind. It just gave me a great deal of satisfaction to play. I enjoyed playing with and against other kids; I enjoyed competing. It's still the thing that turns me on most about football."

He is asked what it is like for a yearling ballplayer to go from the carefree spirit of college to the murderous tension of the pros.

He laughs and says, "That's the misconception people have. Actually, it's quite the opposite. The day before the game at college, you just thought about

247

"There have to be islands for me to visit away from the football field. And if those islands happen to include helping people and helping yourself, well, that's all I can ask."

the team you were going to play. The morning of the game, everything was quiet and still. There wasn't much talking, and the pregame meal was eaten in almost complete silence.

"So then you get here to the pros, and the night before the game, the guys go out and have dinner together and fool around a little bit . . . you know, relax. The morning of the game, there's still a lot of joking. That never happened in college, and at first it was difficult to adjust to. It was something I hadn't experienced before.

"It's really an awesome situation for a young guy just out of school. There are so many things to be concerned about that, as a quarterback, you just can't throw as much as you'd like to. I know when I'd go back to pass, I'd keep wondering if I had called the right play, and half the time I wondered if I'd called it correctly. It's always tough to do anything when you're worrying about something else.

"And it was funny to think that here I was, after all those years, getting paid for doing this. I remember that once at training camp somebody dropped a pass and a coach yelled, 'Catch the ball. That's what you're getting paid to do.' That was the first time I even thought of it that way. Pride had always been the only motivator before, and now all of a sudden money was one too—although I really do believe that to be a good football player, you have to love the game.

"This is a beautiful game. Maybe sometimes it's a little cruel, but, then, so is life. The thing about this game is that it plays so heavily on team things. You work together. I help you. You help me. I love it."

Isiah Robertson, the Los Angeles Rams' sensational linebacker, was a rookie the same year as Plunkett. For him the learning process was different.

"The only thing hard about pro football," he says, "is learning what they expect of you. When I came to the Rams out of Southern University, I think I had the power and self-control to do anything they wanted. But for a month or so, I couldn't tell what was expected of me. The problems went away when I discovered my role. I think that's the way it is for a lot of young dudes.

"And I'll tell you about another reality. Pro football is not a sport. It's a business. If you don't look out for yourself, you're going to get pushed all over the place. Now that I understand that—I didn't know it before—I'm a better football player."

There is an unpretentious honesty about Robertson. He does not answer all questions—some he responds to with just a smile—but when he does answer a question, he is brutally honest.

"The most important things in a coach," he says, "are that he be fair and that you be able to talk to him. I can get along with a man like that. That's why Tommy Prothro [the Rams' coach] and I haven't had any problems. A part of his thing, see, is learning by repetition and that's fine with me. Since I've been here, we've been taught to learn not by thinking but by repeating. The idea is that there's no time to think in football, and if you try to, why, as a linebacker, you're more than likely to make a mistake. I can dig that. So I just go out there, and I play it aggressively, which means I don't wait for things to happen. I make them happen. You just go after people. You don't worry about anyone's feelings."

There is bravado in the words of Isiah Robertson. But it is a bravado that is not false . . . and not unique. Being honest is the rule, not the exception, among pro football players. When somebody asks you how good you are, you tell him. And suppose you say you are very good, but you aren't? You won't be saying it for long. Sunday is show and tell.

Here are a few examples of that bravado:

Joe Namath, Jets' quarterback: "The best quarterback in pro football? [Laughing.] You're talking to him."

Roman Gabriel, Rams' quarterback: "I'm a born athlete. I think I could be pitching today in the majors, and if I were, I might be the best-hitting pitcher in baseball."

Dick Gordon, Bears' wide receiver: "The finest wide receiver should get the finest salary, don't you think?"

Alan Page, Vikings' defensive tackle: "If you don't believe you're the best, the chances are you aren't. I believe in my ability. I have to."

Tim Rossovich plays middle linebacker for the San Diego Chargers. He eats wineglasses, light bulbs and spiders. He sets himself on fire. He leaps out of second-story windows. He backflips into whirlpools. He sleeps on the floor only, with his head pointing north and his feet south, "so the magnetic waves run head to toe and the body is revitalized."

He says, "A lot of preposterous, outrageous things have been written about me, and all of them are true."

He is pro football's answer to Ripley, a living believe-it-or-not.

He really *has* set himself on fire. At least a half-dozen times too. Once he showed up at the door of a party at a friend's apartment in flames. The friend and another guest put out the fire with blankets. Rossovich was unperturbed. He scanned the room and said, "Sorry, I must have the wrong apartment." And then he left.

He sits in a booth in a health food restaurant in San Diego and talks about his favorite subject: himself.

"I live my life to enjoy myself," he says. "I can't explain the things I do much beyond that. I have more energy than I know what to do with. I can't sit around. I need only four hours' sleep. I get bored. So I go looking for fun. Now, I know a lot of what I do is silly—trying to cheer other people up, to cheer myself up, to get some attention—but none of it is done to hurt anyone, including me."

And with Tim Rossovich it is not all play and no work. It is, incredibly, all play *and* all work. His energy is seemingly limitless. In summer camp he will run until he literally drops. Then he'll sign autographs for as long as anyone with a pencil is around.

"I really enjoy being with kids," he says. "I don't think I'm above them at all. In fact, that's one of the reasons I wear my hair long. The young people can associate me with something good and positive and not something radical and violent.

"I'll even go to the kids sometimes. I remember how shy and nervous I was about approaching a big-name athlete. So I go to them.

"I'm concerned with the way young people are being treated today. For the most part, they're ignored, which is wrong. So they react in some radical or violent way—which is also wrong. What you have, really, are two sides both too proud to give in. People are sitting back waiting for someone else to do something. Well, being in my position with some notoriety and all, I can do something for them. Maybe just a little, but a little is better than nothing."

He plays middle linebacker the way you would expect him to—with violent abandon.

"I love to hear that *woosh* that comes when I really hit someone on the field," he says. "Linebacking is a powerful position. There's something happening on every play. You get a chance to be where the ball is. You can hit someone on every play. And me, I'm the quarterback of the defense. I'm in charge. I stand right up there in the center and tell the guys behind me and in front of me what to do. It's a great feeling of power. It's a whole lot different than defensive end [where Rossovich played during most of his first three seasons with the Eagles].

"Maybe it was just coincidence, but when I moved into the middle, I began to change as a person. It's like, it brought something out from deep inside me that I didn't know I had. That's when I began to get away from clowning all the time. I had new feelings about things going on in the outside world. Oh, don't get me wrong. I still like seeing all the stories in print. I like being called a wild man . . . and, you know, I think that deep down most people really envy me that. I think they'd like to do what I do. I'm free. I do what I like when I feel like it. Most people spend eight hours a day sleeping, eight working, a couple commuting, a couple eating, an hour in the bathroom—that's their whole day. What do they do to enjoy themselves? But when people read about me, they're not just reading about another football player. They're reading about a man having a good time living life. Maybe that'll help them some . . . wake them up a bit.

"See, the thing is, I love this game. Love it. I intend to go on playing for a long time . . . at least until I'm thirty-five. Where else can men that old get together and still act like kids?"

Where indeed. In an important team meeting when he was with the Eagles, Rossovich was asked a question. He opened his mouth, and a sparrow flew out.

At USC, he suffered an infection that put him in a coma for four days. When he awoke, he went to the coach, John McKay, and asked to be reinserted into the lineup. Doctors made the mistake of telling him he wasn't fully recovered, and he began racing around the locker room, bashing his head against steel lockers. "Look!" he shouted. "I can play!"

And yet for all the madness, Rossovich is surprisingly establishmentarian in his attitudes about teamwork and football.

"I respect authority," he says. "I've never been fined for anything. My objective is to be the best football player I can, not to make waves. When the coaches in Philadelphia told me to get a haircut, I got one. Not happily, but I got one.

"I don't really know who set the image of football, but I don't think there should be an image. It shouldn't matter what a guy wears or how long his hair is. What should matter is what you say and do. All long-haired people don't protest and blow up buildings. I don't think some guy up in the stands says, 'That player's got a crew cut. He must be good.'

"Guys like Dave Meggyesy were wrong to put the knock on football. Some things in it are dehumanizing, but that's no reason to knock the sport. Professional football can make you a better person, teach you to react better to any crisis. It can teach you responsibility, teach you to be levelheaded, to make split-second decisions.

"It is brutal at times. But I don't go out there to beat up a guy. I play to get respect for myself, because you have to have that. And I play for the respect of my teammates. For me to hear a teammate saying 'Good job' is more important than fans yelling or sportswriters writing. Only the team guys know. They realize what you do for the team. You break your fingers. You bleed. That's the thing about football that Meggyesy missed—the whole thing about working together and being together.

"I think a lot about the game. Excelling physically can give you more excitement than anything—more than closing a business deal or making a killing in the stock market. Physical victory is so satisfying. A guy who makes a million dollars will idolize somebody like a football player. The guy's richer and smarter, and he can do more things, but there he is, wanting my signature on a piece of paper.

"Right now, my basic goal is achievable. I want to be the best middle linebacker in pro football. If I work hard at it, play as hard as I can, do everything possible, yet am never considered the best, I will be at least partially content knowing I did all I could. But there would always be that doubt—did I go far enough? Maybe I'll never know.

"Admit it. I'm not a crazy, like you thought I'd be."

The old J. B. was Jim Brown, charging across the playing fields of the NFL for nearly seven miles of yardage, a record that may never be broken.

The new J. B. is John Brockington. Like Brown, he is a fullback; like Brown, he runs over people.

Brockington was a first-round draft choice of the Green Bay Packers in 1971, but not everyone agreed with the choice. Jim Murray of the Los Angeles *Times* wrote: "When the Green Bay Packers drafted an Ohio State fullback on the first round, lots of people were surprised. They didn't think the pros wanted anybody who could only run three yards."

It may be said that the success of John Brockington was hard to figure—unless you had an adding machine. In his first season as a pro, Jim Brown gained 942 yards. In his first season as a pro, John Brockington gained 1,105 yards.

He looks at the world through rose-colored glasses—not because he needs them, but because they happen to match his red-and-purple shoes and his electric-pink shirt—and he says, "You've got to have a goal, a motivation, in everything. And mine in pro football is to have ten big seasons. I'm not sure what that means in terms of statistics, but I'll know the big ones without having to look at any column of numbers."

A half-dozen years ago, another Green Bay fullback, Jim Taylor, said of being a pro, "What it all comes down to is not your ability—although that has to be there—but how bad you want it. I reached the peak of my profession because I set goals. This whole generation doesn't want to set goals."

Brockington is a contradiction to that generalization, but he does not give himself all the credit. "I have confidence," he says, "but it also comes down to a couple of other things: like luck and if God likes you or not. So far I'm batting a thousand on both scores."

The second of three children of a postal worker and a domestic, he grew up in New York City. The first four years were spent in the dying neighborhood that surrounded Yankee Stadium. After that, the family moved to Canarsie, a Brooklyn neighborhood.

"I wasn't really a part of the ghetto life," Brockington says, "but I could have gotten into anything I wanted to. I stayed straight and got into sports. I never felt deprived. My mother worked hard to take care of us.

"My dad? There's not much to say about him. He was a nice cat, but he was weak. His friends influenced him too much. A lot of people were getting hooked on drugs then. He drank. He couldn't handle it . . . and no one knew it more than he did. It hurt our family life."

His mother and father were separated when he was in elementary school. His involvement with sports began then. "Sports helped make me a whole person," he says.

He sits beneath a poster that says BREAK THE HATE HABIT. WHAT SANE PERSON NEEDS THAT NOISE. SO HOW DO WE TURN IT OFF? WITH LOVE. START TODAY, LOVER.

"I'm not a militant guy," he says. "I can get as burned up as the next cat when I see somebody being railroaded by our system. But I think we have to work within the system . . . that's where the changes have to be made. It's like, I want to teach history at the secondary school level but, shoot, I look at these history books, and they're just behind the times. They haven't even caught up to the cold war. Now I want these books to be better, and I'll work to try to make them so. The self-defeating thing would be to destroy the books, which is what a lot of radicals would suggest. This is just an example. My point is that, if nothing else, the books do provide a foundation for other books, for better books.

"A lot of things have to be updated and upgraded. The entire school system now is too established in the old ways. Somehow we've got to break out of them and make education a reflection of the seventies and not some other decade. I'll tell you, the refusal to change can hurt you in football too. We lost my final game as a player for Ohio State in the Rose Bowl, but I think we could have won if we just hadn't stuck to the rigid patterns. The trouble with not changing is that when you fall behind, you have no way of catching up. And that, my friend, is bad news."

Yesterday they were called heroes. Today they are called antiheroes.

They dress the way they feel like dressing. They let their hair grow. They endorse things besides razor blades. They say what they think.

Calvin Hill was a divinity student at Yale. Now a running back for the Dallas Cowboys and part-time divinity student at SMU, he says, "The church is a lot of people more interested in helping themselves than in helping others. They just want to make money."

Lance Rentzel used to get his hair cut every two weeks. Now he looks like Prince Valiant. A wide receiver for the Los Angeles Rams, he says, "On our team, at least, hair has ceased to be an issue. There's no reason why the length of it should be a matter of anything other than personal taste. If I were a coach, I wouldn't tell a guy with a crew cut that he had to let his hair grow."

Terry Bradshaw posed for a fashion spread in *Harper's Bazaar,* a magazine primarily for women. Some of his teammates told him to expect some needling. Bradshaw bristled. He said, "When I'm out there in the huddle, I'll do the needling."

Roman Gabriel, the Rams' quarterback, directed his team to an important victory that followed an uninspired loss and then announced that his coach of one and one-half seasons, Tommy Prothro, had become a "coach" for the first time during the week before the win. Later, Gabriel asked, "If you can't say it like it is, why say anything?"

Gone are the "if-you-can't-say-anything-nice-don't-say-anything-at-all" days.

The impala is an animal of impeccable grace, wide on the front flanks, narrow on the back flanks, tall and stately at rest, fluid in motion.

Gene Washington of the San Francisco 49ers is an impala. He does not move so much as glide, and when he runs, there is effort only in the bodies of his pursuers. In the catch-me-if-you-can-game that wide receivers play, he is unexcelled.

"I enjoy playing football," he says, "but to me life is more than that. For a black it has to be. There are too many problems out there for me not to stick my head out of this football world."

When he was at Stanford University, Washington was a co-founder of Interact, an integrated organization "designed to promote contact and understanding between Stanford students and minority groups living in ghetto areas near the campus." To some the action was boldly innovative. To others it was a compromise, a sellout.

Gene Washington says that Interact was a good thing. He says, "I don't think everybody has to be a radical in order to improve the lot of the black man in this country. . . . I feel that I have my own way of progressing and at the same time making things better for my family as a whole. I don't think anyone should impose his values on me. I feel in my own mind that what I've been doing is right.

"My experience at Stanford was interesting. I really think the administrators there are very knowledgeable people. There were some things I didn't like, but the good outweighed the bad by quite a margin. That's all you can ask. The important thing is for the black man to find pride and strength in his own community. Then we will grow from that base."

A couple of years ago, the San Mateo, California, Elks Club was planning an Elks–49ers golf match. They invited all the 49ers players, including the blacks. But the racial policies of the national Elks Club were clear-cut, and they had been reiterated in the organization's convention in San Francisco earlier that summer. There was to be only one color among Elks Club members.

Gene Washington was enraged—not by the national rule, but by the local invitation. "They have a right to their rules," he said, "just as we blacks have a right to say, 'We won't participate with you.' Any black with pride or self-respect wouldn't give them the time of the day. I don't want to participate with the Elks or any other bigots. The Elks invited us because we are 49ers, and I say the hell with them. If I can't participate when I want to, then I'm not interested in participating when they want me to. I want the freedom of choice in either case."

A freedom of choice was his when he graduated from high school in Long Beach, California. There can be no higher tribute to his intellect than to say that his collegiate decision came down to a choice of three schools: Stanford, Princeton and Harvard. He had been the president of his senior class in a school that was 90 percent white, an athlete once seen reading Hamlet in the locker room during the halftime break of a basketball game.

"All I've ever wanted," he says, "is to be my own man. That was true in high school and at Stanford, and it hasn't changed now. I want to be recognized for what I do in this sport, of course, but I also want to be recognized as a human being. I like the changes that have happened in sport. Television had a lot to do with them—television and guys like Jimmy

Brown and Joe Namath, who brought individuality to everyone's attention and who were so good that people said, 'Hey, maybe we should bend their way a little bit.' "

In a team game, oddly enough, individuality is vitally important. "Know thyself" is the prerequisite to relating to others.

Says Carl Eller, "I have exceeded goals—or limits or whatever they are—that I set at one time, early in my career. By surpassing things I didn't think I could attain, I know more of what I can do.

"And that's the way it is in life too. It has to come from within. You can't rely on other people to make you a better person. You should more or less analyze yourself in a situation and ask yourself, 'Am I being realistic? Am I going about this right? Am I thinking?' The more I know about that inner me, the more I can cope with the people around me."

Willie Lanier nods and says, "The best thing that's happened is that people are thinking about themselves. We are all together for the same goal—for winning, for the Super Bowl—but we are individuals, and we each have different mental and physical hurts . . . and we can respect that."

Don Maynard was born in 1937.
Steven Tannen was born in 1948.
They came together on the New York Jets, one a wide receiver, the other a cornerback.

In their stories are the then and the now of the professional athlete.

Don Maynard was originally drafted by the New York Giants. In 1958 he seemed to be a man before his time. He arrived at the Giants' training camp out of Texas Western, wearing long sideburns and cowboy boots. Said one writer, "[He had] an independence that caused a personality rift with some of his teammates." Used only occasionally, Maynard was released at the end of the season.

The addendum to the story of Don Maynard is that he was signed by the fledgling New York Titans of the American Football League in 1960 . . . and went on to become one of the greatest pass receivers in pro football history.

Steve Tannen came out of the University of Florida in 1970. His sideburns were long; his hair was long. He arrived at the Jets' camp at Hofstra, New York, and no one even noticed him, except to put him in the starting lineup.

These days, there is nothing unusual about sideburns and long hair and mustaches (Tannen has a mustache now too). What is unusual is what Tannen does when he is not playing football—that is, besides raising horses, trading cattle and running a boutique in Gainesville, Florida, called Tuesday Morning. Steve Tannen writes poetry. Here is some of his work.

To Win

To win you must forget yourself
Tolerate the worst of fears
Denounce all other goals you've set.
To win to face the foe
Declare belief in confidence
Thinking no alternatives.

To win to be the best
To put yourself above the rest.

You can't just think
You've got to know.
To know you're going to win
Can mean to some
The fact that you've
Already won.

Big Pro Ben

It's been ten years for Big Pro Ben
They cheer him now
They cheered him then.
He takes the ball, Big Pro Ben,
He takes the ball around the end.
Watch him weave,
Watch him run.
Then it happens
Knees are done.
Big Pro Ben was made of steel
Now older knees that start to feel
The pain of countless leaps and bounds
The pain the tearing muscle sounds
The pain of every cut and fake
The pain the ligaments must make
The pain of crossing each yard line
The pain of scoring one more time
The pain of exercise and fun
The pain of egos
One by one.

Lollipop

I'd hate to be a lollipop
Perched on a stick
Hands and legs extended
For someone's lousy lick.
I'd rather be a roller skate
With someone else to follow
At least I'd be a major chore
For anyone to swallow.

The poet laureate of pro football sits by his locker, his feet propped up against the wire mesh. It is the morning before a game, and he is writing poetry on a steno pad.

"I write," he says, "when the mood hits me." Later, after the game is over, he says, "It's very hard to write poetry about sports, because it must be spontaneous. I'll sit down and write something whenever the feeling hits me . . . late at night most times, but often just before a game, on those mornings when you're in the locker room just waiting for it to begin."

He began writing poetry when he was in high school after the death of a close friend in Vietnam. "It was a very upsetting experience for me," he says. "The cemetery was right behind our house, and after the burial I wanted to leave some token on the grave. So I went home and wrote a poem, and that night I climbed back over the fence and left the poem there at the grave. After that I wrote a lot of poetry. And in writing it I've gotten to know me a whole lot better."

On Pride

To be proud
  Does it mean to cry at defeats
    Does it mean a victory laugh
      A handshake to a beaten foe
        A vow to overcome?
Or can a proud one give excuses
Can he jest with teary eyes
Can he boast of better men
Can he hope for victory?
How do you tell a proud man's stare
What kind of clothes do proud men wear
What kind of signs do proud men bear?
You name callers beware
I tell you pride is everywhere
You use the word too
Cheaply.

The one-dimensional football player is dead. He was killed by sensitivity and, yes, by kindness. And in some cases he was killed by the green phantom called the dollar bill.

For richer (more likely) or poorer, the modern athlete is a man who cares what happens to others and to himself. He is more concerned with social problems than his older brothers were. He is a man who feels.

As Archibald MacLeish said, "*The crime against life, the worst of all crimes, is not to feel.*"

PHOTO IDENTIFICATIONS

1: No. 51 Ken Avery, No. 32 Franco Harris, No. 12 Terry Bradshaw
2–3: Detroit versus Cincinnati
4–5: Minnesota versus Detroit
6–7: Tom Darden
18–19: Calisthenics
20–21: Isometrics
22–23: Weight lifting
24: Whirlpool
25: Sound treatment
26–27: Football field, California Lutheran College
29, top: Playbook study; bottom left: Spare time; bottom right: Chow
30: Warm-up run
30–31: Weight check
31: Penalty laps
32–33: Taping
34–35: Reminders
36–37: Scrimmage
38–39: Classroom
40: Scrimmage
41: Formations
42, left: Camp followers; right: Pulleys
43: Rope maze
44–45: Night study
46–47: Player cut
49, top: 1. Larry Hand, 2. Sam Gruneisen, 3. Larry Brown, 4. Mike Curtis; bottom: 1. Ben Davis, 2. Ken Burrough, 3. Charlie Sanders, 4. Bob Griese
50–51: No. 25 Ron Shanklin, No. 33 Joe Greene, No. 21 Otto Brown
52–53: No. 10 Fran Tarkenton, No. 81 Carl Eller
54: No. 64 Manny Sistrunk, No. 63 Doug Van Horn, No. 53 Greg Larson, No. 11 Randy Johnson
55: Larry Jackson
56: No. 60 Ben McGee, No. 62 Ed White
57: No. 70 Russ Washington, No. 87 Rich Jackson
58–59: No. 11 Randy Johnson, No. 61 Charlie Harper, No. 75 Jethro Pugh, No. 67 Pat Toomay
60: No. 59 Charlie Weaver, No. 1 Mike Adamle, No. 62 Ed Mooney
61, top: No. 78 Wayne Walton, No. 75 Jethro Pugh; bottom: No. 54 Chip Myrtle, No. 77 Lyle Alzado, No. 20 Mike Garrett, No. 65 Lloyd Voss
62–63: No. 12 John Brodie, No. 74 Larry Hand, No. 79 Cas Banaszek
64: No. 32 Mike Curtis, No. 65 Randy Beisler
65, top: No. 73 Ron Yary, No. 83 Jim Mitchell; bottom: No. 51 Ken Avery, No. 32 Franco Harris, No. 12 Terry Bradshaw, No. 66 Bruce Van Dyke
66: No. 44 Donny Anderson, No. 68 Gale Gillingham, No. 36 Bill Thompson
67: No. 50 Ken Iman, No. 77 Ron East, No. 85 Chuck Dicus
68, left: No. 51 Dave Manders, No. 14 Craig Morton; right: No. 75 Forrest Blue, No. 57 Steve Kiner
69: No. 76 Roland Lakes, No. 70 Bob Hyland, No. 78 Wayne Walton
70–71: No. 65 Lloyd Voss, No. 34 Fritz Seyferth
72: Franco Harris
73, top: No. 32 Mel Phillips, No. 25 Roosevelt Taylor, No. 24 Mel Farr; bottom: No. 50 Ron Porter, No. 31 Charlie Haraway
74: Tom Matte
75: No. 40 Pete Banaszak, No. 44 Marv Hubbard
77: No. 75 Winston Hill, No. 76 Dave Rowe, No. 32 Emerson Boozer
78–79: No. 76 Burt Askson, No. 68 L. C. Greenwood, No. 23 Mike Wagner, No. 59 Jack Ham, No. 34 Tom Nowatzke

80, top: Edgar Chandler: bottom: No. 51 Dick Butkus, No. 55 Doug Buffone
81: No. 42 Altie Taylor, No. 58 Wally Hildenberg
82, top: No. 50 Paul Naumoff, No. 45 Dick Gordon; bottom: No. 54 Chuck Howley, No. 55 Lee Roy Jordan, No. 16 Scott Hunter
83: No. 51 Dick Butkus, No. 54 Ed Flanagan
84: No. 57 Frank Nunley, No. 20 Mike Garrett
85: No. 52 Skip Vanderbundt, No. 32 Mel Phillips, No. 19 Billy Lefear, No. 89 Milt Morin
86–87: No. 2 Jon Staggers, No. 43 Carl Lockhart, No. 21 Otto Brown
88: No. 33 John Fuqua, No. 37 Tom Casanova
89, top: No. 42 Charlie Taylor, No. 76 Bennie McRae; bottom: Mike Carter
90: No. 27 Gary Garrison, No. 52 Fred Forsberg
91, left: Larry Wilson; right: No. 38 Larry Smith, No. 20 Charles Greer
92–93: No. 44 John Outlaw, No. 25 Frank Pitts, No. 42 Don Webb, No. 41 Larry Carwell
94: Bob Trumpy
95: No. 74 Bob Lilly, No. 89 Otis Taylor; bottom: Roy Jefferson
96, top: No. 44 John Outlaw, No .85 Don Herrmann; bottom left: Eldridge Dickey; bottom right: Denver wide receiver
97: Gene Washington
98–99: No. 30 Ken Brown, No. 89 Milt Morin, No. 58 Jim Sniadecki
100: No. 89 Alvin Reed, No. 50 John Garlington
101: Jim Mitchell
102: No. 84 Joe Robb, No. 18 Roman Gabriel
103, left: No. 9 Sonny Jurgenson, No. 56 Len Hauss; right: No. 84 Bill Stanfill, No. 12 Roger Staubach
104: No. 53 Mike Lucci, No. 12 Joe Namath, No. 44 John Riggins
105: No. 19 Bill Munson, No. 76 Rocky Frietas, No. 70 Jim Riley, No. 66 Bob Kowalkowski
106: No. 15 Mike Phipps, No. 82 Royce Berry
107, left: Bobby Douglass; right: Archie Manning
108–109: No. 87 Lionel Aldridge, No. 77 Ron East, No. 66 Rick Redmond, No. 80 Kevin Hardy, No. 82 Steve Delong, No. 16 Dennis Shaw, No. 62 Dick Hart, No. 74 Donnie Green, No. 51 Bruce Jarvis, No. 61 Jim Reilly
110, top: Bobby Douglass; bottom: Bill Kilmer
111, left: Len Dawson; top right: Daryle Lamonica; bottom right: John Brodie
114–115: Paul Trepinski (official)
116: Walt Parker (official), No. 72 Cal Snowden, No. 12 Bob Griese
117: Norm Schachter (official)
119: Frank Sinkovitz (official), No. 43 Carl Lockhart, No. 14 Craig Morton, No. 19 Lance Alworth
120, top: John McDonough (official), No. 51 Dick Butkus; bottom: Gerry Hart (official), No. 86 Jim Mitchell, No. 64 Andy Maurer, No. 27 Phil Wise
122: Hank Stram (coach), Jack Reader, Tony Veteri, Tom Kelleher (officials)
123: Joe Connell
124: Gerry Hart (official), No. 76 Rocky Frietas, No. 72 Bob Heinz
126: Art Deemas (official), No. 53 Mike Lucci, No. 50 Paul Naumoff
127: Don Wedge (official), No. 83 Chip Glass, No. 35 Bo Scott
129, top left: Dick Dolack (official); left: No.

88 Charlie Sanders; top right: Tony Sacco (official), No. 50 Mike Oriard
132: Dick Jorgensen (official), No. 63 Willie Lanier, No. 61 Curly Culp
133, left: No. 7 Tom Bell, No. 34 Fritz Graf (officials), No. 12 Joe Namath; top right: Dick Jorgensen; bottom right: Burl Toler
136–37: Jack Maitland
138: No. 21 Billy Parks, No. 41 Willie Williams
139: No. 29 Walt Sumner, No. 50 John Garlington, No. 41 Tom Matte
140, top: Jack Snow; bottom: Ed Podolak
141: No. 36 Steve Owens, No. 50 Mike Taylor, No. 42 Altie Taylor
142–43: No. 27 Gary Garrison, No. 41 Alvin Wyatt
144: No. 12 Roger Staubach, No. 75 Deacon Jones
145, top: New Orleans huddle; bottom: No. 76 Walter Rock, No. 80 Roy Jefferson, No. 55 Tom Stincic
146: Bob Bell
147: Larry Wilson
148–49: No. 16 Jim Plunkett, No. 72 Diron Talbert, No. 79 Ron McDole
150: Cleveland No. 44 Leroy Kelly, New York No. 44 Richmond Flowers
151: Charlie Taylor
152–53: No. 20 Rocky Bleier
154–55: No. 16 Jim Plunkett, No. 87 Claude Humphrey, No. 77 Tom Neville
156: Ricky Harris
157: Oscar Reed
158: No. 31 Charlie Evans, No. 32 Jack Pardee
159, left: Frank Gallagher; above: Jeff Van Note
160, top: No. 15 Tom Blanchard, No. 56 Carl Gersbach, No. 87 Dick Kotite; bottom: No. 76 Harry Schuh, No. 45 Jim Bertelsen, No. 65 Tom Mack
161, top: Mike Phipps; bottom: Myron Pottios
162–63: No. 41 Tom Matte, No. 84 Mark Thomas
164, top left: Weeb Ewbank; bottom left: Tom Prothro; right: No. 12 John Brodie, No. 75 Jethro Pugh
165: Sonny Jurgenson
166: No. 12 Terry Bradshaw, No. 32 Franco Harris
167: Lance Rentzel
168, left: Jim Kiick; right; Ken Bowman
169, left: Alden Roche; right: Bob Griese
170: No. 84 Carroll Dale, No. 42 John Brockington, No. 72 Dick Himes, No. 68 Gale Gillingham, No. 81 Rich McGeorge, No. 57 Ken Bowman, No. 62 Bill Lueck, No. 71 Francis Peay
171: Len Hauss
172, left: Larry Woods; top right: No. 33 Willie Ellison, No. 88 Alan Page; bottom right: No. 25 Jerry LeVias, No. 50 Ed Beard
173: John Riggins
174: No. 30 Ron Johnson, No. 54 Chuck Howley
175: top: Bobby Douglass; bottom: Ken Houston
176: bottom: Errol Mann
177: No. 80 Henry Reed, No. 71 Dave Tipton, No. 16 Bill Nelsen
178–79: No. 63 Doug Van Horn, No. 77 Bill Brundage
180: Gus Otto
181: No. 10 Fran Tarkenton, No. 53 Mick Tinglehoff, No. 64 Milt Sunde, No. 73 Ron Yary
182: Scott Hunter
184: Bob McKay
185: No. 84 Rich Houston, No. 85 Don Herrmann
192, top: No. 30 Carl Garrett, No. 58 Jim

255

Files; *bottom:* Cleats for artificial turf
194: Equipment room
196, *top:* Fred Heron; *bottom:* cleats for grass
199: No. 88 Charlie Sanders, No. 53 Fred Carr
200, *top:* Individually tailored shoulder pads; *bottom left:* Modified pneumatic-hydraulic helmet; *bottom right:* Older helmet
202: Padding placed under ankle wrapping
203: Ankle protection
204: Taping table
205: Locker
206: Fran Tarkenton
210–11: No. 32 Walt Garrison, No. 67 Larry Stallings
212: Jim Kiick
213: Gale Gillingham
214: Pete Athas
215, *left:* Leland Glass; *right:* Chuck Howley

216: No. 75 Jethro Pugh, No. 16 Dennis Shaw
217: Shoulder bandaging
218, *top:* Joe Namath (left), Emerson Boozer (right)
219: Bill Brundage
220: No. 51 Dick Butkus, No. 55 Doug Buffone, No. 25 Dave Hampton
222, *top:* Jerry Moore; *bottom:* John Watson
223: Carl Noonan
224: Larry Gardner
225: Ice treatment and whirlpool
226: No. 51 Bruce Jarvis, No. 52 Ron Kadziel, No. 42 Don Webb, No. 85 Julius Adams, No. 50 Jim Cheyonski, No. 71 Art May, No. 30 Wayne Patrick
229: Ralph Neely
230: No. 55 Doug Buffone, No. 18 Jerry Moore
231: John Unitas
232, *top:* Joe Profit; *bottom:* Viking injury

233, *left:* No. 84 Bill Stanfill, No. 75 Manny Fernandez, No. 12 Joe Namath; *top right:* Mike McCoy; *bottom right:* L. C. Greenwood
234: Bob Lilly
235: Jerry Sherk
236, *top:* Ice pack; *bottom:* Bob Gresham
237: Ken Bowman
238, *top:* Fran Tarkenton; *bottom:* Tom Matte
239: Tom Keating
240: Carl Eller
242, *top:* Calvin Hill; *bottom:* Gene Upshaw
243: Willie Lanier
244, *top:* Tim Rossovich; *bottom:* Ernie McMillan
245, *top:* Steve Tannen; *bottom:* Terry Bradshaw
246: John Brockington
247: Jim Plunkett
248, *top:* Merlin Olsen; *bottom:* Calvin Hill

PHOTO CREDITS

Ken Heyman: 18–47, 194, 196 bottom, 200, 202, 203, 204, 205, 217, 224, 225
Richard Raphael: 1, 49 bottom 3 & 4, 65 bottom, 68 right, 72, 74, 80 top, 85, 88, 95 bottom, 98–99, 104, 107 right, 110 top, 120 top, 133 left & top right, 139, 141, 148–49, 154–55, 161 top, 166, 176 bottom, 180, 218 bottom, 226, 233 bottom right, 234, 238 bottom, 247
Tony Tomsic: 2–3, 4–5, 6–7, 49 top 1, 56 top, 60, 65 top, 69, 73 bottom, 77, 80 bottom, 81, 83, 84, 92–93, 96 top & bottom left, 103 right, 105, 111 left, 114–15, 117, 120 bottom, 122, 123, 124, 127, 129, 132, 133 bottom right, 136–37, 140 bottom, 145 bottom, 154, 157, 168 right, 169 right, 175 top, 177, 181, 184, 185, 192, 215 left, 229, 232 top, 233 bottom left, 237, 238 top
Charles Aqua Viva: 90, 108, 109
John E. Biever: 94, 107 left, 182
Vernon J. Biever: 66, 97, 152, 159 left, 169 left, 170, 199, 213, 220, 228, 233 top right, 246, 253
Dave Boss: 67, 91 right, 106, 160 bottom, 172 right bottom
Clifton Boutelle: 103 left, 151
Dave Cornwell: 49 bottom 4, 55
Timothy Culek: 100, 159 right
Melchior DiGiacomo: 49 top 3, 50–51, 52–53, 54, 58–59, 61 top, 70–71, 86–87, 89 top, 110 bottom, 159, 160 top, 171, 172 left, 178–79, 214, 215 right, 218 top, 219, 232 bottom
Malcolm W. Emmons: 49 bottom 1, 168 left, 175 bottom, 206, 230
Paul Fine: 75
James F. Flores: 57, 61 bottom, 68 left, 140 top, 144, 145 top, 164 left bottom, 189
George Gellately: 73 top, 82 top, 102, 126
Rod Hanna: 146, 243
Skip Heine: 240
Fred Kaplan: 49 top 4, 64, 89 bottom, 96 bottom right, 111 bottom, 164 right, 172 top right, 173
John E. Martin: 245 bottom
National Football League Properties, Inc.: 49 bottom 2, 101, 142–43, 161 bottom, 162–63, 222, 236, 239
Larry Nighswander: 245 top
Darryl Norenberg: 76
Jack O'Grady: 62–63, 176 top
Russ Reed: 242 bottom, 244 top
Frank Rippon: 222 bottom
Ronald Ross: 78–79, 231
Russ Russell: 82 bottom, 95 top, 119, 138, 174, 216, 242 top, 248 bottom
Robert L. Smith: 116
Jay Spencer: 212, 223
R. H. Stagg: 49 top 2, 236 top
Vic Stein: 167, 248 top
George Tiedeman: 150
Herb Weitman: 147, 196 top, 210–11, 244 bottom